Two Hundred Years of Flight in America

A Bicentennial Survey

Two Hundred Years of Flight in America

A Bicentennial Survey

Eugene M. Emme, Editor

PARTICIPANTS:

Michael Collins
Thomas D. Crouch
Frederick C. Durant, III
Edward C. Ezell
Paul A. Garber
R. Cargill Hall

Richard P. Hallion
Thomas P. Hughes
Donald S. Lopez
Robert L. Perry
Roger Pineau
Richard K. Smith

AAS History Series, Volume I

A Supplement to Advances in the
Astronautical Sciences

Second Printing, May 1979
Third Printing, September 1981

ISBN 0-87703-091-X (Hard Cover)
ISBN 0-87703-101-0 (Soft Cover)

Published by:

Univelt, Inc.
P.O. Box 28130
San Diego, California   92128

Printed and Bound in the U.S.A.

A BICENTENNIAL HISTORY PROGRAM

This volume is essentially the proceedings of
the first history symposium held in the National
Air and Space Museum on November 4, 1976. It
was proposed and developed by the History Committee of the American Institute of Aeronautics and
Astronautics. It was cosponsored by the National
Air and Space Museum, the Society for the History
of Technology, and the American Astronautical
Society.

It is dedicated in published form to the continued pursuit and broader appreciation of the full
history of flight in American History and its global
influences. Any perspectives it affords may prove
of even greater interest a hundred years from now.

FOREWORD

At the time this day-long program on "Two Hundred Years of Flight in America" was proposed as a Bicentennial endeavor by Eugene Emme and the History Committee of the American Institute of Aeronautics and Astronautics, we of the Smithsonian were on the final countdown for the long-awaited opening of the new National Air and Space Museum, which was dedicated by President Gerald Ford on July 1, 1976. Nevertheless, we welcomed this timely and appropriate proposal.

With the additional sponsorship of the Society for the History of Technology and the American Astronautical Society, the conference proved most stimulating. Further, it provided a splendid opportunity for over a hundred historians of flight, including members of the museum staff, to join in this worthwhile historical enterprise. We are now indebted to the American Astronautical Society for this publication, the first in its History Series.

The National Air and Space Museum, as a national center for aerospace education, is a logical place to hold such a symposium. Our collection of air and space craft contributed to the history that was discussed during "Two Hundred Years of Flight in America." The Museum's library, with over 20,000 bound volumes and an extensive photograph archive, is a resource that sustains and enhances historical interest. We hope that students and scholars alike may profit from reliving past dreams of a future that is now, as we contemplate our own future in a dynamic and ever more accessible universe.

The Air and Space Museum embodies the Smithsonian's long-standing interest in flight, which dates from the year of the Institution's founding. Indeed, the very basis for the scientific tradition of the Smithsonian, as envisioned by its creator, was to provide for "the increase and diffusion of knowledge among men." In 1861, the first Secretary of the Smithsonian, Joseph Henry, persuaded President Abraham Lincoln that balloonist Thaddeus Lowe be permitted to demonstrate the capabilities of the balloon for military observation. The demonstration took place on the present site on the Mall.

In 1876, the aeronautical collection of the Smithsonian was initiated when a group of kites was obtained from the Chinese Imperial Commission at the close of the Centennial Exposition in Philadelphia.

The third Secretary, Samuel P. Langley, was an established "astrophysicist" in today's terms. He studied the problems of heavier-than-air flight and experimented with unmanned and manned winged craft between 1887 and 1903. Two of Langley's steam-driven "aerodrome" models flew more than a half mile (one kilometer). Langley provided bibliographical information to many others, including the Wright brothers, on the science of aeronautics. Langley's astronomical studies led to the creation of the Smithsonian Astrophysical Observatory, now the Center for Astrophysics, in Cambridge, Massachusetts.

The Smithsonian's interest in flight continued with Secretary Charles D. Walcott, Langley's successor, who was instrumental in the 1915 creation of NASA's forerunner, the National Advisory Committee for Aeronautics.

Only a year later, the Institution began its 29-year association with Robert H. Goddard as he experimented with liquid-fuel rockets. Goddard's work was initially supported by Secretary Charles Abbot from the Hodgkins Fund, an endowment for the "increase and diffusion of more exact knowledge in regard to the nature and properties of atmospheric air." Goddard's two classic papers on his research were published as Smithsonian Reports in 1919 and 1936.

With commitment to the study of flight so apparent in the Smithsonian's history, we were especially pleased to host the jointly-sponsored program on "Two Hundred Years of Flight in America". I commend these proceedings to those with a love for this most challenging and dramatic area of twentieth century science and technology.

Michael Collins

Director

National Air and Space Museum

PREFACE

This volume was intended to be more than a mere proceedings of a rather remarkable historical venture. The table of contents outlines the scope of this day-long program held in the magnificent theater of the new National Air and Space Museum, one immersed, as it were, in a giant building filled with the glorious as well as the not well-known early artifacts and art documenting the sweep of man's history of flight from past dreams to realities and the future.

It contains the full papers upon which each of the authors couched their oral presentations. An introduction attempts to give broader perspectives to the history of flight in America, and to include the salient commentary by an eminent historian of technology and by the first and now Historian Emeritus of the National Air and Space Museum. Biographical sketches of all participants has been included in an aphabetical listing. And a list of illustrations and an index has been provided to enhance ready reference.

To the editor, this program on "Two Hundred Years of Flight in America -- A Bicentennial Survey," was a unique happening at the right time and in the right place. Most of all we are indebted to Michael Collins, Director of the National Air and Space Museum, for enthusiastically solving the matter of where this program would take place. Impetus for this program sprouted out of some anticipation of the opening of this great new museum atop a former parking lot of the headquarters of the National Aeronautics and Space Administration. A request from the NASM for consultation with the History Committee of the American Institute of Aeronautics and Astronautics in 1975 only augmented the idea. The thrust of this idea was in some way to engage historians in making a special contribution to the take-off of the Nation's museum dedicated to the history of flight as a Bicentennial event. In the meantime, the proposed "Two Hundred Year" program had garnered endorsements but did not fit the conference formats of either the Society for the History of Technology or the American Institute of Aeronautics and Astronautics. Added to the proposal made to Michael Collins was the offer of Phillip Bolger, president of the American Astronautical Society, to publish the proceedings in the AAS Series. Here it is.

Special acknowledgments are in order for attempting
to make this volume a worthy reference. First, Horace Jacobs,
director of the AAS Publications Program, a non-profit effort,
deserves highest thanks. Indeed, this volume is to become the
first in a new American Astronautical Society History Series.
This will make available substantive historical works on aerospace technology beyond the commercial and academic literature. With regard to illustrations we are first obligated to
the authors, as well as to the following for special efforts:
Les Gaver and his staff in NASA headquarters; John Giannetti,
prime mover in the Bicentennial creation of the Indian Queen
Tavern Museum in Bladensburg, Maryland; Arthur Renstrom of
the Library of Congress; and Frank Winter and Colonel John
Tucker of the NASM regular and volunteer staff, as well
as Grace Bogart Reeder, formerly reference librarian in NASA.
Credits are given with each illustration.

Last but not least, toleration of various institutions for the time borrowed enabling most participants to
engage in this project beyond their personal hours, deserves
tribute. We shall have a hundred years before the next one
of this kind in any case.

                              Eugene M. Emme

                              NASA Historian

                              Washington, D.C. 20546

January 30, 1977

TABLE OF CONTENTS

PART THREE: ASTRONAUTICS

PART FOUR: COMMENTARY

HISTORY COMMITTEE OF THE AMERICAN ASTRONAUTICAL SOCIETY

    Eugene M. Emme, NASA Historian, Chairman
    Philip H. Bolger, Department of Transportation, former
        AAS President
    Tom D. Crouch, Curator/Astronautics, National Air and
        Space Museum
    Frederick C. Durant, III, Assistant Director/Astronautics,
        National Air and Space Museum
    Mitchell R. Sharpe, Historian, Alabama Space and Rocket
        Center

BIOGRAPHICAL SKETCHES OF PARTICIPANTS

Michael Collins: Director, National Air and Space
    Museum, Smithsonian Institution. Astronaut pilot
    of Gemini X in 1966, and of the Command Module of
    Apollo 11. Graduate of the U.S. Military Academy,
    becoming a test pilot in the U.S. Air Force. He
    served briefly as Assistant Secretary of State
    before coming to the NASM in 1972. Major General
    in the USAFR. Author of highly acclaimed memoir,
    Carrying the Fire: An Astronaut's Journey (1974).

Tom D. Crouch: Curator, Astronautics Department, NASM,
    adjunct professor of history, University of Mary-
    land. Ph.D. in history from Ohio State University.
    Historian with Ohio State Historical Society, where
    he wrote The Giant Leap on flight in Ohio from the
    Wright brothers on. Winner of the AIAA History
    Manuscript Prize for 1976 for "The Aeronautical
    Community and the Problem of Heavier-than-Air
    Flight, 1885-1905."

Frederick C. Durant, III: Assistant Director, Astronautics
    Department, NASM. Graduate chemical engineer from
    Lehigh University, U.S. Naval Aviator and test pilot
    during World War II, and thereafter with Arthur D.
    Little, Inc., Bell Aerosystems, and AVCO Corp. Past
    president of the American Rocket Society and the
    International Astronautics Federation. Fellow of
    AIAA, AAS, BIS, and DGLR. Author of numerous
    articles, including "Rockets" and "Space Exploration"
    in the Encyclopedia Britannica, and co-editor of
    First Steps Into Space (1975).

Eugene M. Emme: NASA Historian since 1959, founder and
    current chairman of history committees of AIAA, the
    National Space Club, and the International Academy
    of Astronautics (co-chairman). Ph.D. in modern Euro-
    pean history from the University of Iowa. CPT grad-
    uate, then with Army Air Forces contract schools,
    and Naval Aviator and historical officer during

World War II. Professor of History at Air University
and director of Air War College Graduate Study Group
(1949-57), Office of Research at OCDM (1958-59).
Author of "German Air Power, 1919-1939," Air Power
and International Politics--A Bibliography, Aeronautics and Astronautics, 1915-1960, and A History
of Space Flight; editor of The Impact of Air Power,
The History of Rocket Technology, and NASA historical publications to 1973. Founding member of the
Air Force Historical Foundation, the National Space
Institute and Society for the History of Technology.

Edward C. Ezell: Historian, consultant, and author of
numerous technical histories, including "The Partnership: A History of the Apollo-Soyuz Project" and
a preliminary history of the Viking Project. Ph.D.
in the history of technology from Case Western Reserve University, dissertation on "Search for a Light-
weight Rifle: The M14 and M15 Rifles," and taught
at Butler, Case Institute, North Carolina State,
and Sagamon State universities. Author of numerous
articles on the history of technology, and co-editor
of the AIAA History Newsletter.

Paul A. Garber: Historian Emeritus, NASM. Employed by
the Smithsonian Institution since 1920, serving as
first curator of the artifacts of flight in the
Museum of Transport and the National Air Museum,
precursors to the NASM. Authored numerous works of
the Smithsonian and was unflagging in his search for
artifacts and memorabilia. His dedication was an
inspiration in the genesis of the NASM and its
collections, and the history of flight nationally.

R. Cargill Hall: Historian, Jet Propulsion Laboratory,
California Institute of Technology, since 1967.
Graduate of San Jose State with M.A. in political
science. Historian with Lockheed at Sunnyvale,
prior to joining JPL. Winner of the first two
Goddard Historical Essay prizes in 1962 and 1963.
Author of Lunar Impact: A History of Project Ranger
(in press), editor of proceedings of I.A.A. History
Symposia, III-VI (in press), and numerous articles
on history and international space law.

Richard P. Hallion: Curator, Science and Technology
Department, NASM, and adjunct professor of history,
University College, University of Maryland. Ph.D.

in history from the University of Maryland, and his
dissertation was on"Legacy of Flight: The Guggenheim
Fund for the Promotion of Aeronautics"(in press),
winner of the AIAA History Manuscript Award in 1975.
Author of Supersonic Flight: Breaking the Sound
Barrier and Beyond, and co-author of "Out of the
Past," a monthly chronology in Astronautics and Aeronautics magazine of AIAA. Now writing a history of
the NACA/NASA Dryden Flight Research Center.

Thomas Parke Hughes: Professor, Department of History and
Sociology of Science, University of Pennsylvania.
Ph.D. in modern European history, University of
Virginia, and has taught the history of technology
at the University of Wisconsin, M.I.T., Johns Hopkins
University, and Southern Methodist University. Author
and editor of numerous articles and books, including
his prize-winning biography of Elmer Sperry, and
Medicine in Virginia. He was editor of volumes on
Changing Attitudes Toward American Technology, Lives
of Engineers, and several in press. Among his
stimulating articles are "Technological Momentum,"
"The Railway: A Technological Frontier," "Problems of
Technological Innovation," and "ENIAC: Invention of
a Computer." Serves on numerous boards and councils,
and is a member of the historical advisory committees
of NASA and ERDA. A founding member of the Society
for the History of Technology.

Donald S. Lopez: Assistant Director, Aeronautics Department, NASM. B.S. in Aeronautics from the California
Institute of Technology, and graduate of U.S. Air
Force Test Pilot School. Became an ace flying P-40
fighters with General Chennault in China, and flew
in combat tour in F-86's in Korea. Assistant Professor of Aeronautics at the USAF Academy before
retirement from Air Force, when he became systems
engineer on Apollo-Saturn Launch Vehicle and the
Skylab Workshop. He is a charter member of the
Society of World War I Aviation History, and of the
American Fighter Aces.

Robert L. Perry: Member of senior staff of the RAND Corporation, Santa Monica, CA. Was civilian historian
for the U.S. Air Force after 1952: chief historian
at the Wright Air Development Center in Dayton, and
also at USAF Space Systems Division in Los Angeles.
Author of numerous official histories on aircraft
and rocket systems, R&D management and policy, and

systems development. Also author of RAND studies
and AIAA papers on variable-sweep aircraft and
aerospace technology, as well as "The Atlas, Thor,
Titan, and Minuteman" in The History of Rocket
Technology. Past member of the NASA historical
advisory committee.

Roger Pineau: Captain, USNR, Director, Naval Memorial
Museum, Navy Yard, Washington, D.C. He was, while
on the staff of the NASM, assigned the task of
preparing the NASM balloon exhibit, the first prepared in 1971-72 for the new building. Graduate of
the University of Michigan and the George Washington
University Law School, he became a Navy Japanese
translator during World War II, and was assigned to
the U.S. Strategic Bombing Survey. For ten years
was an assistant to the late Rear Admiral Samuel
E. Morison, USNR, in preparation of the History of
U.S. Naval Operations in World War II volumes. Was
detailed as Naval Aide to the President on six Far
East missions. Co-author, translator, or editor on
numerous volumes, including The End of the Imperial
Japanese Navy, and The Japan Expedition: Personal
Journal of Commodore Matthew C. Perry. He is
author of the catalog of a Smithsonian exhibit on
The Japan Expedition, 1852-1855, and Ballooning,
1782-1972, an outstanding catalog of the NASM
exhibit.

Richard K. Smith: Historian, Washington, D.C. Combined
graduate study with sea duty as Merchant Marine
officer, and received Ph.D. in history from the
University of Chicago. Author of dozens of articles
and the following books: First Across: The U.S.
Navy's Transatlantic Flight of 1919 (winner of the
AIAA History Manuscript Award for 1972), The Airships
AKRON and MACON: Flying Aircraft Carriers of the U.S.
Navy, and editor of The Hugh L. Dryden Papers, 1898-
1965, A Catalogue. He is the American literary editor
of AIR International, published in London.

INTRODUCTION—PERSPECTIVES ON THE HISTORY OF FLIGHT IN AMERICA

"EARTH RISE"

Historic view of Spaceship Earth by the first men to voyage to the Moon, the crew of Apollo 8, in December 1968.

I

INTRODUCTION

PERSPECTIVES ON THE HISTORY OF FLIGHT IN AMERICA

Eugene M. Emme

"If there is any twentieth century
aspiration which corresponds to that of the
nineteenth century for the conquest of the
air, it is perhaps that of the conquest of
space with the early goal, travel to the
moon..." (1953)[1]

"The opportunities of this age are
their own inspiration. They provide us with
the potential of travelling into space, of
investigation of the moon and Mars, then
more. But these individual projects are
only segments of the real mission -- to contribute to the welfare of mankind." (1961)[2]

-- Hugh Latimer Dryden (1898-1965)

To some savants, perspectives on American history
seemed surprisingly animated during the Bicentennial Year
just concluded. As an inter-disciplinary study of man's
past experience, "history" appears not to have been vogue in
the curricula of most American schools. Recent happenings,
always dynamic to be sure, also have not been congenial to
the labor of professional historians ever pressed to reflect
upon all of man's past. A vast array of scientific and technological innovations have had a cummulative impact upon
individuals, their institutions, and society as a whole during the twentieth century. Among the seminal aspects of
rapid change have been electronics, the automobile, nuclear
energy, and biological science. Historians as well as
scientists and engineers, not to neglect politicians,
generals, diplomats, artists, and others, have been challeng-
ed by the accelerated pace and breadth of change during the
past four decades. To most busy Americans, history can wait.

Among the major innovations altering the realities
of the twentieth century was the coming and utility of man's

unprecedented capacity for flight above the surface of the earth, first with ever-improved winged aircraft, and, just two decades ago, with spacecraft for his instruments and himself in earth orbit, and increasingly into the far reaches of our solar system. The opening of the National Air and Space Museum, which this volume hopefully augments, was a most timely presentation to help assess some of the dimensions of that which has already taken place. Millions of visitors already have confirmed they appreciate much of that of which they were already aware has not been neglected historically. Yet the history of aerostatics, aeronautics, and astronautics beyond fragile memories of participants and ready artifacts and documentation remains a challenging task to fully assay and comprehend.

To get our mental time-clocks ready to consider the history of flight for the past two centuries, as well as to stamp a vintage on this volume, one might start with some perspectives on 1976. Reflection upon major events in the very recent past helps lend perspectives on the ancient past.

To a contemporary columnist, George F. Will, "the most newsworthy event during the Bicentennial Year" was the landing of the American Viking spacecraft on the surface of the planet Mars on July 20, 1976.[3] Placing two automated laboratories upon our neighboring planet, appeared symbolic of great future significance, not just another space mile - stone. Apparently no other member of the news media reflected upon 1976 in accord with Mr. Will, although actual discovery of any evidence of life forms on Mars would have certainly changed the impression. Viking had no heroes like Apollo.

Exactly seven years before Viking I sent its first picture of the reddish Martian landscape and its pink sky, two of the Apollo 11 astronauts walked on the surface of the moon in 1969. Man's first landing on the moon was a dramatic event. Remember the other five Apollo lunar landings?

Just seven months before Apollo 11, the crew of Apollo 8 had made man's first voyage to the moon at Christmas time in 1968. They orbited it ten times, and expressed their impression of the beauty of planet Earth as viewed from above the "dirty beach sand" appearance of the lunar surface. It was a memorable impression despite the fact that color pictures of the whole earth had been taken from space before. But the eyeball account by the crew of Apollo 8 could prove the turning point of man's relative view of his own homeland planet. May it be considered as significant as Galileo's first sketches of the craters on the moon when he first viewed them with a telescope in 1609? Galileo helped trigger the first "new world" and all that it meant for the rise of critical science and unfettered speculation.

Single events appear to give new perspectives with the passage of time. They ever motivate curious scientists, innovative engineers, and explorers adventuring within the limits of technology giving them access to untouched places, not to ignore the philosophers and others attempting to give meaning to it all. With TV, came "instant history"?

A leading American historian of technology, Melvin Kranzberg, editor of Technology and Culture, has suggested that man's landing on the moon in 1969 will be regarded in the distant future as the outstanding event of the twentieth century. This was also expressed by Arthur Schlesinger and others at the time of Apollo 11. But Kranzberg submitted a catchy limerick to aid the school children five centuries from now in their history class. In the twenty-fifth century, Kranzberg suggested, when the school children were going to be asked to name the greatest historical event in the twentieth century, "even the stupidest kid in the class" will answer:

"In nineteen-hundred and sixty-nine,
Neil Armstrong leaped for all mankind."[4]

Who does not remember the first historical date in American history, one anchored by the limerick about Columbus "in fourteen-hundred and ninety-two" and the "ocean blue"? Professor Kranzberg has helped to explain the meaning of the space program, but he did not suggest where the school children of the twenty-fifth century would be attending classes. One might speculate about colonies in space. Students of aerospace technology in history would recall that the twenty-fifth century belonged to the futuristic comic strip hero of the 1920's, Buck Rogers. Each era of flight history has its dreams and its spectacular accomplishments.

HISTORICAL ROOTS

Well known from the legend of Icarus and the drawings of Leonardo da Vinci, flight by birds early stimulated envy and the idea of flight by man with wings. Recent discovery of the largest flying creature in prehistoric North America seems of more than antiquarian interest. Fossil remains of flying reptiles of the late Cretaceous period, known as "pterosaurs," have been found from sparrow size to wing spans of several meters in Wyoming, Oregon, Kansas, Arizona, Alabama, and Texas in North America, as well as in China, Germany, and Jordan. In 1972, the remains of three large pterosaurs were discovered in Big Bend National Park in West Texas. With a mean estimated wing span of 15.5 meters (over fifty feet), and similar in shape to the tailless Northrop YB-49, "flying wing" of 1945, these new Texas pterosaurs are considered by far the largest flying creatures presently known.[5] Most palentologists seem agreed that pterosaurs were gliders for their remains show no attachment for wing muscles. <u>Homo Erectus</u>, or man, appeared much later. In 1901, interestingly, Samuel P. Langley considered prehistoric flying reptiles. They most closely approximated the wing span and weight ratio of his project of making his successful powered model a man-carrying "Aerodrome."[6] At the same time, the Wright brothers, as is known, observed the use of wing tips for flight control by sea gulls, the distant descendants of the pterosaurs. Once the Wrights perfected their controllable glider, while learning to fly it, the powered glider soon became an airplane. As Charles Gibbs-Smith and others have noted, the Wright brothers put together the ideas of many before them and made it work. They had to build their own wind tunnel to obtain reliable aerodynamic data. And, they made four successfully-controlled powered flights on December 17, 1903.[7]

The first flights made by man were accomplished with aerostatic balloons, first by the Montgolfier brothers in France. After the first unmanned demonstration on June 5, 1783, on October 15, Pilatre de Rozier made a tethered ascent and, in November, with Marquis d'Arlandes, made a free flight balloon voyage of over five miles. Mankind had at long last flown, not like a bird, but as a crowning achievement for all of mankind. Within a year after the "balloon craze" burst in France and around the world, an American had built a balloon. Peter **Carnes** of Bladensburg, Maryland, constructed and demonstrated his 35-foot diameter multicolored hot air balloon on June 19, 1784. Apparently, Carnes had tested it before a few friends, perhaps as early as June 10. But his public flight in Bladensburg, duly cited in the newspapers of its day, has not been a part of the published historical record.[8] Significantly, the history of flight in America can be said to have begun the same year that the confederated thirteen American states were recognized as an independent nation.[9]

Five days after his unmanned demonstration, Peter Carnes persuaded a thirteen-year-old boy to ascend in his tethered balloon on June 24, 1784. Who was the first American aeronaut? You will read more about him in the next chapter, but his name was Edward Warren. The only useful history of <u>The First Century of Flight in America</u>, by Jeremiah Milbank, Jr., which resurrected the Warren flight in 1943,[10] has been out of print for many years. For our perspectives on this volume, then, the history of actual flight during the nineteenth century was all balloons except for several gliders and models leading to the coming of the airship and the airplane.[11] And balloons remain with us yet today.

Upon reflection, this bicentennial survey of flight in America could well have begun in the 1750's with the kites and publications of Benjamin Franklin, as well as his moving commentary on witnessing the first balloon ascensions much later in Paris in 1783.[12]

FIRST BALLOON ASCENSION IN AMERICA

On June 19, 1784, Peter Carnes raised his
unmanned balloon in a public demonstration at
Bladensburg, Maryland. (I-1 - Courtesy of the
Indian Queen Tavern Museum, Bladensburg, Md.)

7

When Michael Collins opened this program, he correctly observed that the bicentennial of flight in America would not occur until 1984, if the balloon flight of Edward Warren of Bladensburg was our take-off date. However, it seems not inappropriate to turn the time-clock back further, and look briefly at several of Benjamin Franklin's earlier interests for launching our historical perspectives.

In 1751, Benjamin Franklin, as a Philadelphian printer, published the first known volume in North America containing an illustration of a pyrotechnic skyrocket (I-2). He published, in the German language for five-hundred Pennsylvania subscribers, a reprinting of a seminal pietist religious work by Johann Arndt. Freely translated, it was titled "True Christianity" (Die Vier Bücher vom wahren Christentum).[13] According to theologian Ernst Benz, who resurrected this illustration in our space era in 1963, the 1751 Pennsylvania reader of Arndt's work of 1628, was admonished to consider a skyrocket as a symbol of Christianity itself. A rocket in flight was striving to reach Heaven, dedicated with total faith by consuming all of its inner resources through "the suffering of fire" until it reached its highest point nearest Heaven.[14] The illustration also showed, to the left, a rocket failure for those lacking true faith.

Professor Benz's fascinating article on "Franklin and the Mystic Rocket" was brought to the attention of the NASA Administrator, James E. Webb, by historian Arthur Schlesinger, Jr., then a special assistant to President John F. Kennedy. Schlesinger made the notation: "You may be entertained by an 18th Century religious interpretation of the rocket."[15] If the mystical interpretation of the rocket had changed by 1963, the technology of rocketry likewise bore little kinship with the ancient art of black powder pyrotechnics. As is well known and elaborated elsewhere, the sky rocket was to become adjunct to the traditional fireworks in America in annual celebration of Independence Day, July 4, 1776. Even Robert H. Goddard, who was to revolutionize rocketry in the twentieth century by first launching a liquid-fuel rocket on March 16, 1926, fired a dozen skyrockets on the 4th of July, 1903.

The powder rocket had, in the meantime, made minor markings on American history by the Congreve "war rockets" used by the British Army in 1814 -- "the rockets' red glare" over Fort McHenry in Baltimore harbor, the battles of Bladensburg and New Orleans, and even the firing of the Nation's Capitol. During the Civil War, President Abraham Lincoln just barely escaped severe injury in the explosion of a rocket at the Navy Gun Factory. Lifeline rockets saved many lives from ships floundering off shore, and, for a time, were used for harpooning whales. But the gunpowder rocket, like the balloon

Ich steige und
läubere mich.

THE "TRUE" ROCKET

In Benjamin Franklin's printing in 1751, of Die
vier Bücher vom wahren Christentum by Johann Arndt. (I-2 -
Courtesy of the Library of Congress.)

9

for purposeful flight other than up and downwind, had little relationship, if any, to the technology leading to large intercontinental ballistic missiles or to space flight. Thomas Parke Hughes commented that a long view must be taken in the history of technology, and particularly in the study of transportation. It must be noted that Robert H. Goddard, as well as Konstantine Tsiolkowsky of Russia, and Hermann Oberth of Translyvania, all looked to space mobility prior to theoretically determining that only liquid-fuel chemical rockets would provide adequate thrust for space mobility. Only the American, Goddard, constructed and flew a rocket. The liquid-fuel rocket made a major contribution to the history of the twentieth century, even to altering the location of Heaven from above the Earth to somewhere beyond the solar system?[16]

The same year Benjamin Franklin published Arndt's volume, in 1751, he also published the first pamphlets on his basic scientific work, Experiments and Observations on Electricity. Probably in June 1752, Franklin flew his famous kite in conducting his experiment in "drawing lightning from the Clouds." He proved that lightning was generic to the static electricity experiments then in vogue. Franklin's kite experiment was duplicated by others in France and England, and his Papers were translated into Italian, German, and Latin. Franklin wrote in his autobiography that it was his kite experiment that "engag'd the public Attention every where."[17] Apparently Franklin did not write a first hand account of his kite experiment. But he wrote elsewhere about the practical need for protecting buildings from lightning and how to ascertain whether clouds were electrically charged. Franklin's curious and practical thoughts and actions can hardly be neglected to initiate a history of the roots of science, of engineering, and of flight in America. Even the Wright brothers, as Paul Garber has pointed out, flew their first glider as a kite.

During the nineteenth century, the romantic but limited capabilities of the balloon demonstrated that it was just as impossible to navigate in the air from one place to another as it was to fly to the moon. Science-oriented fiction permitted imaginative writers to modernize the old dream of flight in air-space, at least free as a bird. Early science-fiction Americana seems to have been rather neglected.[18] Two now better-known examples are inescapable. Jules Verne's From the Earth to the Moon (1865), followed by Around the Moon (1870), were published together and became an international classic. He combined the age-old dream with high drama and considerable technical realism, with the pivotal exception of the infeasible giant cannon to impart the needed velocity to escape the gravity of the earth. Professor Robert Goddard confessed being influenced by Verne's classic, to the extent that he wrote a rocket launching section for it, and never published. He kept space thoughts to himself.

First expression of the idea of a man-made satellite of the earth appeared about the same time. It was The Brick Moon by Edward Everett Hale, a Boston clergyman and later a chaplain of the U.S. Senate. It appeared in serial form in The Atlantic Monthly (1869-70), and was not illustrated. Hale used an inertical device for launching his populated "brick moon," which served as a communications, weather observation, and scientific satellite. It was frequently reprinted but apparently not in Europe, according to the late Willy Ley.[19] But Hale's novel contained the first known explanation of an earth satellite's flight since Sir Isaac Newton illustrated his laws of motion by showing that if a cannon ball would be given sufficient velocity above the denser atmosphere, it would not come down to earth when it was attracted by the force of gravity.[20] With the "discovery" of the Italian astronomer, G. Schiaparelli, that there were canali apparent on the surface of the planet Mars, a rash of Mars-oriented fiction appeared after 1877.

Space travel dreams were to be further deferred in becoming realities by the coming of the practical airplane. The problem of heavier-than-air flight with wings had remained difficult. It awaited combining a light-weight internal combustion engine with Leonardo's "air screw" for locomotion as well as reliable data on the dynamic flow of air for wings with adequate lift, and pilots with controls and skill in operating such a craft. In the 1890's came the successful hang gliders of Lillienthal and others, and the stable Aerodrome model of Samuel P. Langley. By 1908, the improved Wright Flyer was demonstrated and was considered the superior "flying machine" in Europe and the United States.

The history of practical flight in America really begins in the twentieth century, which our examination of some of its roots makes evident. The early airplanes mainly replaced the balloons at county fairs, and performance was to be improved. Subsequent chapters treat slices of the evolution of flight during only the first three-quarters of the twentieth century. Further overall perspectives seem required, other than a great deal happened in a very short period of time since the first powered and controlled flights by the Wright brothers at Kitty Hawk, North Carolina.

As aerospace technology grew useful, it was to be considerably shaped and influenced by the overall historical environment in which it thrived.

THE HISTORICAL ENVIRONMENT

From the powered-glider of the Wrights at Kitty
Hawk in 1903, to NASA's Space Shuttle aborning for the 1980's,
and from Russia's missile-launched sputnik challenge in 1957,
to the achievements of hundreds of useful satellites, Apollo,
Viking and other space probes -- the accelerating rate of
change in the technology of flight, as well as its broadening
influence upon society, has come to characterize the overall
history of aeronautics and astronautics.[21] Flight technology
wrought within several generations shrank the time-distance
size of the earth and its relative place in the solar system.
Techniques of war and peace, as well as scientific inquiry
into universal nature, have been given new meanings.

In the late 1950's, just as man anticipated flight
into space soon, the large jet air transport revolutionized
global transportation for anyone with the price of a ticket.
Intercontinental military power as well as global-legged
statesmen, scientists, politicians, artists, scholars, and
tourists quickly made their mobility felt in world affairs.
Communication, weather, and scientific satellites gave immediate sense of a planetary community. As aerospace technology
was increasingly of dedicated utility to nations and individuals, it nurtured new industries, research establishments,
military commands, trade and commerce, not to mention politico-
social concerns and promise for the future. As a backdrop
for the chapters which follow, some perspectives may enhance
a clearer historical view of the total spectrum involved.

The fragile early airplanes essentially remained
the plaything of devoted mechanics, sportsmen, and daring
pilots in the United States until the coming of the first
worldwide war in 1914. As Walter T. Bonney wrote: "In the
years before World War I, literally hundreds of flying machines
were constructed. Scores became airborne, if only in a
faltering sort of way; a very few flew reasonably well."[22] In
Europe, the descent into war had mobilized the most technically advanced nations. Air forces with supporting industry and
research and development emerged. Despite glamorized combat
in the air, military air power could neither prevent nor
break the deadlocked trench warfare on the Western front. But
for the first time, the organized attempt was made to make
airplanes useful on a large scale. In continental isolation,
the United States' first move was the creation of the National
Advisory Committee for Aeronautics (NACA) in March 1915, to
provide policies and recommendations to help overcome the
obvious deficiences of flight technology as seen in Europe.

FIRST AIRPLANE FLIGHT

By Orville Wright, with Wilbur Wright at wing
tip, at Kitty Hawk, North Carolina, December 17,
1903. (I-3 - courtesy of NASM)

In 1916, the First Aero Squadron, the entire aerial
capability of the U.S. Army Signal Corps, was assigned to
support the punitive campaign against Pancho Villa in northern
Mexico. It destroyed itself by its own operations in the
field. At this same time, German Zeppelin and Gotha bomber
raids had been conducted on London, but the allied air forces
over the trenches in Europe had achieved no decisive results
other than denying uncontested air action by the enemy. Many
specialized aircraft types had appeared in fighters, bombers,
observation, and training aircraft. After the United States
entered the conflict in 1917, American Army pilots exclusively
flew in European aircraft in the heroic individual air combat
highly publicized. Despite the ambitions of American industry
wood-wire-fabric aircraft, as well as the Liberty Engine,
proved difficult to design and mass manufacture from scratch,
and transport to Europe. The war was over before the massive
American buildup could be brought to bear. In 1918, military
air power had yet to prove itself, and mainly because of its
incapacities. Its potentialities in the future seemed evident to airmen, but nothing succeeds like demonstrated success.
Two decades later, the testing of military air power again
began in the crucible of war. It began with the German
blitzkrieg and the Battle of Britain, and once again the U.S.
had over two years to prepare for a conflict. It began at
Pearl Harbor.

In the peace of 1919, aviation institutions survived but were to be altered in the demobilization. The nascent aircraft industry underwent wholesale collapse. The Army and Navy air services had an over-abundance of obsolete aircraft. Military airplanes were not well suited for commercial or private operations, with the exception of the JN-1 Standard and the JN-4 Jenny trainers. This will be covered more in detail in later chapters.

The 1915 charter of the National Advisory Committee for Aeronautics (NACA) -- "to supervise and direct the scientific study of the problems of flight, with a view to their practical solution..." -- proved viable. NACA's odd-dozen-man in-house support group became the Langley Memorial Aeronautical Laboratory when its first wind tunnel became operational in 1920. By that time, the Army Air Service had long ago moved its testing unit from the Aircraft Proving Ground at Langley Field, Virginia, to Dayton, Ohio, while the Navy had moved its flying boats to Norfolk. NACA's Office of Aeronautical Intelligence in Washington, with a branch in Paris, digested all wartime advances and maintained European sources. Thus the NACA broadly defined the foci for its own fundamental aerodynamic research. With modest resources, the leaders of the NACA generated a passion about NACA's "business of research," a non-political virtue enabling it to survive intact through the Great Depression and World War II. The NACA because of the klout of its presidentially-appointed members was to evolve a mission for its in-house laboratory of support for the military services and all of American aviation. Its scientific and engineering knowledge time and again proved useful, and its published reports gained international fame.[23]

In 1916, the NACA had recommended that flying the mail be initiated. Public service by aeronautics was early manifested. Air mail operations began in 1918 by the Army under the Post Office Department. The next year, the Post Office itself took over flying air mail. By 1926, flying air mail was contracted out to air carriers until 1934. Because of conflicts of interest, President Roosevelt cancelled all air mail contracts, and assigned the Army Air Corps the task. Ten Army fliers were killed in accidents between February 20 and March 10, 1934. Air mail was gradually restored to contract operations, and the New Deal decreed that government mail be flown by air. These vicissitudes of aeronautical application for communication were to be spared in the space age. The policy decisions on governmental-private operations were to be debated and hammered out prior to the existence of a practical technology for communications satellites.[24]

During the 1920's the U.S. Army Air Service repeatedly made a series of successful demonstrations of the increasing capability of the airplane. Most notable were the sinking of German warships off the Virginia Capes, "mock air raids" on New York City, aerial surveys, and long distance flights. Brig. General "Billy" Mitchell emerged with his trenchant campaign for an independent air service, challenging the Army General Staff and the U.S. Navy. For this he **was ultimately court-martialled for military insubordination,** not lack of vision. In 1925, however, there was no immediate aerial threat to the security of the United States. Technical progess in aeronautics would ultimately confirm some of "the wild blue yonder" prognosis Mitchell had championed. After the Washington Naval Treaty Convention of 1922, the U.S. Navy had available cruiser hulls with which to program aircraft carriers to increase the role of aviation in the fleet. As is discussed later, the Navy also became interested in the large rigid airship as an airborne aircraft carrier. Meanwhile, commercial air transportation, general aviation, and sport flying was much in evidence, and without much Federal action but considerable newspaper commentary.

Retaining our overall perspectives on the historical environment, the year 1926 was pivotal. President Coolidge created the Morrow Board to answer some of the claims which had been raised by "Billy" Mitchell. The Morrow Board made recommendations that led to the Air Commerce Act of 1926. It was legislated that American aviation clearly had both a military and a civilian sector. Created were Assistant Secretaries for Air in the Army, Navy, and Commerce Departments. Secretary of Commerce Herbert Hoover, himself an engineer by the way, was responsible to foster air commerce, establish airways and aids to navigation, license pilots and certify aircraft for air worthiness, and investigate accidents.[25] This was an important milestone in the history of Federal organization with regard to aeronautics.

1926 was also the year that Professor Robert H. Goddard successfully launched the first liquid-fuel rocket. Like the Wright brothers, Goddard was not federally funded. His demonstration was not publicized but it was indicative of a virgin technology that was to attain its first practical application in wartime in the German V-2 ballistic rocket of World War II. Because of his "moon rocket man" publicity in the New York Times in 1920, Goddard kept his broad scale thoughts about space mobility, as is well known today, to himself. The role of individuals in the history of technology should not be neglected. This, Professor Thomas Hughes submits in Chapter IX. Robert Goddard is well identified in various of the major exhibits of the National Air and Space Museum.

FIRST LIQUID-FUEL ROCKET

Robert H. Goddard with his rocket just prior to
launching at Auburn, Massachusetts, March 16, 1926.
(I-4 - Photo by Esther Goddard, courtesy of NASA)

The solo trans-Atlantic flight to Paris of Charles
A. Lindbergh in the Spirit of St. Louis, May 20-21, 1927,
provided great stimuli to American aviation. A man-made
happening, pumped up in the public mind by a twenty-odd-hour
wait for the answer to the publicized question -- "Where is
Lindy?" -- kept millions of Americans tuned in on their radios.
The great future of aviation was instantly more widely accepted as inevitable by many who had not previously given it a
serious thought. Only the Russian sputnik in October 1957,
and the landing of Armstrong and Aldrin on the surface of the
moon in July 1969, were events comparable to Lindbergh's
singular triumph. In 1927, however, manufacturers were
ready to replace all the worn out war-time surplus Jennies
and Standards with aircraft for everyone as Henry Ford had
done for the automobile.[26] An aviation boom preceded the
crash on Wall Street in 1929, which was to slow things down.
NACA's Langley Laboratory remained the center of aerodynamic
research in the United States. Its basic work on air foils
was augmented by streamlining of cowlings for air-cooled
engines, and filleting, as well as other practical suggestions for industry. It proved the inefficiency of the trimotor, and the best location for efficiency for wing-mounted
engines. A few of the most important concepts for military
aircraft were not initially publicized. NACA did not design

16

CHARLES A. LINDBERGH
Arrival with the Spirit of St. Louis at the Navy
Yard, Washington, D.C. June 11, 1927. (I-5 - NASA)

aircraft. It was the industry that developed the cantilever-wing, monocoque-fuselage, all-metal airplane which revolution-ized commercial and military aviation. It came to be symbol-ized by the Douglas DC-3 airliner and the Boeing B-17 bomber and their offspring. In the early 1930's, American aero-nautics was second to none.

Once again, the European cockpit of world politics presented additional challenges to which American aerial responses would eventually be forthcoming. If Charles A. Lindbergh's flight stimulated aviation in general in the late 1920's, it was the coming of Adolf Hitler to rule in Germany that proved the greatest stimulant to progress in military aviation in the late 1930's. Early in 1933, the new Third Reich set in motion the revival of German military power with an accelerated aircraft construction program, at first of available types and later to advanced models. Germany had been prohibited from having a military air force under the terms of the Treaty of Versailles so that Hitler's decision was as much political as strategic in nature. As Hugh L. Dryden once said: "Germany set out to build a bigger and better NACA, and to a large extent it did."27 When war in Europe was avoided at the Munich appeasement in 1938, the German Air Force achieved its first and greatest strategic victory as Britain and France were humbled because of their apparent deficiencies in military air power. The American

17

aircraft industry was brought out of its post-depression doldrums by British and French orders. Colonel Lindbergh, living in Europe, regularly reported on progress in European air rearmament to General "Hap" Arnold, chief of the Army Air Corps. In November 1938, Lindbergh wrote the Chairman of the NACA, Dr. Joseph Ames, that the design and attainment of a 500 mph airplane was essential if the U.S. was going to overcome its deficiencies in military aviation as compared to Europe, particularly in Nazi Germany. Dr. Ames replied to Lindbergh, who was also a member of the NACA, that "there is now a new atmosphere in Washington. It has been likened to a state of 'peace-time war.'"[28] Ames invited him to take part in NACA's creation of additional laboratories. It was also in 1938, at the urging of General Arnold, that the very first Federal contract for the development of a rocket, one to assist aircraft on take-off or landing, was made. This went to the California Institute of Technology, where Prof. Theodore von Karman was to inspire outstanding contributions to the history of flight, later instituted in the Jet Propulsion Laboratory.

Several major decision in 1940 were to influence the course of the history of aerospace technology. Immediately after the fall of France in May, President Roosevelt called for the production of "50,000 airplanes" in the United States. Industry and airmen gulped, for "FDR" meant annually. In June, the creation of the National Defense Research Committee was approved, later called the Office of Scientific Research and Development (OSRD). It provided for the mobilization of scientists out of uniform. Vannevar Bush, Chairman of the NACA and later head of OSRD, fashioned a technical committee system similar to NACA's. But NACA retained sovereignty over aeronautical research. And finally, Roosevelt made the unpublicized decision to develop an atomic bomb before Nazi Germany. The Manhattan Project under the Army Engineers got that task. It does appear that these pre-Pearl Harbor decisions relating to technology might be more fully understood with regard to the history of flight. Even the Battle of Britain, it would appear, must now be reexamined since the British had broken the German transmission codes. Without tactical early warning, the "narrow margin" victory of the Royal Air Force might not have happened.[29] At minimum, it offers a severe contrast to what happened at Pearl Harbor on December 7, 1941.

Briefly stated here, the course of World War II witnessed a revolution in the art and science of conflict in the air, on the land, on the sea, and, in the homeland of the participating nations within range of enemy aircraft. The United States, except for the Japanese Fugo balloon, was to be spared any assault except on Hawaii and Alaska. It was a wholesale revolution. It was outlined in bold relief by one bomber and one bomb for each atomic attack upon Hiroshima and Nagasaki in August 1945. The "atomic age" was merely the first synonym coined to describe the technological impact of vehicles capable of exploiting air-space and outer space. The "air age," the "jet-atomic age," the "jet-set age," the "missile age," and the "space age" -- these were among the leading labels generated within two eventful decades after World War II. Aerospace technology thus had attained the influence of directly helping shape the historical environ-ment on virtually a global scale.[30]

MOMENTUM AND INTERACTIONS

Daniel J. Boorstin, the Librarian of Congress, has astutely observed: "Technology creates momentum and is irreversible. Nothing can be uninvented..."[31] It was the beginning of space flight in the history of mankind, coming as it did within a dozen eventful years after the end of World War II, which was to assume a historical trajectory of its own. But the convergence of the practical technology for space flight was coupled with interrelated developments of considerable significance of their own in history. There was the revolution in aeronautics, both military and commercial, by the jet-propelled aircraft capable of transoceanic flights without refuelling. The large liquid-fuel rocket was to be upgraded in thrust seriously when, in 1953, it could appear to carry smaller thermonuclear warheads at intercontinental ranges. At the same time, the international scientific community proposed that small, unmanned earth satellites be launched to augmented the worldwide experimentation planned for the International Geophysical Year in the 1957-58 period. A few perspectives seem required to help sort out in general terms the concurrent and complex interactions involved before the "space era" began.

Mobilization of science had been intensified during World War II. The American wartime contribution of the atomic bomb made the great fleets of four-engined propeller-driven bombers with TNT payloads instantly obsolete for a total war in the future. Companion were a host of ingenious OSRD innovations: the proximity fuse, families of guided missiles for all military services, and legion electronic devices in-cluding upgraded radar and computers.[32] These were more than matched by those innovations of Nazi Germany: the first oper-ational turbo-jet and rocket-powered aircraft, snorkel sub-marines, the V-1 "buzz bomb," and the large, supersonic, liquid-fuel ballistic rocket in the V-2. German wartime innovations appeared too late to counter the overwhelming might of conventional Allied ground and air power. The V-2, a costly yet imprecise weapons system launched in large num-bers, could not be countered until its launching sites almost

LAUNCH OF BUMPER-WAC

U.S. Army captured V-2 was mated to JPL Wac
Corporal to achieve a record altitude of 244 miles,
from White Sands, New Mexico, February 29, 1949.
(I-6 - NASA)

two-hundred miles distant from point of impact were neutral-
ized. German innovations were prime spoils of war, and were
available to the victor nations. Key engineers of the large
interdisciplinary team who had developed the V-2 chose to
serve as "prisoners of peace" in the United States. The U.S.
launched the first of its transferred V-2's from the White
Sands Missile Range in New Mexico on April 16, 1946, which
was just the beginning of a notable sounding rocket program
for high altitude scientific research. The Soviet Union
launched its first V-2 in October 1947, which was the same
month that Captain Charles Yeager made the first supersonic
flight by man in the AAF-NACA-Bell X-1 rocket-powered
research airplane at Muroc, California.[33] On February 29,
1949, a V-2 with a Jet Propulsion Laboratory Wac Corporal
rocket as a second stage, called a "Bumper Wac," reached a
record altitude of 244 miles over White Sands. No one in
high places was interested in space flight for it had no
immediate military utility. And,no rocket could possibly
loft a heavy atomic bomb to ranges better served by jet aircraft in the works to replace the B-36.

A so-called "cold war" between the United States and the Soviet Union erected itself all too quickly after the end of World War II. The U.S. had demobilized its wartime forces wholesale and offered to internationalize atomic energy under the newly-created United Nations. The new "air age" geography of great circle air routes around the world made small by the relative swiftness and directness of the airplane was evident, first by military airlift during the war, and then afterwards by commercial airlines. But an "iron curtain," as Winston Churchill called it, from the Baltic to the Black Seas was clanged down by the Kremlin in contiguous Eastern Europe. A Communist China began to arise in Asia. In the United States, the new Department of Defense endorsed the creation by the new U.S. Air Force of a global Strategic Air Command (SAC) and a Continental Air Command for homeland defense. Both were to be weaponed as soon as possible with jet aircraft, and likewise the Navy's aircraft carriers. In 1947, the first serious proposals to launch an earth satellite, perhaps by 1951 -- the Navy Bureau of Aeronautic's "Earth Satellite Vehicle," and the USAF's "World Circling Spaceship" of Project RAND -- were considered "too far out" and never got out of the Pentagon, a fate similar the long-range ballistic missile at this time. The U.S. had an overwhelming bomber superiority in the B-36, except in the eyes of the U.S. Navy. In 1947, lest one forget, the first UFO reports of the modern era appeared, and received as much unscientific media publicity as the growing rivalry among the armed services competing for defense dollars in peace time.[34] The heroic Berlin Airlift began in 1948.[35]

After the USSR tested its first atomic device in 1949, the American monopoly of atomic energy was rudely shattered. Military realities of the "cold war" assumed mushroomed concern. President Truman directed the development of the hydrogen or thermonuclear bomb, one considered to be a thousand times more destructive than an atomic bomb. Steps toward collective security in the North Atlantic Treaty Organization (NATO) in Europe, were also enhanced by Communist aggression in South Korea in June 1950. Mobilization of science and technology was intensified. Appearance of the Soviet Mig-15 swept-wing fighter over the Yalu River in north Korea proved almost a match for the comparable U.S. F-86. Another indicator of Soviet progress in flight technology was the deployment of V-2-type missiles along the NATO front, so the U.S. Army concentrated its rocket R&D at Redstone Arsenal in Alabama, while the U.S. Air Force stepped up its work on "pilotless aircraft" on the Navaho and rocket engine development. Feasibility of thermonuclear warheads came in 1953.

Perspectives should not be slighted by historians on the general technological momentum of which aerospace developments were an important part, and particularly as it contributed to general social influences. Suffice it to say here that emergent was a vast array of practical devices including television and solid-state circuitry, the boom in labor-saving equipments including computers, creature comforts in air conditioning and automated household appliances, not to ignore improved anti-biotics and eventually "the pill." These cummulative advances on a broad scale were part and parcel of the evolution of what became known as "the affluent society," to which the jet airliner gave global legs. In the year 1958, it was the first year that the total number of transatlantic air passengers exceeded the number of sea passengers. The jet airliner conquered the ocean liner within several swift years and tourists found the world a very small place. Even private aviation boomed beyond expectations.

At the same time, however, a potential for doomsday, which was erected as a deterrent to an all-out thermonuclear war, became a reality with jet bombers by 1955, and next by long-range ballistic missiles in the early 1960's. When the Soviet "Bison" heavy-jet bomber first appeared in 1955, an aircraft comparable to the American B-52, "Air Power" hearings grabbed the spotlight on Capitol Hill. In the meantime, President Eisenhower had approved the ICBM program in 1954, and the IGY satellite project in 1955, the latter to launch a scientific experiment in outer space for international science and not to interfer with the urgent ballistic missile program. Intermediate-ranged ballistic missiles (IRBM's) of both the Air Force and the Army were approved, along with the Navy submarine-based Polaris. As it turned out, it was the Soviet Union which placed its IGY test satellite atop an ICBM rocket and launched Sputnik I on October 4, 1957. Though it was no great surprise to the R&D community, it was a rude shock to the American people that the "backward" Russians had achieved a first in the technology of flight. What was most evident, however, was that the USSR possessed a rocket capable of launching a TN weapon at intercontinental ranges. The "missile race" and the "space age" became twin concerns at the same moment of history, which was to account for some of the confusion which reigned in the post-Sputnik environment in the United States.

PHASES OF THE SPACE ERA OF FLIGHT

In the central entrance hall of the National Air and Space Museum are the prime artifacts and replicas identifying the "Milestones of Flight." Without being critical in the slightest, one might raise a basic question: Have most of the several millions of visitors of all ages noted the replica of Sputnik I in that Hall? It is only about the size of a beach ball. Or, nearby, just above the Apollo moon rock have these visitors noted the replica of the first U.S. earth satellite, Explorer I? And, one might wonder, just how the Apollo generation of American youth come to appreciate the significance of two very small, ancient, and now de-orbited satellites in American history? If the first Russian Sputnik was to prove historically significant, why was a civilian space agency, the National Aeronautics and Space Administration, later known worldwide as "NASA," created by the White House and the Congress during the heyday of the "cold war"? If a Manhattan Project was created to develop the atomic bomb, why not a similar organization for space?

Why did it happen, when NASA was thirty months old, that the second American President in the space era of mankind, John F. Kennedy, set in motion his decision that American astronauts would be landed on the surface of the moon before 1970? This decision was essentially made before the first American flew in an up and down space flight, Alan Shepard on May 5, 1961. This first Mercury mission seemed to enforce a momentum to mount a priority and open enterprise making a manned lunar mission a national goal. The approval of the Congress for the Apollo program imperative came six months before the first American orbited in space.

As the Soviet Sputnik became the historic catalyst for organizing a full-spectrum U.S. space program at the outset, it was the first flight by any man in space that was to initiate the second phase of the space era, the race for the moon. The first man to circle the earth in space was a Major in the Soviet Air Force, Yuri Gagarin, who, on April 12, 1961, set in motion the second phase of the space age which peaked when Apollo 11 astronauts, Armstrong and Aldrin, first stepped upon the surface of the moon. A few perspectives on the beginning of the space era of flight during the past two decades seem in order. Such are by way of introduction to Chapters VII and VIII, both of which treat well the manned and instrumented aspects of astronautics.

The initial phase of the so-called "space age" was to be greatly influenced by military priorities with regard to the ballistic missile crisis. Army General James Gavin

called the impact of Sputnik I as a "technological Pearl
Harbor." Yet it was the sheer novelty of the first orbital
flight by a man-made object that had widespread impact. It
aroused scientific interest in space flight on a wide scale
and appealed to imaginative minds on the prospects of exploring the universe. Circling the earth every 96.2 minutes at
18,000 mph, Sputnik I was an indentifiable flying object that,
despite its size, erected the long-held query about mankind's
place in the universe. Thus the space implications of Sputnik
were sustained. It was additional to the central military
concern posed by the missile birth of the rocketry making
space flight possible. On August 26, 1957, five weeks before
Sputnik I, the USSR had announced that it had successfully
tested a multi-stage ICBM, which the Soviet satellite clearly
confirmed. For the first time in American history, a potential enemy genuinely possessed a basic technology to inflict
massive nuclear destruction directly upon the North American
heartland. An operational ICBM had to be assumed ready soon.

Sputnik I, above all else, stimulated an unprecedented news media orgy, fanned by "expert" opinions expressed
from all sectors of aroused concern, and daily animated by
cartoonists in the press, by all manner of ready commentators
and was not ignored by the Kremlin. Several White House
spokesmen inflamed the public dialogue by ill-informed
disparaging comments, one comparing the sputnik to "a hunk of
iron," another expressing extreme disinterest in "the basket-
ball game in outer space." Yet, it was to take about four
long months before the first U.S. earth satellite was launched.
Until it was, even President Eisenhower would find it
difficult to explain why the USSR had a larger ICBM rocket
apparent with Sputnik, or why he had sought to keep space out
of the armament race by deciding that the Vanguard satellite
would not utilize a military rocket in the name of international science.[36] Long after the space era entered the second
phase, former President Eisenhower insisted: "What was more
important than keeping space peaceful?"[37]

Army spokesmen pointed out right after Sputnik I,
that it could have been possible to have launched a simple
satellite, one without a scientific payload, with its Jupiter-
C a year before October 4, 1957. The Air Force sought to
demonstrate its Atlas ICBM rocket in a full-range test as
soon as possible. "Bird watchers" on the beach near Cape
Canaveral now reported every rocket failure or presumed
success, including Vanguard which could not seem to get off
the launching pad into orbit. None of the first generation
of large rockets ever worked very well in their gestation.
In his first post-Sputnik address, President Eisenhower said:
"What the world needs now is not a giant leap into space, but
a giant step toward peace."[38] He did successfully convey
confidence in U.S. military superiority in October 1957, and

for the future. Indeed, there was never to be proven a
"missile gap" during the Eisenhower Administration, or
in the early 1960's, which was contrary to some of the campaign oratory in the elections of 1960. The one thing that
the sputniks achieved was to accelerate R&D for the second
and third generations of ICBM's.

Sputnik II was orbited on November 3, 1957. It
dramatically carried a little Russian dog. The Senate Preparedness Investigating Subcommittee under Lyndon B. Johnson,
Senate Majority Leader, now initiated open hearings from
mostly military witnesses on "Missiles and Satellites." The
unclassified hearings were programmed on live TV. Edward
Teller and Wernher von Braun were the only two all-out space
advocates in the entire series of hearings into 1958. Many
questions were asked by the Senators as to why the sputniks
had happened. The Soviet technological drive, including
ballistic missiles, since 1947, was more than confirmed.[39]
Upon reflection and re-reading the record, Congressional
leaders and the President, politics aside, publicly appeared
to agree that national security tasks took immediate prece-
dence over initial space deficiencies, a premise which seems
often tilted by Lyndon B. Johnson"s later leading role in
helping to shape the legislation for the national space program[39] Speeding the Atlas ICBM development, along with both
the Army Jupiter and Atlas Thor IRBM's for early deployment
to NATO sites, the ready-alert status of SAC's bomber forces,
and early warning for continental air defenses to include
Soviet ballistic missiles -- these were among the prime sub-
jects of high concern during 1957 on Capitol Hill. Congressional oversight dug deeply into Pentagon management practices
permitting a "missile mess" and to avoid another "technological surprise" such as the sputniks. On space, launching of
the first American satellite would not be accelerated by
starting a new program. The President had already directed
that the Army Jupiter-C team as a backup satellite launching
system should Vanguard fail in future attempts. The Army
satellite was assigned an IGY scientific experiment, one
devised by James A. Van Allen. It is interesting to note that
during November 1957, there were 414 sightings of "UFO's," a
record frequency.[40]   On November 27, the President had
suffered a "mild stroke," placing responsibility on his staff.

Immediately after Sputnik II, President Eisenhower,
requiring objective and dispassionate advice, had appointed
James R. Killian, President of M.I.T., as his Science Adviser.
Killian would also chair the President's Science Advisory
Committee (PSAC), which also would report directly. Killian's
first task was to appoint panels in PSAC to assist in sorting
out roles and missions in the Pentagon's R&D. Both the Army
and the Air Force had vocal space champions, who openly
claimed R&D jurisdiction because of apparent competence in

rocketry and related technology. Reconnaissance and communications satellite systems appeared to have military implications for the near future, while manned space flight was considered the key for space operations in the distant future. Creation of an Advanced Research and Development Agency (ARPA) by the Department of Defense was announced as a means of managing dollar control of duplicative R&D by the military services. In the meantime, ARPA was to serve as an interim focus for selecting earth satellite and space probe projects from among the hundreds proposed after the sputniks. And, the National Advisory Committee for Aeronautics under Chairman James H. Doolittle, who was also Chairman of the U.S. Air Force Scientific Advisory Board, sought to stake out an up-graded mission. It created a Special Committee on Space Technology, under H. Guyford Stever of M.I.T., to make recommendations on how NACA could serve needs for space as it had done for aeronautics for forty-three years.[41]

Scientists in military laboratories and on campuses, increasingly voiced their concern that military priorities in space would not correct the situation which had helped to contribute to the low priorities for the Vanguard, or serve genuine interests in the study of nature in outer space. The American Rocket Society, the Rocket and Satellite Research Panel, and others associated with the International Geophysical Year made proposals for an independent space agency. Dr.

NACA COMMITTEE ON SPACE TECHNOLOGY

Known as the "Stever Committee" after its chairman, members were selected as key representatives of fields in space technology. They are pictured here at a meeting at the Lewis Laboratory in Cleveland in March 1958. Members are identified in Note 41. (I-7 - NACA/NASA)

Lloyd V. Berkner, one of the architects of the IGY and later first president of the Space Science Board of the National Academy of Sciences, described Sputnik, as follows: "From the vantage point of 2100 A.D., the year 1957 will most certainly stand in history as the year of man's progression from a two-dimensional to a three-dimensional geography. It may well stand, also, as the point in time at which intellectual achievement forged ahead of weapons and national wealth as instruments of national policy. The earth satellite is a magnificent expression of man's intellectual growth -- of his ability to manipulate to his own purpose the very laws that govern his universe."[42] Scientists who had used rockets as research tools, starting with the captured V-2's, remained vocal on making sure that whatever space organization might be established would include fundamental scientific missions. This also included the international aspects of science in which a military aegis might be a constraint.

On December 6, 1957, the Vanguard TV-3 test launch blew up on the pad at Cape Canaveral. It had been billed in the press as the American answer to the Soviet sputniks although only if everything worked perfectly would a grapefruit-size test satellite gain an orbit. Its crash downward to the pad through flames and smoke was also carried on live television. The crisis continued. Panels of PSAC debated Christmas-week 1957 in the Executive Office Building on how best the U.S. space program might be organized to serve all national needs. Difficulties would arise if the space mission was assigned to either the Army or the Air Force. Minimal disruption by giving all space responsibility to ARPA of the Defense Department seemed not the lasting answer and it had the main virtue of serving national defense above service interests. The thought early arose that perhaps the NACA, with its demonstrated experience in dealing with the military services, industry, and academe might be the best focus to get the non-military space program started. There was no clear-cut recommendation to make to the President yet, at least until a Vanguard or an Army Jupiter-C team, both under pressure, succeeded in launching the first U.S. satellite. Meanwhile, the Atomic Energy Commission and the NACA both stepped up their planning to make their cases for a share of the space program. The Congress too became impatient.

With the launching of the first U.S. earth satellite by an Army Jupiter-C on January 31, 1958, Explorer I, the way was now opened to organize the national space program. Everyone seemed to breath a sign of relief that America had finally started flight in space almost four months after Sputnik I. President Eisenhower asked Dr. Killian to come up with a recommendation. The Organization and Management division of the Bureau of the Budget prepared a staff study on space organization. PSAC panels on space and organization made

LAUNCH OF <u>EXPLORER I</u>

The first American satellite was launched by
an Army Jupiter-C with Jet Propulsion Laboratory upper
stages, at Cape Canaveral, January 31, 1958 (I-8 - NASA)

recommendations. Two presentations were made by PSAC space
panelists, one to the National Security Council, the other
to the Cabinet. Eisenhower attended both. On March 5, 1958,
the recommendation was made to the President, which he approved,
that a non-military space program would be instituted in
a "reconstituted NACA," leaving space projects of military
interest within the Department of Defense. While the houses
of the Congress organized special space committees to review
White House legislative recommendations, two key papers now
moved swiftly to completion in the White House: First, was
the Administration bill to submit to the Congress by early
April 1958. Secondly, the President's Science Advisory
Committee drafted a rationale, one entitled "Introduction to
Outer Space," which was issued on March 26, with a foreword
by President Eisenhower. PSAC called it a "space primer,"
and indeed it was very well received across the nation. Most
important, however, it served to explain what space exploration meant to the long term interests of the nation and of
mankind. Four factors gave "urgency and inevitability to
advancement of space technology: (1) the compelling urge of
man to explore the unknown; (2) the need to assure that full
advantage is taken of the military potential of space; (3)
the effect of national prestige of accomplishment of space
science and exploration; and (4) the opportunities for
scientific observation and experimentation which will add to

our knowledge of the earth, the solar system, and the universe."
On April 2, President Eisenhower sent a message to the Congress
indicating his legislative intent to create NASA, leaving to the
Department of Defense those elements of the space program for
national security needs. Late in the afternoon of April 2, the
White House's space bill was transmitted to the Congress, and
the next day a bill to reorganize the DOD was transmitted. Both
bills were not introduced in both houses of the Congress until
April 14, after the traditional Easter recess.[43]

      Sufficient to our overall perspectives here, the
legislative process on Capitol Hill clearly endorsed, as a
national decision, the intent of the legislation sent up to
it by the White House. The preamble of the National Aeronautics and Space Act of 1958, retained Eisenhower's intent:
"It is the policy of the United States that activities in
space should be devoted to peaceful purposes for the benefit
of all mankind." But the workings of the Senate Special
Committee on Space under Lyndon B. Johnson were certainly to
beef up authorities given the new space agency in the legislation, made certain that the White House coordinate all
space matters through a National Aeronautics and Space Council
in the White House, and provide for international cooperation.
In this, Johnson was aided by the House Committee under John
W. McCormack. The important perspective is that within a
year after the beginning of space flight, the United States
had legislated that space affairs had the broadest possible
significance. This was comparable to the slower-paced but
similar recognition given to aeronautics in the Air Commerce
Act of 1926 some twenty-three years after the Wright brothers'
first flights, and seven years after the end of World War I.[44]
President Eisenhower signed the so-called "Space Act" on July
29, 1958. NASA Admistrator T. Keith Glennan and Deputy Dryden
were confirmed in August, and NASA acquired responsibility to
complete non-military space projects underway in the services
and plan and initiate a space program for its own sake. This
is elsewheres elaborated in some detail.[45] But NASA did
carve out a place for itself in history which was to be wholly
based upon its ability to mobilize talent and resources toward
agreed-upon goals. Its open information policy and its very
strong support from the Congress proved hallmarks for its
success in achieving that which it set out to do.

      While the second phase of the era of space flight
was to be dominated by the Apollo commitment, which is likewise evident in Chapters VII and VIII, it proved to be one of
the greatest peacetime engineering enterprises which has yet
to be duplicated by anyone else.[46] Life on "spaceship Earth"
was never to be the same again. The dynamism of new knowledge
from nature in outer space raises new scientific questions and
new demands for technology and new blessings and new problems.

No conclusion that the challenge of space flight remains anything other than an endless frontier for mankind seems valid
from historical perspectives.[47] For this appreciation we surely
are endebted to the Bicentennial Year and the National Air
and Space Museum for prodding our reflections.

POSTSCRIPT PERSPECTIVES

The history of flight in America began with the kite
of Benjamin Franklin in 1751 and the balloon of Peter Carnes
in 1784. Not until the twentieth century did aeronautics
eventually have significant cultural influence on a broad
scale beyond random transportation of things and people. Then
came astronautics which had an unprecedent impact upon the
thoughts and ways of mankind within a few swift years. The
kindergarden phases of man's initial venture into outer space
proved at once to be a revolutionary tool of basic science, a
national instrumentality for power and prestige, a prod for
both international cooperation and competition, and, a viable
projection of man's historic quest to explore the furthest
reaches of his accessible environment.

Prospects for the so-called "space shuttle" as a
genuine space transportation carrier suggests confirmation of
the "space travel" dreams of the 1920's in the 1980's. Until
anything happens, however, often some of the earlier thoughts
about the possible meaning of the space era of mankind offer
appreciations. A half dozen years before the sputniks,
Arthur C. Clarke, the philosopher and professor of the British
Interplanetary Society, wrote in his prescient volume,
The Exploration of Space, as follows: "Fifty years from now,
instead of preparing for the conquest of the planets, our
grandchildren may be dispossessed savages clinging to the
fertile oases in a radioactive wilderness. We must keep the
problems of today in their true proportions: they are of vital
 -- indeed supreme -- importance, since they can destroy civilization and slay the future before its birth. But if we can
survive them, they will pass into history, and the time will
come when they will be as little remembered as the causes of
the Punic Wars. The crossing of space -- even the sense of
its imminent achievement in the years before it comes -- may
do much to turn men's minds outwards and away from their
present tribal squabbles."[48]

Just as mankind's space enterprise got underway,
the NACA Special Committee on Space Technology submitted its
final report during NASA's first official month, October 1958.
In its introduction, it was said: "Scientifically, we are at
the beginning of a new era. More than two centuries between
Newton and Einstein were occupied by observations, experiments,
and thoughts that produced the background for modern science.

New scientific knowledge indicates that we are already working in a similar period preceding another long step forward in scientific theory. The information obtained from direct observation in space, of environment and of cosmological processes will probably be essential to, and will certainly assist in, the formulation of new unifying theories. We can no more predict the results of this work than Galileo could have predicted the industrial revolution that resulted from Newtonian mechanics."[49]

And at the outset of the space era of flight, sage Hugh L. Dryden observed: "We must understand that the kind and magnitude of the program that our national interest requires will cost hundreds of millions of dollars each year for years to come. I know that some knowledgeable people fear that although we might be willing to spend a couple of billions for space technology in 1958, because we still remember the humiliation of Sputnik last October, next year we will be so preoccupied by color television, or new style cars, or the beginning of another national election campaign, that we will be unwilling to pay another year's installment on our space conquest bill. For that to happen -- well, I'd just as soon we didn't start. Fortunately for the sake of our children's future if not for the protection of our own skin, I do not think we are that grasshopper minded..."[50]

Will mankind succeed in finding a destiny in outer space?

REFERENCE NOTES for Chapter I, "Introduction":

1. Hugh L. Dryden, "The Next Fifty Years," Aero Digest
(July 1953), offprint copy of text, p. 6. This was written
when he was the Director of the NACA. Dryden saw his first
airplane in 1910, and was fond of saying in later years that
he and the airplane grew up together. Most recent biography
is the author's, "Astronautical Biography: Hugh Latimer Dryden,
1898-1965," Journal of the Astronautical Sciences, vol. 25
(April-June 1977), in press.

2. As quoted in Shirley Thomas, Men of Space, vol. 2
(Philadelphia: 1961), p. 87.

3. Statement of George F. Will, on CBS-TV program, "Agron-
sky and Company," January 1, 1977, WTOP-TV (Washington, D.C.,
7-7:30 p.m.), which apparently did not appear in any of Mr.
Will's columns. He more recently received a Pulitzer Prize.

4. Melvin Kranzberg, "Historical Perspectives on the
Space Program," Georgia Tech Alumnus, vol. 51 (Spring 1973),
p. 8.

5. Douglas A. Lawson, "Pterosaur from the Latest Cretaceous of West Texas:Discovery of the Largest Flying Creature,"
Science, vol. 187 (March 14, 1975), pp. 947-48, and cover
comparing wing span of Pterosaur to YB-49 aircraft and Condor;
Cf. William M. Stokes, Essentials of Earth History: An Introduction to Historical Geology (Englewood Cliffs, N.J.: 1966),
p. 277.

6. Samuel P. Langley, "The Greatest Flying Creature,"
Annual Report of the Smithsonian Institution for 1901 (1902),
pp. 648-58. Langley used the term "pterodactyl," meaning "a
brother to dragons," which most closely resembled the wing
area-weight ratio of his Aerodrome model. He also clearly
distinguished between soaring and flapping birds. Cf. M. J.
B. Davy, Interpretative History of Flight, "Flight in Nature,"
(London: 1945), pp. 1-2 -- a classic work.

7. On the Wrights, Charles Gibbs-Smith of the Victoria
and Albert Museum in London is the world's authority on the
airplane before 1910. See his chapter XI, "The Invention of
the Airplane," in The History of Flight (New York: 1954), pp.
223-34; and, "The Wright Brothers and the Invention of the
Practical Aeroplane, 1899-1905," in Aviation: An Historical
Survey (London: 1970), pp. 94-104; Walter T. Bonney, The
Heritage of Kitty Hawk (New York: 1962); and Paul A. Garber,
The National Aeronautics Collection (Smithsonian Institution
Pub. 4255: 1965), pp. 32-40.

8. Best authoritative account of Peter Carnes' balloons
is John M. Walton, "A Brief History of the George Washington
House," (Unpublished manuscript, Prince Georges County, Md.,
1974), pp. 3-9. The Indian Queen Tavern Museum, Bladensburg,
Md., the former residence of Carnes, was restored as a Bicentennial Project of the State of Maryland, and was also

known as the "George Washington House."

9. Jeremiah Milbank, Jr., The First Century of Flight in America (Princeton, N.J.: 1943), p. v. Newspaper account of Warren's flight in the Maryland Journal and Baltimore Advertiser, June 25, 1784, is reproduced in J. Jobe (ed.), The Romance of Ballooning (NY: 1971), p. 41.

10. Milbank, pp. 21-23. Milbank's singular work helped to stimulate numerous works. See Courtney G. Brooks, "American Aeronautics as Spectacle and Sport," Ph.D. Dissertation, Tulane University, 1969, 241pp.; and Tom D. Crouch, "The American Aeronautical Community and the Problem of Heavier-than-Air Flight, 1885-1905," Ph.D. Dissertation, Ohio State University, 1976, winner of the AIAA History Manuscript Prize for 1977.

11. Cf. Francis Trevelyn Miller, The World in the Air: The Story of Flying in Pictures, 2 vols. (N.Y.: 1930); Alvin M. Josephy (ed.), The American Heritage History of Flight (N.Y.: 1962).

12. See Chapter II. On Franklin, see Abbott L. Rotch, "Benjamin Franklin and the First Balloons," Proceedings of the American Antiquarian Society, vol. 18 (April 1907), pp. 259-75, as cited in Brooks, pp. 2-3; Milbank, pp. 4-10, 23-29.

13. Johann Arndt, Die Vier Bücher vom wahren Christentum. (Philadelphia: 1751), p. 868. Franklin's edition was from the Leipzig edition of 1728, over a century after Arndt first published it in 1612, from whence the illustration came.

14. Ernst Benz, "Franklin and the Mystic Rocket," The American-German Review (June-July 1963), pp. 24-26.

15. Memorandum from Arthur Schlesinger, Jr., to James E. Webb, July 23, 1963, copy in the NASA Historical Archives. The author is endebted to Mr. Webb for routinely making a copy of this memorandum, with a copy of Benz's article, available to the NASA History Office.

16. See E. Emme, A History of Space Flight (N.Y.: 1965), and (ed.), The History of Rocket Technology (Detroit: 1964).

It is antiquarian, but should be noted here, that the first mention made of use of a signal rocket in America was by Captain John Smith on July 8, 1608. During his exploration of the Chesapeake Bay, he anchored his ship at an Indian village near present-day Hampton, Virginia, location of the NASA Langley Research Center. Smith later wrote: "In the evening we fired a few rakets [sic], which flying in the ayre so terrified the Salvages [sic], they supposed nothing impossible we attempted, and desired to assist us." John Smith, The Generall Historie of Virginia, New England, and the Sumner Isle (London: 1624), as cited in draft manuscript by the NASM's Frank Winter, "U.S. Pyrotechnology Before World War I," p. 1.

17. The Autobiography of Benjamin Franklin, ed. by Leonard W. Labaree, R.L. Ketchum, H. C. Boatfield, and Helene H. Fineman (New Haven, Conn.: 1964), Text and editor's notes, pp. 240-47; and "Introduction," by the editors, pp. 1-40.

REFERENCE NOTES (I - Continued)

18. A rich body of Americana has been neglected on all the hoaxes, science fiction, and imaginary hardware conceived for flight during the nineteenth century, a conclusion very usefully developed by Barbara Wood, "Early American Thought on Space Science and Technology," NASA Historical Note No. 97, September 1969, 61 pp.

19. Emme, Space Flight, pp. 83-94. European rocket buffs of the 1920's very thoroughly unearthed all possible history of gunpowder rocketry and imaginary space travel, as was evident in Willy Ley's editions with numerous printings of Rockets, Missiles, and Space Travel, between 1949-1968. Only in the last edition, in 1968, did Ley include E. E. Hale's The Brick Moon. The late Mr. Ley came to the U.S. in 1935.

20. Outstanding discussion and documentation of Sir Isaac Newton's illustration of orbital flight is, Sir Bernard Lovell, The Origins and International Economics of Space Exploration (N.Y.: 1973), pp. 1-3. Early scientific mathematics of trajectories was developed by artillerists. See the classic work, A. R. Hall, Ballistics in the Seventeenth Century (N.Y.: 1952), 181 pp.

21. I have drawn freely from my "Perspectives on Space Exploration," Aerospace Historian, vol. 11 (January 1960), pp. 83-94; "Historical Perspectives on Apollo," Journal of Spacecraft and Rockets, vol. 5 (April 1968), pp. 369-82; and, "Space and the Historian," Spaceflight (BIS), vol. 11 (November 1973), pp. 411-17.

22. Bonney, p. 141.

23. On founding and early years of the NACA, see Bonney, pp. 172-89; Jerome C. Hunsaker, "Forty Years of Aeronautical Research, 1915-1955," Smithsonian Report for 1955 (Washington: 1956), pp. 241-71, and Final Report of the NACA (Washington: 1958), pp. 3-27.

24. Arnold E. Briddon and E.A. Champie, FAA: Historical Fact Book -- A Chronology, 1926-1963 (Washington, DC: 1965), pp. vii-2.

25. Briddon and Champie, pp. 1-9. It is pertinent to compare the National Aeronautics and Space Act of 1958, which organized the U.S. space program (it created a civil NASA and left military space matters to the Department of Defense). This is best contrasted in Arthur Levine, The Future of the Space Program (N.Y.: 1975), as he drew from his doctoral dissertation on the NACA.

26. Cf. R. T. Jones, "Recollections from an Earlier Period of Aeronautics," American Review of Fluid Mechanics, vol. 9 (1977), pp. 1-17; and, "Fifty Years of Flight: How Lindbergh's 33 Hours Changed the World," series of articles in Saturday Review (April 16, 1977), pp. 6-42.

27. Hugh L. Dryden, Testimony, "Hearings... NASA Authorization .....," U.S. Congress, House Committee on Science and Astronautics, Pt. 1 (February 4, 5, 7, 1964), pp. 16-20.

28. Letters, from C. A. Lindbergh to J. Ames, Chairman of the NACA, November 9, 1938 (3pp.), and November 28, 1938 (18 pp.), and Ames' reply of December 7, 1938 (1p.), in NASA Historical Archives.

29. F. W. Winterbotham, The Ultra Secret (N.Y.: 1974), pp. 67-87, and particularly the Foreword by Sir John Slessor, pp. 12-14. This is far from a satisfying historical treatment but it is most suggestive. It was my pleasure to discuss the reciprocal aspects of the British-German air contest and particularly the turning points of the Battle of Britain with Lord Dowding, when he came to the Air War College to lecture in 1951. Fortunately, the Germans did not know how close it was.

30. E. M. Emme (ed.), The Impact of Air Power: National Security and World Politics (Princeton, N.J.: 1959), passim. Recent years have been devoted to study in detail with access to newly available documents with regard to the coming of the sputniks and the subsequent "space race" aspects of the Cold War. This will be elaborated in a forthcoming volume.

31. Daniel J. Boorstin, "Tomorrow: The Republic of Technology," Time, vol. 109 (January 17, 1977), pp. 36-38.

32. James P. Baxter, 3rd, Scientists Against Time (Boston: 1947), the overall treatment of the OSRD histories, known as the Science In World War II Series; Vannevar Bush, Pieces of of the Action (N.Y.: 1970), an outstanding memoir.

33. Richard Hallion, Supersonic Flight (N.Y.: 1972), and on Soviet rocketry and space initiatives, see Nicholas Daniloff, The Kremlin and the Cosmos (N.Y.: 1972).

34. No evidence has yet been found to show that any satellite proposal reached the White House during the Truman Administration. Early U.S. satellite proposals are best covered in R. Cargill Hall, in The History of Rocket Technology, pp. 67-93.

35. The breadth of the acceleration of technological advances, particularly with regard to aerospace technology, may be surveyed by skimming a mere chronology. See Aeronautics and Astronautics, 1915-1960 (Washington: 1961), pp. 63-93.

36. Best summaries of the impact of the Soviet sputniks, those without over-drawn hindsight, are: William Manchester, The Glory and the Dream: A Narrative History of America, 1932-1972 (N.Y.: 1974), "Beep Beep," pp. 787-813; Constance McL. Green and Milton Lomask, Vanguard: A History (Washington: 1971), pp. 185-212, and the foreword by Charles A. Lindbergh, pp. v-viii; Enid Bok Shoettle, "The Establishment of NASA," in Knowledge and Power, edited by S. A. Lakoff (N.Y.: 1960), pp. 162-270. Much remains to sort out of the significant unpublicized or classifed reactions within the Federal establishment, as well as the role of the mass news media worldwide and of the Kremlin, for genuine historical treatment. Herbert F. York's Race to Oblivion: A Participant's View of the Arms Race (N.Y.: 1970), neither a memoir nor a history, offers very useful insights, pp. 106-146.

37. General Eisenhower repeated this statement three times with increasing emphasis during an interview by Constance McL. Green and E. M. Emme , Gettysburg, PA, November 8, 1966, which was not recorded. He, while President, often said: "We have no enemies on the Moon."

38. On November 7, 1957, Public Papers, D.D. Eisenhower, 1957, p. 230.

39. U.S. Senate, Committee on Armed Services, Preparedness Investigating Subcommittee, Hearings...on Satellite and Missile Programs, November 27, 1957-January 23, 1958. Mr. Johnson later chaired the Senate Special Committee on Space and Astronautics, and, after passage of the National Aeronautics and Space Act of 1958, was the first chairman of the standing Senate Committee on Aeronautical and Space Sciences. With his space age role as Vice President and President, Lyndon B. Johnson had the longest space involvement of any high elected official.

40. Paris Flammonde, UFO's Exist (N.Y.: 1976), p. 288, which attempts to be a sober summary. Compare David R. Carlson, "UFO's: The Air Force and the UFO," Aerospace Historian, vol. 21 (December 1974), p. 214, and I. Habana and J. Weverbergh, UFO's From Behind the Iron Curtain (N.Y.: 1975), 302pp.

41. See Robert Rosholt, "NACA's Reaction to Sputnik," An Administrative History of NASA (Washington: 1966), pp. 34-36. Much newly-available evidence elaborates more meaningfully the reasons for the ultimate success of the NACA strategy to become the nucleus of NASA. The so-called "Stever Committee" on Space Technology served to animate the entire NACA organization during its agency-wide visits, and also clearly demonstrated NACA's ability to inter-relate with the R&D community with regard to mounting a space program. Its impact was felt during its existence, not when it submitted its final reports after NASA was already in being.

Photograph (I-7) shows the following members (right to left), as follows: Wernher von Braun (ABMA), Abe Silverstein (NACA Lewis), Dale R. Corson (Cornell Univ.), Hugh L. Dryden (NACA Director), Carl B. Palmer (NACA, Committee Sec'y), J.R. Dempsey (General Dynamics), Robert R. Gilruth (NACA Langley), H. Julian Allen (NACA Ames), Milton U. Clauser (Ramo-Wooldridge), Samuel K. Hoffman (NAA Rocketdyne), W. Randolph Lovelace (Lovelace Clinic), Hendrik W. Bode (in back, Bell Tele. Lab.), Abraham Hyatt (Navy BuAer), Colonel Norman C. Appold, USAF (arm on table, ARDC), and Edward R. Sharp (NACA Lewis). Not present were James A. Van Allen (Univ. of Iowa) and William H. Pickering (JPL).

Paralleling steps of NACA to assume a central role in the civil portion of the national space program, was the involvement of a central role in the Department of Defense by the U. S. Air Force. Best available summaries are John T. Greenwood, "The Air Force Ballistic Missile and Space Program," Aerospace

(41 continued) Historian, vol. 21 (December 1974), pp. 195-197; and Thomas Sturm, The USAF Scientific Advisory Board, 1944-1964 (Washington, D.C.: 1967), pp. 80-88.

42. Lloyd V. Berkner, "The Impact of Sputnik," Foreign Affairs, vol. 36 (January 1958), pp. 221-31, reprinted in Impact of Air Power, pp. 849-55.

43. President Eisenhower wanted both bills passed as soon as possible, and the Congress moved quickly on the space bill.

44. The legislative process is partially summarized in Alison Griffith, The National Aeronautics and Space Act (Washington: 1962), and Enid Bok Shoettle, "The Establishment of NASA," op.cit. A fuller history would seem desired.

45. See Rosholt, Administrative History, pp. 40-48, and passim. It is interesting to note that NASA Administrator Glennan always carried a copy of the Space Act, which was to be cited chapter and verse in his discusions in NASA and in the Pentagon on what and how things should be done to fulfill NASA's charter.

46. On the historic decision of President John F. Kennedy to send Americans to the moon "before this decade is out," announced on May 25, 1961, see Emme, "Perspectives on Apollo," Journal of Spacecraft and Rockets, vol. 5 (April 1968), pp. 377-380, John M. Logsdon, The Decision to Go to the Moon (Chicago: 1976, a revised edition).

47. Thoughts on the long-term future of astronautics from a historical point of view have elsewhere been stated: "Astronautics and the Future," Impact of Air Power, pp. 844-848, and "The Challenge of Space," in Melvin Kranzberg and Carroll Pursell (eds.), Technology in Western Civilization, vol. 2 (N.Y.: 1968), pp. 673-86. Prognosis is not the historian's province. Also note, Sir Bernard Lovell, The Overall Picture and the Future," The Origins and International Economics of Space Exploration (N.Y.: 1973), pp. 88-89.

48. Arthur C. Clarke, The Exploration of Space (New York: 1951), p. 194.

49. NACA/NASA Special Committee on Space Technology, "Recommendations Regarding a National Civil Space Program," October 28, 1958, p. 2.

50. Hugh L. Dryden, speech to the Air Force Association, April 20, 1958, in NASA Historical Archives.

PART I—AEROSTATICS,1784-1976

I I

BALLOONING IN THE UNITED STATES
FROM STRAW TO PROPANE

Roger Pineau*

A buoyant review of the history of ballooning from
its inception in France to its appearance and development in the United States, including the present
state of aerostation.

The flight of birds has ever been for man an object of envy and
emulation. When his slow-moving muscles proved inadequate for flight, he
looked to forces of nature for assistance, and found it at his own hearth.
The upward swirl of smoke led to his conquest of the air through aero-
station--the art of operating craft that are lighter than air.

The magnificent new National Air and Space Museum highlights man's
aerial progress from aeronauts to astronauts and beyond. Do not miss any
part of it. To understand the early days of man's airborne ventures
serves to heighten appreciation of his vast accomplishments in a mere
two centuries.

It is curious that during man's long yearning to be airborne, fire
and non-porous fabric--the two basic elements of a hot-air or fire bal-
loon--had been available for centuries. Not until 4 November 1782, however, were they successfully combined. On that day--194 years ago this
very morning--Joseph Michel Montgolfier, a French paper manufacturer,
filled a taffeta container with hot air and watched ecstatically as it
rose to the ceiling. Until that moment, no man-made inanimate device had
ever, of its own power, arisen from the earth.

*Captain Pineau, director of the Navy Memorial Museum, is a translator,
editor, and author of books and articles on the Japanese side of World
War II; and was curator of an early NASM exhibit "Ballooning, 1782-1972."

In June 1783 Joseph and his brother Etienne first demonstrated a fire balloon publicly in their hometown of Annonay. Two months later, Professor Jacques Alexandre Cesar Charles publicly launched an unmanned hydrogen balloon at Paris.

On 21 November 1783--a momentous date in man's conquest of the air--Jean Pilatre de Rozier and the Marquis d'Arlandes rose over Paris in history's first aerial journey. By adding straw to a fire pot hung beneath the open neck of a Montgolfier balloon, they stayed aloft twenty-five minutes and traveled about five miles.

Most amazingly, a mere ten days later, on 1 December 1783, Professor Charles and an assistant arose from Paris in a hydrogen balloon. Those two balloons--embodying all the essential elements of today's balloons--were developed from concept to materialization within one year, and without unfortunate incident. They revolutionized the thinking of the day, and the future of mankind.

That first manned hydrogen balloon, of 1 December 1783, was aloft for two hours and landed twenty-seven miles from Paris, just at sunset. Professor Charles, her designer and one of the two passengers, decided to go up again, alone. The lightened vehicle shot to a chilling ten thousand feet, but scientist Charles jotted his observations: severe cold, considerable fright, earaches, and the unique experience of seeing two sunsets in one day.

He wrote of that day, "Nothing can approach the joy that possessed me." Yet in all his remaining thirty years, he never ballooned again. That one day was enough.

This new thing--ballooning--caught the public fancy and spread all over Europe. It soon crossed the Atlantic to the fledgling United States where aerostation and its farreaching offspring have outsoared the wildest dreams of the Montgolfier brothers.

In the 1780s Benjamin Franklin was our minister to France. At one of the first balloon launchings a cynical observer remarked, "Of what possible use is it?" Said Franklin, who foresaw many possibilities for aerostats, "Of what use is a newborn babe?"

Franklin wrote at length to scientific friends about the early balloons. His observations were widely distributed and read in America.

FIRST MANNED AERIAL ASCENT IN AMERICA

- JUNE 24, 1784, near Baltimore, Maryland

This recent rendering of the first tethered-balloon flight of Edward Warren was drawn by Susan Hart. Peter Carnes had made several demonstrations of his balloon before Warren's historic ascent.

(II-2 - Courtesy of the Indian Queen Tavern Museum of Bladensburg, Md.)

George Washington said, "The tales of these balloons are marvelous, and lead us to expect that our friends at Paris, in a little while, will come flying thro the air, instead of ploughing the ocean to get to America."

Balloons were also seen through the eye of Thomas Jefferson, who got involved with aerostation prospects. He worked out statistics and made sketches of the 1783 vehicles, and enumerated their probable uses, including transportation over dangerous terrain, intelligence, science, and discovery.

The first ascension of a balloon of any kind in this hemisphere took place 10 June 1784, just north of what is today the nation's capital. *The Maryland Gazette* reported, "Mr. Peter Carnes, a gentleman of Maryland, distinguished in the law, made an experiment, in the vicinity of Bladensburg, of one of these new aerostatic balloons."

Lawyer Carnes was thirty-five years old, and the hot-air balloon was thirty-five feet in diameter. So successful was the unmanned and tethered Bladensburg demonstration that he put on another at Baltimore two weeks later.

At Baltimore, after several unmanned ascents, Edward Warren, 13, volunteered to go up. He "behaved with the steady fortitude of an old voyager." He acknowledged the loud applause "of the gazing multitude below" by a wave of his hat.

At Philadelphia, in July, Carnes tried for a free-flight ascent from the prison yard, where high walls could afford wind protection. At takeoff, the balloon banged into a wall, knocking Carnes from the basket, and freed of its passenger, the balloon zoomed and burst into flames. America's first balloonmaker then and there gave up aerostation and resumed the practice of law. Of little Edward Warren—first American to ascend in a balloon—the record speaks no more.

The first American to be airborne in sustained free flight was Dr. John Jeffries, a Boston-born Harvardian and royalist, who escaped the revolution by moving to London. There he became interested in studying the "upper air," and paid one hundred guineas for a ride with the French aeronaut Jean-Pierre Blanchard on 30 November 1784. Blanchard's balloon bore the motto *"Sic itur ad astra"*—this way one goes to the stars.

Next Dr. Jeffries paid seven hundred pounds to fly with Blanchard across the English Channel from Dover to France. Even so, Blanchard tried various and devious means to avoid having to share the honor. He schemed, for example, to increase his own launch weight by wearing a lead-lined vest. In best slapstick tradition, however, Blanchard's Dover tailor exposed the treachery by mistakenly delivering the telltale garment to Dr. Jeffries's hotel room.

The unprecedented flight occurred on 7 January 1785. They managed to reach France only by divesting the balloon of all extra paraphernalia-- including wine and cognac--and themselves of clothing and the contents of their bladders. Incidentally, they carried the first airmail letters, one of which still exists.

Although various schemes and experiments with small balloons were reported in America, it remained for the Frenchman Blanchard to make the first successful free ascent in this country. He came here in 1792, after an imposing series of European firsts, including the channel cross-ing and ascents from the Netherlands, Germany, Belgium, Warsaw, Vienna, and Prague, for a total of forty-four flights. His forty-fifth took place on 9 January 1793 at Philadelphia. Blanchard selected Walnut Street prison (where Peter Carnes had tried nine years earlier), as the launch site.

Admissions were two or five dollars, but the paying crowd was small, as most of the city's fifty thousand population watched from outside the walls. President Washington greeted the aeronaut, and gave him a pass-port letter, as Blanchard spoke no English.

The audience included four future Presidents: Adams, Jefferson, Madison, and Monroe, and many other distinguished people, for Philadelphia was then the capital and Congress was in session.

At 1009 the hydrogen-filled balloon was ready, and Blanchard cast off. Forty-six minutes later he landed fifteen miles away in New Jersey. There he was surrounded by suspicious farmers who looked askance at an airborne visitor speaking an outlandish tongue. President Washington's laissez-passer relieved the tension. After reading it and sharing Blan-chard's wine, the natives carted him and his balloon back to Philadel-phia that same day.

For two years he toured this country trying in vain to recoup his

FIRST AERIAL VOYAGE IN AMERICA - 1793

On January 9, 1793, Jean Pierre Blanchard of France
made a premier free-flight balloon ascension from the
Walnut Street Prison Yard in Philadelphia, which was witnessed by President Washington, his entire Cabinet, and
many others. Blanchard's hydrogen-inflated balloon reached
an altitude of 5,813 feet, and was carried by a north-
west wind over the Delaware River, landing 15 miles from
point of ascension in 46 minutes. He was accompanied by
a little black dog.
(II-3 - From a woodcut by Charles R. Gardner, courtesy of
of the National Air and Space Museum.)

finances by displaying the balloon. He also showed a depiction of the channel crossing in which Blanchard struggles to keep the balloon aloft while a relaxed Dr. Jeffries idly consumes cognac. It is ironic that Blanchard carried a prospective fortune in his pocket. Philatelists still seek the Washington letter, first airmail carried in the United States.

After Blanchard, a manned ascent was not tried again in this country for more than twenty years. Instead, unmanned balloons with firework displays commanded American attention.

Eugene Robertson, another Frenchman, made his ballooning debut here in July 1825 from Castle Garden (now Battery Park) in New York City, with General Lafayette as guest of honor. Robertson stayed here several years, making numerous ascents and conducting various experiments, sometimes with a lady passenger. These included studies of the peculiarly lively and stimulating effects of drinking champagne at high altitudes. His greatest contribution to American aeronautics, however, was in training this country's first professional balloonist, Charles Ferson Durant, an ancestor, appropriately enough, of this museum's own Frederick C. Durant.

Charles Durant went to France with Robertson and studied there for several years before returning to the United States. In September 1830, he rose from Castle Garden in the first flight by an American in this country. In his twelfth and last ascent--from Boston in September 1834-- he was carried out to sea by one current of air, and returned to shore by another.

Durant was farsighted about the uses of balloons for upper air studies, for charting inaccessible places, and as a means of escape from besieged cities. He designed the first specifically aeronautical instrument-- an altitude barometer resistant to jarring and inversion. Despite the brevity of his aeronautic career, he greatly influenced ballooning in the United States. His enterprise seemed to open the skies for a burgeoning of American aeronauts.

The next quarter of a century saw a number of native balloonists and exploits, and 1835 was a banner year. In April, Richard Clayton sailed 350 miles--from Cincinnati to Munroe County, Virginia--in nine and a half hours. John Wise made his first ascent in May from Philadelphia. In July, Clayton carried some unofficial mail from Cincinnati, and landed a hundred miles away at Waverly, Ohio.

That same year, one Edgar Allan Poe wrote a burlesque on ballooning, "The Unparalleled Adventure of One Hans Pfaal." In that story lunar voyage problems are studied and solved with great care for detail, including a sealed gondola, the earth's appearance from the sky, upper-air atmospheric conditions, and other matters of scientific interest.

Nine years later, readers of the 13 April 1844 *New York Sun* were startled to learn that eight aeronauts led by Monck Mason--who had once ballooned from London to Germany--had just landed in South Carolina, after a three-day aerial voyage from England. This unsigned article proved to be pure hoax, also sprung from Poe's fertile imagination.

Signor Muzio Muzzi announced ascents in Italy which never materialized, but in 1839 finally exhibited a model balloon with directional control. He came here and, on 16 October 1844, obtained the first United States patent pertaining to aeronautics. It described a gas balloon with inclined planes on either side to provide directional force during ascents and descents. His model evoked approval, but an aerostat's limited supply of ballast severely limits its number of ascents and descents, consequently limiting dirigibility. The fate of Muzzi's experiment is not known, but he is important as one of the few inventors in the 19th century with a working model for aerial navigation, and his idea no doubt inspired others.

A noted French aeronaut, M. Petin ascended from New Orleans on Christmas in 1852, and had to be fished out of Lake Pontchartrain. After a workshop intruder damaged his last balloon the discouraged aeronaut returned to France.

When Alexander Morat came to New Orleans in 1858, he already had sixty flights to his credit. While aeronauts back in France made news by ascending on horseback, Morat and S. S. Smith went up astride alligators. *The Daily Picayune* for 9 February reported: "The alligators, it is supposed, were never so high before; but Messrs Morat and Smith have been high often."

In 1859 Smith ascended at New Orleans for Washington's birthday and observed a cannonade honoring the occasion. Impressed by the sight, he proclaimed the balloon an unexcelled observation point for artillery fire.

The idea was not new. Montgolfier, Franklin, and others had written of it as early as 1782. The French had a special reconnaissance balloon corps in the 1790s.

Balloons were considered for use in Florida's Seminole War of 1840, but it ended before they were put in the field. The same thing happened in 1846 when John Wise proposed to bombard Vera Cruz from balloons. So military balloons had been thought of and used before, but such utterances as Smith's served further to bring them to public attention as something more than objects of wonder and pleasure.

John Wise, the 19th century's foremost American exponent of aerostation, made his first ascent in 1835 at the age of twenty-seven, and pursued that calling until age seventy-one when he ascended from St. Louis only to disappear over Lake Michigan.

As others had before him, Wise experienced the parachuting effect of a partially deflated balloon. In experimenting with this phenomenon in 1839 he conceived the idea of a rip cord to empty the bag of all gas immediately upon landing. This invention reduced the danger of being dragged helplessly along the ground by an untoward wind. Wise's introduction of inexpensive domestic muslin as a balloon fabric brought aerostation within popular reach.

On his 230th ascent, from St. Louis in July 1859 with aeronaut John LaMountain and two others, Wise traveled 809 miles in twenty hours and landed at Henderson, New York. In August 1859 Wise carried the first official mail by air from Lafayette, Indiana, to Crawfordsville. His combined interest in science and ballooning produced valuable experiences and observations which he published in 1873.

After brief Civil War service, Wise returned to his own ballooning enterprises. In 1873 *The New York Daily Illustrated Graphic* financed his building a huge balloon for an Atlantic crossing. When Wise quarreled with the backers and withdrew, his assistant, Washington H. Donaldson, took off in the balloon with two novices on 6 October, heading for Europe. They landed in the Catskills several hours later.

Thaddeus Sobieski Constantine Lowe, even from his first ascension, at Ottawa in 1858, was another aeronaut dedicated to crossing the Atlantic. Within a year he had backing to build a 104-foot-diameter gas bag. It was to be launched in November 1859 from New York's Crystal Palace, but the gas company could not inflate the balloon enough for takeoff. In 1860 he moved to Philadelphia, where sufficient gas was promised, but the balloon burst during inflation.

Joseph Henry, first Secretary of the Smithsonian Institution, persuaded Lowe to prove his "prevailing-wind theory" by taking off from some western point and landing on the Atlantic coast. Accordingly, Lowe took off from Cincinnati in the early morning of 19 April 1861. Nine hours and a thousand miles later he landed near Unionville, South Carolina. So hostile was his reception that he took off again, and landed at nearby Pea Ridge. Hostilities between the states had broken out just a week earlier and Lowe was saved from rough treatment as a Yankee spy only by the local hotelkeeper who just happened to have made a tethered ascent with him the preceding year.

During the Civil War, balloons were used by both sides, but mostly by the north, which had a total of nine professional aeronauts. Each approached war service in his own way, with James Allen of Providence in the lead. He packed up two balloons and set off for Washington on 19 April 1861, just four days after President Lincoln's call for troops. On 9 June his larger balloon was inflated from a gas main and towed to a farm about a mile north of the Capitol for an experimental tethered ascent to five thousand feet.

On 9 June the army asked John Wise the cost of a military balloon and aeronaut. He offered a balloon to army specifications in two weeks for $850, and said his services would be gratis. His appointment as military balloonist was announced on 1 July. He completed the first military aircraft built to army order, and delivered it to Washington seventeen days later. The basket floor was of sheet iron to protect against enemy gunfire. Wise advocated a field generator for hydrogen, but the $7000 cost was prohibitive.

Wise inflated his balloon at the D.C. Armory (on the very site of this NASM building) and started for Manassas early on 21 April—the day of McDowell's rout in the first Battle of Bull Run—with an army wagon detail of twenty soldiers to expedite his move. They walked the balloon out Pennsylvania Avenue, through Georgetown, across the aqueduct bridge, along the C&O Canal, and into Virginia. Only halfway by noon, and with

LOWE'S TRANSATLANTIC BALLOON

Photograph of test inflation in August
1860 of Thaddeus Lowe's "Great Western,"
which burst when he was to attempt crossing
from Philadelphia on September 7, 1860.
(II-3 - Courtesy of National Air and Space
Museum)

battle sounds audible, the soldiers--to hasten the march--tied the balloon to the wagon, where it lurched against each passing tree. Just short of Fairfax, branches impaled and tore the bag, rendering it useless. When an officer upbraided Wise for failing to use the balloon at Bull Run, he replied, "The balloon part was just about as good as the fighting part."

Wise made repairs quickly enough for aerial observations from Arlington on 24 July. Two days later he was moving across the aqueduct bridge from Georgetown, heading for Ball's Cross Roads (now Wilson Boulevard and Glebe Road) when the balloon got out of control and sailed off toward enemy lines. Sharpshooters shot it down to prevent its falling into the hands of the Confederates.

Neither of these two discouraging incidents were his fault, and Wise continued to plead that a properly instituted and practiced system of aeronautics would produce results. He argued for decent organizations, trained assistants, and proper precautions. He received only violent rebuke and recriminations, despite his having labored without pay or quarters, or even reimbursement for repairs to the balloon which he had built without profit.

John LaMountain volunteered early as a balloonist, sending the Secretary of War a historic disquisition on military ballooning, a plea that the government adopt aeronautics as part of army tactics (with him in charge), and a petition of recommendation signed by leading citizens of Troy, New York. He heard nothing until June when General Benjamin F. Butler, at Fortress Monroe, Virginia, offered him employment as aerial observer with his command. LaMountain arrived on 23 July and began making ascents within two days. These marked the first effective use of observation balloons in the United States Army.

On 3 August 1861 LaMountain secured a balloon to the stern of a small armed transport, *Fanny*, and, moving out into the channel, he inspected enemy positions from two thousand feet in the air. In a sense, *Fanny* was the first aircraft carrier in history. LaMountain's last ascent from Fort Monroe was made 10 August, after which hydrogen materials were exhausted. Thus, after three brief weeks of service, but having performed freelance operations of real value and importance, he returned north to await further duty.

LaMountain was the first aeronaut to make free reconnaissance ascents across enemy lines, drifting over with a favoring wind, and relying on opposite winds to carry him back. This feat, repeated many times, spoke well for his courage and acute wind sense, but jealous colleagues called it theatrical. He was dismissed from service as the result of a quarrel with Thaddeus Lowe.

Lowe, returning from his April flight into South Carolina, resolved to get into the war. He felt that to sell the army on ballooning he would have to put on an impressive demonstration, and that cost money. To promote funds he made a public ascent from Cincinnati on 8 May, hoping to be carried toward Washington. He landed, instead, in Canada.

When Lowe finally reached Washington, Joseph Henry helped him to get the attention and interest of President Lincoln. On 18 June 1861, just north of the Smithsonian Building, Lowe made a tethered ascent to five hundred feet. From the balloon he sent a telegraph message to the President, describing his observation point and its commanding view of an area nearly fifty miles in diameter. Lincoln was impressed.

President Lincoln's support helped, but Lowe still had many problems in gaining army acceptance of balloons. Like many other aeronauts, he offered his services to the Union, and--against considerable odds and difficulties--he developed the first army air corps in this country. By the end of 1861 seven balloons had been constructed, and twelve hydrogen generators were eventually built. These could inflate a balloon in three hours, on an average consumption of 1,600 pounds of acid and 3,300 pounds of iron filings. In normal weather an inflation lasted two weeks.

In November 1861 Lowe had a coal barge remodeled to serve as a balloon boat, and named it *George Washington Parke Custis*. The vessel was 122 feet overall, shallow draft, flat deck, and had ample stowage space, making her ideal for balloon operations. Towed by tug to otherwise inaccessible vantage points, she was useful in observations for Hooker's division at Budd's Ferry, Virginia, and served the balloon corps during the Peninsular Campaign.

The balloon service proved its merit with observations that correctly allayed fears of enemy attacks on Washington, as well as by successfully directing artillery attacks. Two Union balloons were responsible for

McClellan's victory at the Battle of Fair Oaks.

Through no fault of its own, the corps did not last the war. This novel service was limited in scope and did not achieve results commensurate with its potential or the abilities of its chief, had he been properly supported and encouraged. It operated with creditable success, however, and was a direct influence in leading the British army to adopt aeronautics. This first American air service deserves an honored place in the annals of United States military history.

Confederate forces also realized the importance of aerial observation, as evidenced by their persistent efforts to shoot down Union balloons. Southern aeronauts promptly offered to serve the Confederacy, and their balloons were soon being sighted by Yankees. On 14 June 1861 a Confederate balloon was seen beyond Chain Bridge in the direction of Leesburg Pike.

Because ballooning materials were limited, the Confederates were never able to field an effective air arm, but they tried. In April 1862, Captain John Randolph Bryan, twenty-one, made several bold ascents at Yorktown in a tethered hot-air balloon. His first flight drew heavy menacing enemy fire during the slow descent. Thereafter the balloon was hauled down by a team of six artillery horses at full gallop. On Bryan's last ascent a soldier's foot got caught in the control rope, and he was rapidly being drawn toward the windlass when a comrade cut the rope. This promptly freed foot and soldier, but it also freed balloon and Bryan, to drift toward Union lines. After hairbreadth escapes from the enemy, from a river dunking, and from friendly rifle fire, he came safely to an orchard where he slid down the tether cable and tied the collapsing balloon to an apple tree.

Captain Langdon Cheves of Savannah provided the Confederacy with a gas balloon made of dress silk. This gave rise, so to speak, to a romantic but erroneous legend that southern ladies had sacrificed their gowns to the cause. Ever since known as the silk-dress balloon, it was inflated at Richmond, carried by rail to the battle area, and first raised at the battle of Gaines' Mill on 27 June 1862. From his own balloon, Lowe reported at eleven that morning, "About four miles to the west of here the enemy have a balloon about 300 feet in the air."

CIVIL WAR ASCENSION

Professor Lowe ascends over Northern Virginia in
this historical Brady photograph.
(II-4 - Courtesy of the National Air and Space Museum)

When the action moved away from the rail line the silk-dress balloon was tethered to steam tug *Teaser* for transport. Poor *Teaser* ran aground in the James River on 4 July 1862, was taken under fire by ships *Monitor* and *Maratanza*, and abandoned by her crew. The balloon thus fell into Union hands. The Smithsonian eventually came into possession of a remnant from this Confederate balloon. Passage of time and the rubber-naphtha varnish, which made the fabric impermeable, have not dimmed the color of this historic dress material.

A second "silk-dress" balloon was built at government expense, piloted by Charles Cevor, and saw duty in the Charleston area. It escaped in July 1863 and was carried away by a high wind.

Public interest in ballooning burgeoned during the rest of the century, with ascensions for sale at circuses, fairs, and other such gatherings. Professional ballooning prepared the way for an air-minded nation in the 20th century. One pre-Civil War idea that persisted, and does to this day, was the dream of a transatlantic balloon crossing.

In the four brief years of his ballooning career, which began with aerial acrobatics in 1871, Washington H. Donaldson established himself as a leading aeronaut of his time. Aside from the usual risks of the profession, Donaldson attracted attention in May 1873 with a paper-balloon ascent in which he traveled ten miles. (Shades of the Montgolfiers, and forefloater of Japan's remarkable paper balloons of World War II.) He joined P. T. Barnum's Hippodrome in July 1874 and made forty-five ascents in six months.

On 19 October 1874 Donaldson made his ninety-eighth ascent in Cincinnati, with an aerial wedding. Fifty thousand spectators cheered the garlanded balloon and its nuptial party of six. His last ascent was made the next year from Chicago, with one passenger. They were apparently forced down by a sudden Lake Michigan storm, and only the body of the passenger was found.

Unquestionably the foremost proponent of ballooning in the United States during the last half of the 19th century was Samuel A. King, who made his first ascent in 1851 at Philadelphia. In 1860, from King's balloon over Boston, William Black took the first aerial photograph in this country. King's distinctions include a record of more than four hundred and fifty ascents.

One of King's many contributions to ballooning in America was the drag rope. First used in Europe in 1836, the drag rope acted as a stabilizer to keep the balloon within a fairly constant distance from the ground. Any part of the rope dragging on the ground relieved the balloon of that much burden. If the balloon rose, the rope burden increased the ballast; as the balloon neared the ground, its rope load was lightened.

Of numerous balloon competitions, the most notable was the Gordon Bennett Cup races, first won by the United States in 1906. The coveted trophy was retired--upon three successive wins--by this country in 1928, and again in 1932. The only other entrants to ever retire a trophy were Belgium and Poland, and the hard-fought competitions were discontinued after 1938.

It has been estimated that by 1859 more than three thousand ascensions had been made in the United States, and that some eight thousand people had been airborne. These numbers were multiplied many times over in the remaining years of the century.

Just as in the early days in Europe, so too in America ballooning caught the female fancy. Foremost American woman balloonist of the 19th century was Mary H. Myers who, as "Carlotta, the lady aeronaut," performed throughout the northeastern states and Canada from 1880 to 1891. She probably made more ascents than any other woman in history.

Aerostats continue to this day to attract such fearless ladies as Connie Wolf, who holds several ballooning records; artist as well as balloonist Vera Simons; and the Reverend Dr. Jeanette Piccard. She was the first woman to enter the stratosphere, preceding Valentina Tereshkova into that rarefied zone by twenty-nine years. Dr. Piccard, on high-altitude flights with her equally famous husband, Jean, always carried a bit of angelfood cake "because one never knows whom one might meet up there."

Long before man climbed Mt. Everest, its altitude was surpassed by manned balloons, and many of the early flights--beginning in 1803--were made exclusively for scientific purposes. Most were in hydrogen balloons, but in 1808 two Italian astronomers used a hot-air balloon to reach twenty-five thousand feet. That record endured 163 years, until

EXPLORER II - 1935

Army Air Corps-National Geographic stratosphere
balloon ready for launch from the Black Hills, South
Dakota. Crew of Orvil A. Anderson and A. W. Stevens
established official world record of 72,395 feet, which
endured until Navy's Strato-Lab High III in July 1958.

(II-5 - U.S. Air Force Photo)

June 1971 when propane-burning balloons rose above thirty thousand feet.

After several high-altitude scientific experiments had ended in disaster and death, two Frenchmen questioned the need of risking human life in this fashion. In 1892 they pioneered the use of unmanned instrument-bearing balloons which burst at a given altitude, parachuting the instruments to safety. This use of sounding balloons led to discovery of the stratosphere. Worldwide use of weather balloons for meteorological research followed a 1906 international conference on the subject in Paris. With the addition of a lightweight radio transmitter, our weather service has been using such balloons for daily observations since 1937.

The four main types of scientific balloons in general use today are: Expandable, Zero-pressure, Super-pressure, and Tethered. Their modern uses by numerous organizations are as varied as the patterns, sizes, and colors of the balloons of yesteryear. An idea of modern developments may be had by a glance at some of the principal organizations concerned with scientific ballooning.

The Office of Naval Research sponsors or is involved in about 25 percent of the approximately five hundred major balloon experiments that are lofted each year.

The Air Force Geophysical Laboratories are the largest federal user of scientific balloons for experimental measuring, sampling, and testing in the upper atmosphere.

The National Center for Atmospheric Research, sponsored by the National Science Foundation, serves as focal point for a vigorous and integrated national research effort in the atmospheric sciences. Some thirty-seven universities have joined to provide balloon operations and service to users of all disciplines for atmospheric and cosmic research.

The Environmental Research and Developmental Administration, with Air Force cooperation, conducts a monthly sampling for radioactive debris in the upper atmosphere. It is the only interhemispheric program in operation.

The Advanced Research Project Agency is concerned primarily with tethered balloons and their various applications, such as sensor platforms to provide long-time, on-station coastal surveillance against pollution or enemy action, air defense, communications relays, and related functions.

There are many private users as well. Balloon manufacturers provide whatever is needed in the way of sizes and configurations. The balloon makers of today have far more to work with and are no less ingenious than their 18th- and 19th-century precursors. A brief dozen years ago the workhorse of high-altitude experimental balloons was of three million feet capacity, and measured about two hundred feet in diameter at altitude. Today there are regular scientific ascents with balloons of thirty-five million cubic feet. Last June, in Palestine, Texas, a 52.6-million-cubic-foot balloon was sent up. Last month, October, one of seventy million cubic feet was launched. At altitude this balloon will be 580 feet in diameter. To get an idea of what that size means in concrete terms, consider that the Washington monument has a volume of about one million cubic feet. One such balloon could theoretically contain seventy Washington monuments!

Balloons raise heavy scientific payloads to altitudes of 150,000 feet and more, some thirty miles, and maintain them there for hours of experiments on everything from weather observation to the monitoring of x-rays.

Many high-altitude balloons have been used to gather information needed for space probes. The testing of space suits, for example, was the main purpose of the highest manned balloon flight ever achieved. In May 1961, Commander M. D. Ross and Lieutenant Commander Victor A. Prather rose from the deck of aircraft carrier *Antietam*. An eighty-story-high balloon system carried them to 113,740 feet. The record set that day may well last forever, but tragedy struck when Prather slipped from the rescue helicopter and was drowned. We should honor the memory of all aeronauts--early and recent--who gave their courage, their skill, and in some cases their lives to the furtherance of learning about the air, and space, and outer space.

Balloons are not confined in their scientific uses to mere altitude and payload records. They do other fantastic things as well. In 1965 a three-million-cubic-foot balloon launched in Manitoba descended thirty days later in the Greek Peloponessus. In 1966 a GHOST (Global HOrizontal

Sounding Technique) balloon launched at Christchurch, New Zealand, circled the earth in ten days at an altitude of 42,000 feet. Another GHOST balloon remained aloft for more than a year

A hundred years ago James Glaisher, an early scientific aeronaut, wrote:

> . . . the balloon . . . in its present form is useless for commercial enterprise, and so little adapts itself to our necessities that it might drop into oblivion tomorrow, and we should miss nothing from the conveniences of life. But we can afford to wait, for already it has done for us that which no other power ever accomplished; it has gratified the desire natural to us all to view the earth in a new aspect, and to sustain ourselves in an element hitherto the exclusive domain of birds and insects. We have been enabled to ascend among the phenomena of the heavens, and to exchange conjecture for instrumental facts, recorded at elevations exceeding the highest mountains on earth.

He went on to say that the great Lavoisier (coiner of the name hydrogen) had started to list the potential uses of the Montgolfier discovery, and had suddenly stopped, appalled in some measure at the multitude of applications of the balloon.

Lavoisier was right. It is appalling in *any* measure to consider the numerous uses to which balloons have been put, and their wide variety—everything from auto tires to cartoon talk containers, and from kiddie toys to contraceptives. But it is amazing enough to limit our consideration just to aerostats.

In wars—hot or cold—balloons have been used for more than mere observation and artillery spotting. Starting in World War I they were used as barriers to air attacks on important centers, as submarine spotters at sea, and for spreading propaganda behind enemy lines. Much earlier, during the siege of Venice in 1849, the Austrians loaded small montgolfiers with time-fused bombs fixed to fall on the enemy. A fickle wind caused most of the bombs to fall in the Austrian ranks. Such tactical use of balloons was, accordingly, abandoned until World War II when Japan revived the concept ingeniously. Unmanned balloons carrying

FIRST INTERCONTINENTAL WEAPON SYSTEM

     Hundreds of Japanese "FUGO" balloons rode
the jet stream to North America during World War II.
Arrival was kept secret but their incendiaries and
grenades inflicted some casualties.

(II-6 - Courtesy of the National Air and Space Museum)

explosive and fire bombs were sent across the Pacific Ocean, via the jet stream, to dump their cargo upon the United States. And they succeeded.

Their eye appeal has made balloons popular at coronations, fairs, festivals, and all kinds of galas. They helped to dedicate London Bridge in 1831, Brooklyn Bridge in 1883, and London Bridge again in Lake Havasu City, Arizona, in 1971.

In 1952 a balloon safari in Zanzibar produced wildlife observations and photographs obtainable in no other way.

Both hot-air and gas balloons are employed in commercial fishing and marine research.

Use of gas balloons in the logging industry reduces the need for building expensive roads. So successful has this operation been in recent years that the system is being tested for ship-shore logistic possibilities.

In both marine and dry-land archeology, balloons are used to advantage in spotting and plotting prospective sites.

The sheer joy of ballooning continues today as a passenger described it in 1852:

> . . . that peculiar panoramic effect--the distinguishing
> feature of a view from a balloon--which arises from the utter
> absence of all sense of motion in the machine itself. The
> earth appears literally to consist of a long series of scenes,
> continually drawn along under you, as if it were a diorama
> beheld flat upon the ground, and gives one the notion that
> the world is an endless landscape stretched upon rollers,
> which some invisible sprites are revolving for your special
> enjoyment.

As pilots or passengers, thousands of Americans enjoy this thrill each year, and the number is growing. Except for scientific flights, gas ballooning is on the wane in this country. Natural gas and hydrogen-- though still used in Europe--are not generally acceptable, and helium is very expensive for private use. There are only five or six gas balloons registered, and most of them belong to the Balloon Club of America, in Philadelphia; or the Balloon Flyers Club, of Akron.

There are, on the other hand, nearly one thousand hot-air balloons

STRATOSCOPE BALLOON

Launch crew inflates hugh plastic
balloon with helium from four trucks, for
carrying 36-inch telescope to above 80,000
feet to read infrared radiation from the
planet Mars in 1963.
(II-7 - NASA Photo)

privately registered, and their number is growing. A two-place balloon, ready to go, can be bought for about $5000. No longer fueled by burning straw in open fire pots, today's lovely plastic aerostats are kept aloft by occasional blasts of flame from propane burners. The ballooning experience is everything marvelous that has ever been said about it. Do not let an opportunity pass you by.

It may seem a far cry--but it really isn't--from a gleam in the eye of an 18th-century French papermaker to the 20th-century flight at Kitty Hawk of a craft heavier than air. The transition was facilitated by the intermediate achievement of dirigible lighter-than-air vehicles.

Following Kitty Hawk came rapid developments in airplanes, made even more rapid by two world wars, which advanced aeronautic science by decades within a matter of years. From piston engine to jet, then rocket, which thrust us into the age of space, and outer space. Then we ranged into the heavens and visited the Moon, and Mars.

Starting with a small balloon wafted to the ceiling of a room in 1782, and given a mix of audaciously courageous and brilliantly ingenious people all along the way, we have--in remarkably short time--given substance to the prophetic slogan Jean-Pierre Blanchard affixed to his balloon. We have, indeed, gone to the stars, and ballooning was the first giant step along the way.

BIBLIOGRAPHY

AMICK, M. L., compiler, *History of Donaldson's balloon ascensions*.
Cincinnati: Cincinnati News Company, 1875. Negative photostat
in NASM library.

Aeronautic scrapbook of newspaper and magazine clippings, 1784-1905, in
NASM library (629.13,C75,L.A.).

BASSETT, Preston R., "Carlotta, The Lady Aeronaut of the Mohawk Valley,"
in *New York History*, April 1962.

CORNISH, Joseph Jenkins, III, *The Air Arm of the Confederacy*. Richmond:
Civil War Centennial Committee, 1963.

DOLLFUS, Charles, and Henri Bouche, *Histoire de l'Aeronautique*. Paris:
L'Illustration, 1932.

DOLLFUS, Charles, *The Orion Book of Balloons*, translated by Carter Mason
from the French *Les Ballons*. New York City: The Orion Press, 1961.

EMME, Eugene M., *Aeronautics and Astronautics*. Washington, D.C.:
National Aeronautics and Space Administration, 1961.

FREY, Carroll, *The First Air Voyage in America* together with a facsimile
reprint of *Journal of My Forty-fifth Ascension and the First in
America by Jean Pierre Blanchard*. Philadelphia: Penn Mutual Life
Insurance Company, 1943.

GIBBS-SMITH, Charles H., *Ballooning*. London: Penguin Books, 1948.

_____, *Balloons*. London: The Aerial Press, 1956.

GLAISHER, James, F.R.S., Camille Flammarion, Wilfrid de Fonvielle, and
Gaston Tissandier, *Travels in the Air*. Philadelphia: J. B. Lippin-
cott & Company, 1871.

HAYDON, Frederick Stansbury, *Aeronautics in the Union and Confederate
Armies with a survey of Military aeronautics prior to 1861*. Baltimore: The Johns Hopkins Press, 1941.

JEFFRIES, Dr. John, *a Narrative of the Two Aerial Voyages of Doctor
Jeffries with Mons. Blanchard*. London: J. Robson, 1786; New York
City: Aeronautical Archives of the Institute of Aeronautical Sci-
ences, 1941.

Latest World Records, Federation Aeronautique Internationale, 1971.

LOWE, Thaddeus S. C., "My Balloons in Peace and War." An unpublished
manuscript in the NASM library. Written at Pasadena, California,
1911.

MIKESH, Robert C. "Japan's World War II Balloon Bomb Attacks on North
America." *Smithsonian Annals of Flight* No. 9, 1972.

MILBANK, Jeremiah, Jr., *The First Century of Flight in America*.
Princeton University Press, 1943.

MILLER, Frances Trevelyan, *The World in the Air*, two volumes. New York
and London: G. P. Putnam's Sons, 1930.

PINEAU, Roger, *Ballooning, 1782-1972* (an exhibit catalog). Washington,
D.C.: Smithsonian Institution Press, 1972.

STEHLING, Kurt R., and William Beller, *Skyhooks*. Garden City, New York:
Doubleday & Company, Inc., 1962.

TURNOR, Hatton, *Astra Castra*. London: Chapmen and Hall, 1965.

WISE, John, *Through the Air*. Philadelphia, New York, Boston: Today
Printing and Publishing Company, 1873.

I I I

THE AIRSHIP IN AMERICA

1904-1976

Richard K. Smith*

Initially behind European experience, the
dramatic history of American lighter-than-air
ships is surveyed in this concise paper. It
reviews the limited application of the blimps
as well as the early promise of the transoceanic dirigibles which was not to be realized.

Immediately after World War I and for more than a decade
thereafter no other aircraft seemed to hold a greater promise
for transoceanic air transportation than the airship. It was
the only aircraft in the world which possessed the obvious
potential of carrying hundreds of passengers and tons of cargo
over thousands of miles nonstop, and providing all the amenities
of long distance travel as the world had come to understand it
in terms of the Pullman Palace Car, the Wagons-Lits carriage,
and the luxury liners of the Cunard and White Star.

In May 1919, the U.S. Navy's four-engine flying boat NC-4
with a crew of six made the first flight across the Atlantic,
from Rockaway Beach, N.Y., to Lisbon, Portugal. But the NC-4
carried no payload, made five stops en route, two other flying
boats that accompanied her were lost on the way, and the
passage took all of 21 days.[1] A few days later, in June, the
British airmen, John Alcock and Arthur Whitten Brown, took off
from a field near St. Johns, Newfoundland, and 16 hours later
crash-landed in a bog near Clifton, Ireland, to make the first
nonstop crossing of the North Atlantic.[2]

Looking back on his flight in the NC-4 only a few weeks

---

*Dr. Richard K. Smith is the author of First Across! The
U.S. Navy's Transatlantic Flight of 1919, winner of the AIAA
History Manuscript Award in 1972, The Airships AKRON And
MACON, The Papers of Hugh L. Dryden -- A Catalog, and many
articles.

after its conclusion, Lieutenant Commander Albert C. Read said: "Crossing the Atlantic by seaplane will not be profitable commercially soon; the dirigible will accomplish more along this line within the next few years."[3] While Commander John Towers, whose own NC-3 had been forced down at sea during the Navy's transatlantic flight, seconded Read: "The dirigible has a big future; until the seaplane is made larger, the dirigible will have the advantage in overseas flight."[4] And Sir Arthur Whitten Brown remarked with greater pungency: "That the apparatus in which Sir John Alcock and I made the first nonstop air journey over the Atlantic was an aeroplane only emphasizes my belief that for long flights above the ocean the dirigible is the only useful vehicle."[5]

As if to confirm the estimates of these transatlantic airplane pioneers, on 2 July 1919 the Beardmore-built airship R.34 took off from East Fortune, Scotland, and 108 hours and 12 minutes later moored at Hazelhurst Field near Mineola, Long Island. The R.34 had on board a crew of 31, one American observer, one stowaway, two homing pigeons, and a tortoise-shell cat named Woppsie. After four days at Mineola, the R-34 took off and 75 hours later moored at Pulham, England, thus completing the first nonstop flights between Europe and the United States and the first round-trip crossing of the Atlantic by air.[6]

The news media in America and in England were ecstatic over the R.34's flights. The airplane flights of May and June were very interesting, great human achievements and technical demonstrations for 1919, but obviously not anything that could be done on a regular basis, much less provide a passenger service. The New York Times observed: "The R.34 is the pioneer of the air fleets of commerce and pleasure, which in a very few years will make the flight from the New World to the Old, a brief, luxurious, and comparatively tame enterprise. The airplane flights [of 1919] were gallant adventures; the voyage of the R.34 is the real beginning of the new age."[7]

In 1919 there were no difficulties whatsoever in imagining great fleets of airships cruising across the transoceanic air routes of the world by 1929, speeding hundreds of passengers and tons of cargo to their destinations---while airplanes were laboring to hippity-hop along overland routes, lifting small express cargos and special mails from New York to Buffalo to Cleveland to Detroit and finally to Chicago. The airplane would become an airliner some day; but tomorrow certainly belonged to the airship, especially over the oceans.

Americans wanted to share in this great transoceanic airship future, but how? If there was a transoceanic airship "race" shaping up---and many commentators of 1919 thought there was---the United States was so far behind the Anglo-

Europeans in airship technology that it risked being a non-starter.

EARLY AMERICAN AIRSHIPS

The development of the airship in America by 1919 was remarkably stunted. What little had been done by way of continuous effort was owed wholly to the Navy; its interest dated from about 1912 when it sent an officer to Europe to study the airship situation there.[8] But its active prosecution of the subject did not get under way until 1917.[9] Any development prior to this was spotty at best.

The first airship built and flown in America, by August Greth, was in 1903. It was a project that went nowhere.[10] By 1904 Thomas Scott Baldwin was building and flying airships. They were primitive as compared to those in Europe and their only function was to advertise state fairs and commercial expositions and entertain the crowds who attended. Baldwin's greatest contribution to aeronautics was to entice Glenn Curtiss into the aero engine business.[11]

In 1908 the Army procured the first airship on behalf of the U.S. Government. This was a Baldwin-built airship, the SC-1 of 19,500 c.f. (cubic feet) and was powered by a single 20 hp (horsepower) engine.[12] But while the SC-1 was aweing crowds during its trials at Fort Myer, Virginia, in the summer of 1908, in Germany Count Zeppelin was flying his LZ-4 of 530,000 c.f., 446 feet long and powered by two 100 hp engines. More to the point, after its acceptance by the Army the SC-1 was shipped off to Fort Omaha, Nebraska, from where it was carted around the Midwest to fly at state fairs and similar exhibitions. It was finally sold for junk in 1912.[13]

After the SC-1 the Army's interest in lighter-than-air aeronautics regressed to the balloon. After the United States intervened in World War I the Army's interests were absorbed by training thousands of men in the operations of tethered kite balloons, which were vital to artillery spotting on the Western Front. The Army did not operate another airship until 1921, when the Navy turned over about a dozen of its blimps to the Army Air Service.[14]

On 1 June 1915, the Navy had let a contract for its first airship, the DN-1. It staggered into the air at Pensacola on 20 April 1917, two weeks after the United States entered World War I. The DN-1 can be viewed as a fiasco or a "learning experience" and the Navy chose to view it as both. The DN-1's shortcomings became manifest during construction: the combination of an inexperienced contractor with specifications that expected too much from the contemporary state of the art.[15]

BALDWIN'S AIRSHIP "ARROW" - 1904

Thomas Scott Baldwin's "Arrow" was flown over the St. Louis Exposition in 1904, by Roy A. Knabenshue, shown here in a faded photograph.

(III-1, National Air and Space Museum)

In December 1916, five months before the DN-1 flew, the Navy drew up a more realistic specification for a new type blimp based upon the British "Sea Scout" type. One prototype was to be procured. But on 17 February 1917, the eve of the U.S. entrance into the European War, the prototype was multiplied to an order for 16---right off the drawing boards. The result was the single-engine B-ship of 84,000 c.f., an eminently successful little airship.[16]

During the course of the war, the Navy procured 20 B-ships, 10 twin-engine C-ships, and six twin-engine D-ships; but most of the latter came into the inventory after the Armistice of 1918. None of them was sent overseas.[17] In Europe, the Navy established airship bases at Paimboeuf, Guipavas, and Gujan, and about a dozen French airships of various manufactures were used. But only Paimboeuf became fully operable before the Armistice.

RIGID AIRSHIPS

Both the Army and the Navy sought to develop the rigid, Zeppelin-type airship. Whereas the non-rigid blimp was a relatively simple aircraft, the rigid airship was highly complex, demanding sophisticated technology in its design, and needed as extensive industrial base for production. Because of the Navy's obvious requirement for a rigid airship for long-range ocean patrols, it was delegated exclusive responsibility for its technical development. Theoretically, when the Navy finally developed a "successful" rigid airship, the Army would come forward and order a few of the same for itself. Here the working assumption was that a "standard" type could be realized and, once in hand, put into mass production to the benefit of all concerned. This would eliminate "wasteful duplication" and create great "savings." At the root of such thinking was the assumption that a technology possessed of incredible dynamics could be frozen in the same manner as the design of artillery carriages.

It became U.S. policy to initiate the construction of two rigid airships in America and procure two abroad. The war ended before this could be implemented. In 1919 these plans were halved and given reality by the Congress authorizing the Navy to create an airship base at Lakehurst, N.J., to build one airship domestically and to buy a second in England. Meanwhile, the U.S. Army's Air Service had developed a new self-consciousness under the leadership of General William "Billy" Mitchell, the self-styled "prophet of airpower," and initiated a campaign to "retrieve" the rigid airship from the Navy.

When the R.34 flew to America in 1919 the American observer on board was Lieutenant Commander Zachary Lansdowne of the U.S. Navy. Flying eastward on her return to England the R.34's American observer was Lt. Col. William N. Hensley of the U.S. Army Air Service. Once in Europe Hensley set in motion a frantic effort to procure a German Zeppelin for the Army. He tried to buy the Zeppelin L.72, the dirigible that was allegedly designed to bomb New York City.[18] This effort was thwarted by the L.72 being awarded to France as "spoils of war." So Hensley entered into a clandestine contract with Luftschiffbau Zeppelin for the construction of a wholly new and "bigger and better" airship than the L.72.

As it turned out, Hensley was being watched by Anglo-French intelligence services. They turned over their findings to the U.S. State Department. This was embarassing. The legalists "shot down" the Hensley Zeppelin by pointing out that the United States was still technically at war with Germany and his contract with the Luftschiffbau violated the Trading With the Enemy Act.[19] It was a crazy episode; opera bouffe cum Zeppelin! But it illustrated how far Billy Mitchell's "empire of airpower" was prepared to go to obtain a Zeppelin in 1919. It was also a harbinger of events 25 years later when the agents of Project Paperclip scoured a newly-conquered Germany for knowledge concerning innovative technological developments in rocketry and jet propulsion.[20]

The Army Air Service was thus frustrated in its efforts to obtain a "secret Zeppelin." And although by the agreement with the Navy of 1917 the Army had excluded itself from the development of the rigid airship, it was nevertheless free to experiment with other types.

During 1920-21, the Navy turned over to the Army all of its D-type blimps and some of its C-types. And in September 1922 the Army used the ex-Navy C-2 to make the first coast-to-coast flight by an airship. Meanwhile, the Army had procured a hugh semi-rigid airship of 1,240,000 c.f. in Italy. It was called the Roma, a name which it continued to carry, curiously enough, even during its short-lived operations in the United States. On 21 November 1921, at Langley Field, Virginia, the Roma made her first flight in America. But only four months later on 21 February 1922, she went out of control during flight, struck electrical power lines which ignited her hydrogen gas, and hit the ground in a flaming horror. Of the 45 men on board, only 11 managed to survive the holocaust. The Roma disaster provided a dramatic demonstration to Americans of the perils of flying with hydrogen as a lifting gas and made a more than adequate case for the use of helium. And although helium was available at that time it did not exist in sufficient quantity to inflate an airship as large as the Roma.

The Army continued to experiment with the semi-rigid airship, but with no satisfactory results. It later procured the

RS-1, its parts fabricated by Goodyear and assembled in the big airship hanger at Scott Field, Illinois. The RS-1 made its first flight on 8 June 1926 and had a career of minor troubles thereafter. During 16-17 October 1928 she was en route from San Antonio, Texas, to Scott Field when she flew into a wild storm of several hours duration in the vicinity of Memphis which mauled her badly. She finally made it to Scott Field, but there it was discovered that she was so bent out of shape that she never flew again. In 1929 the RS-1 was quietly sold for scrap. Army blimp operations nevertheless continued for almost another decade.

During the interwar years the United States operated five rigid airships. One was procured in England, another in Germany, and three were built domestically. As a result of the Navy being given exclusive responsibility for the development of the rigid airship, these were all U.S. Navy airships. In addition to this technical responsibility the Navy took on a concurrent commitment to assist in the establishment of commercial airship operations in the United States. The first step in this effort was the creation of the Naval Air Station at Lakehurst, N.J., for lighter-than-air operations, and the procurement of the two initial airships. One, the ZR-1 was built in the United States by the Navy and by way of a "learning experience"; the other, the ZR-2, was purchased "off the shelf" in England so as to have an operating vehicle as soon as possible.

The ZR-2 was the British R.38. Unknown to the Americans the R.38 was riddled with technical defects and some major structural faults, and her career was short and dreadful. During the airship's fourth trial flight, 24 August 1921, the R.38 broke up in the air over the city of Hull, her hydrogen ignited and the flaming hull sections fell into the Humber River. Of the 45 men on board only five survived. It was probably just as well that the inevitable occurred here instead of a few weeks later when the Americans would have been flying the airship transatlantic to Lakehurst.[21]

The ZR-2/R.38 disaster had one fortuitous aspect. It served to put diplomatic pressure upon the British to obtain their political assistance in obtaining a genuine German Zeppelin.

THE SHENANDOAH AND THE LOS ANGELES

At the end of World War I, the United States was awarded two German Zeppelins, the L.14 and L.65, by way of "spoils of war."[22] But on 23 June 1919, their German crews deliberately wrecked these and other airships to prevent their passing into the hands of the Allies.[23] This provided the Americans with the opportunity to press Germany to build a wholly new airship, one representative of the latest Zeppelin technology, by way of "compensation" for the two destroyed.[24]

The British and French opposed this. But after the R.38 disaster the British were no longer in a position to oppose and were pressured into supporting the American case, which they did reluctantly. And with as much Gallic ill-grace as possible, the French agreed. The Americans wanted a Zeppelin of 3.4 million cubic feet; French jealousy whittled this down to 2.5 million cubic feet. This was the smallest size capable of flying the Atlantic. On 24 June 1922 a contract was finally signed between the Navy and Luftschiffbau Zeppelin for the airship that would become the ZR-3.

Meanwhile, the construction of the ZR-1's sub-assemblies was proceeding apace and on 28 June 1921 the Lakehurst Air Station with its huge hanger, capable of housing two rigid airships, was formally placed in commission. The components of the ZR-1 were fabricated at the Naval Aircraft Factory in Philadelphia and transported to Lakehurst for assembly.[25] On 24 April 1922 the ZR-1's first main ring was hoisted into position; nine months later her hull structure was essentially complete; and by 20 August 1923 her outer cover had been applied, her gas cells inflated and she was "floated" inside the hanger.

On 4 September 1923 the ZR-1 made her first flight.

The transformation of the ZR-1 from a vague paper conception of 1919 to a flyable airship was accomplished within four years, a work which included the construction of the Lakehurst hanger. When it is considered that prior to 1917 there was very little technical intelligence on the subject of rigid airships in the United States, the construction of the ZR-1 can only be scored as a technological achievement of the first order.

On 10 October 1923 the ZR-1 was formally christened Shenandoah, the name by which she is best recalled. The Shenandoah was essentially a "school ship," the means by which Americans learned how to build and operate rigid airships. But she also had a military mission, and that was to determine how rigid airships could best be used with the Fleet and how effective such operations might be.

The function of the airship in the Navy was to be a high speed "scout cruiser of the air" which could operate with the Fleet and not be dependent upon a shoreside network of expensive hangars in which winds could keep an airship imprisoned for days. This requirement led to an intensive development of the British-conceived mooring mast to which an airship was moored by its nose and was free to weathercock around the mast, 360-degrees.

A mooring mast's tower enclosed piping for water ballast, gas and fuel, and cables for electric power; it provided everything a hanger did except shelter. The Navy erected masts in Florida, Cuba, Texas, California, the state of Washington and in Hawaii. One mooring mast was erected over the stern of the Fleet tanker Patoka and another was to have been built on the tanker Ramapo. There were plans in 1924 for the Shenandoah to make a transpolar flight from Lakehurst to one of the tankers off Greenland where she would refuel, fly over the North Pole to the other tanker offshore of Alaska, refuel and fly on to Washington and California. This flight was cancelled, the Ramapo never modified. And the experience with the Patoka indicated that the versatility expected from mooring to a mast on a ship was fraught with more complications than anticipated. It had once been hoped that a ship could tow an airship from a mast, casting it loose when the Fleet needed its services. But as a result of the two vessels moving in quite different mediums this proved to be hopelessly impracticable. However, it had to be tried before it could be discounted.

Although in 1921 the Navy had flown the blimp C-7 with helium as its lifting gas, the first airship in the world to do so, it was the Shenandoah which taught the Navy and indirectly the world, that however "safe" helium was by virtue of its nonflammability, it was no panacea. Indeed, helium created its own peculiar problems to afflict airship operations. Helium was first discovered on the sun in 1868 by means of solar spectrum analysis. It was not discovered on earth until 1895 when it was isolated from its terrestrial mother gases by means of expensive laboratory processes. It remained frightfully expensive---$2,500 per cubic foot---a laboratory curiousity until 1905 when natural gases in the Texas panhandle were discovered to be unusually rich in helium. This "unusual richness" nevertheless amounted to something less than one per cent of volume. World War I created a need for a nonflammable or "bulletproof" lifting gas for balloons and airships, and in 1917 the United States began developing industrial processes for large scale helium separation. This effort was only getting in gear when the war ended. At the time of the Armistice there was about 150,000 c.f. of helium stacked in cylinders on the piers of New Orleans, consigned to the Western Front.[26]

Helium was safe. But it also possessed substantially less lift than hydrogen.[27] As bad if not worse, it was expensive; so the operator was not only getting less for his money but was paying more for less.

Hydrogen cost about $3 per thousand cubic feet and airship operators were accustomed to taking off with their gas cells 100 per cent full for maximum lift; as the gas expanded with altitude the airship's automatic valves bled off the excess to the atmosphere. If the airship was too light upon landing, the operator simply valved off gas to make her heavy enough for the landing.

Helium was a totally different story. In 1923 it cost $123 per thousand c.f.; and although this was reduced to $50 by 1929 and $25 during the 1930's, its price never became remotely competitive with hydrogen. As a lifting gas, the only thing which made helium attractive was hydrogen's flammability.

The Americans were never permitted to be as free with helium as they had with hydrogen. Airships were not permitted to take off with their cells 100 per cent full; a 10 per cent slackness was mandatory to leave space for expansion at altitude so helium would not be valved off automatically. As an airship burns off fuel it becomes lighter and wants to climb higher. Ordinarily, gas would be valved to correct this situation. But the Americans were obliged to devise a system to generate ballast to replace the weight of the fuel. The Navy developed a means of condensing water vapor from the exhaust gases of the airship's engines which more than replaced the weight of fuel consumed. However, the weight of this water recovery apparatus was substantial, its aerodynamic drag was phenomenal, and its maintenance a constant headache.

Flying with helium assumed an adequate supply of the gas. In the mid-1920's there occurred a nagging helium shortage as the gas fields around Fort Worth lost pressure and the Congress debated the wisdom of funds for a new extraction plant near Amarillo which would tap the helium-rich Cliffside gas site. Until the Cliffside gas could be tapped, stern conservation was the order of the day and severely inhibited flying operations. More than a few American airship operators came to regard "safe" helium as less a blessing than a dark curse.

In her two years of existence the Shenandoah made 57 flights only a total 740 hours. It is likely that these hours would have been doubled had it not been for the helium shortage. Her most sensational flight was in October 1924, when she flew to the West Coast, to San Diego, and to Fort Lewis Washington. When she returned to the East Coast there was a new airship in the Lakehurst hanger: the ZR-3, just arrived from Germany. The ZR-3 had been inflated with hydrogen, which was valved to the atmosphere after her arrival. To make the new airship flyable the Shenandoah's helium had to be transferred to the ZR-3. There was insufficient helium for both. For want of helium the Shenandoah was grounded for the next eight months.

Construction of the ZR-3 (known in Germany as the LZ-126) had begun in the summer of 1922 and she made her first flight on 26 August 1924, the first of five trial flights in Germany. During 12-15 October the ZR-3 made her transatlantic delivery flight from Friedrichshaven to Lakehurst nonstop, a passage of 81 hours and 17 minutes. This was the seventh flight ever made across the North Atlantic; no one would fly it again until Charles Lindbergh in 1927.

On 25 November 1924, after the "transfusion" of the Shenandoah's helium, the ZR-3 flew to Washington, D.C., moored at the Naval Air Station at Anacostia, and here Mrs. Calvin Coolidge christened the airship Los Angeles. The Los Angeles was the only rigid airship in the world to fly with both hydrogen and helium, to provide comparative data on the effect of both gases on the performance of the same machine. With hydrogen the Los Angeles had a gross lift of 168,000 lbs. which included a useful lift of 81,600 lbs. With helium these figures were reduced to 153,000 and 63,100, respectively. The reduction in useful lift may appear drastic; but aside from the lesser lift of helium the Los Angeles' was increased by 4,000 lbs.---two tons---by the water recovery apparatus for conserving helium. This is the equivalent of 670 gallons of fuel she might otherwise have been able to carry. Only with hydrogen was the Los Angeles able to fly the Atlantic; with helium it was out of the question.

The Los Angeles operated for eight months, flying to Cuba, Porto Rico and Bermuda, besides to points within the United States---until she had to give up her helium to put the Shenandoah back in service.

In the summer of 1925 the Shenandoah operated in two minor exercises with the Atlantic Fleet. And in September she took off on a tour of the Midwest. During the night of 2-3 September she was literally torn to pieces by a thunderstorm over southern Ohio. Of the 43 persons on board 14 were killed.[28]

The destruction of the Shenandoah was a national sensation--wholly because of the uproar created by Billy Mitchell, who seized upon the disaster to indulge in the act of public insult and insubordination that resulted in his sensationalized court martial. The name of Billy Mitchell is rarely associated with the airship, and then only obliquely; presumably because it is indiscreet to associate "prophets" with dramatic failures. But as late as 1933, Mitchell was prophesying that the rigid airship would be the long-range strategic bomber of the next war.[29]

The airship was always very close to Billy Mitchell, and for six years the Army Air Service had waged a sometimes bitter behind-the-scenes political struggle to "retrieve" the rigid airship from the clutches of the Navy. Beyond the abortive "Hensley Zeppelin" of 1919, there was also a determined effort

THE LOS ANGELES

Moored to the mast of fleet tanker USS
Patoka, the Los Angeles took part in Fleet
Exercises off the west coast of Panama in
February 1931. (III-2 - U.S. Navy Photo)

to obtain the Los Angeles for the Army. In Mitchell's
"struggle for airpower" the rigid airship question was one of
his greatest frustrations. Small wonder that he should erupt
in such a mindless fashion over the Shenandoah disaster.

With the Shenandoah gone there was only one rigid airship
left in the United States---the Los Angeles. And in a sense
there was none---the Shenandoah disaster had also vented most
of the Navy's helium into the atomosphere. Seven months
passed before sufficient helium was on hand to inflate the
Los Angeles and she did not take to the air again until 13
April 1926. For the next six years the Los Angeles had an
active career, as a training ship and workhorse for developing
a new and more versatile mooring and ground handling system,
as a test bed for new devices to be used aboard the Akron and
Macon. In 1931 she flew to Panama to participate in her one-
and-only Fleet Exercise. On 30 June 1932, after 331 flights
totalling 4,181 hours, the Los Angeles was decommissioned by
way of an economy in deference to the Great Depression, and
never flew again---except at a mooring mast. On 24 October
1939 she was formally stricken and by February 1940 was completely dismantled and sold for junk; the U.S. Treasury gross-
ed $3,667.80 on the sale.

THE AKRON AND THE MACON

The Navy pressed for a replacement for the Shenandoah.
This question was less tortured by a popular outcry against
"murderous airships" than the syllogism: no helium, no airships.
The helium question was answered by new production in Amarillo,
and the airship question was answered by the ZRS4 and ZRS5,
the Akron and Macon.

The Akron and Macon were not only the Navy's first and
last truly naval airships---as distinct from school ships---
but were also significant by way of serving to create an airship building industry in the United States. The Navy had
built the ZR-1 itself by way of an learning experience and had
no desire to do so again; it wanted a private builder---more
than one if practicable---who would create an industrial base
for the state of the art, become a reliable supplier of airships, and have its facilities ready in the event of national
emergency. The Navy assumed that a private builder would,
given a basis by the navy construction, press on to build airship airliners for commerce in transoceanic passenger and mail
services. Operated with a Government subsidy via air mail contracts, these commercial airships would be built to Navy specifications for easy conversion to wartime use, and they would
be manned by crews who were members of the Naval Reserve.

The Goodyear Tire and Rubber Co. was more than ready to
become a builder but required a substantial order before it
could justify the relatively huge capital outlay for the

necessary industrial facilities. It had already created an aircraft subsidiary, the Goodyear-Zeppelin Co., expressly for this purpose.

In 1923, coincident to the completion of the Los Angeles in Germany, Goodyear and Luftschiffbau Zeppelin concluded a partnership by which the North American rights to the Zeppelin patents and all other technical data were made available to the new Goodyear-Zeppelin Co. And more than a dozen of Luftschiffbau's top engineering staff were put at the disposal of the new company. But beyond this point Goodyear could not move until a contract provided the incentive to invest a couple of million dollars in a manufacturing plant.

The necessary incentive was the Akron-Macon contract, awarded on 6 October 1938. The price of the first airship was $5,375,000, the second $2,450,000, for a total of $7,825,000. These prices are very significant because they are the only figures historians have for the actual construction of rigid airships in the United States; they provide the only baseline for what similar costs might have been at any point in time thereafter. As aviation money went in the interwar years, this was a breathtaking sum. The same money would have bought 176 Ford trimotor airliners or about 300 Navy fighter planes. Indeed, even eight years later this sum would have bought more than 60 Douglas DC-3's.

In the midst of the feverish effort to bring the Akron-Macon to fruition, the Navy contracted for a novel---indeed, unique---airship, the ZMC-2. It was not only an all-metal airship, but was probably and remains the largest monocoque aircraft structure in the history of aeronautics. The Metalclad airship was born of the genius of Ralph Upson, a Goodyear airship engineer who saw no future in rubber blimps or the complex redundancies of the Zeppelin-type airship. He went off to form his own company in the early 1920s. His Metalclad was a rigid airship in that it had a rigid hull, although it used ballonets---as does a blimp---to maintain a slight pressure inside its hull. Gas-tightness of hull's manifold riveted seams was maintained by a bitumastic paint applied inside the shell.

The egg-shaped ZMC-2 was delivered in 1929. Of only 200,000 c.f. her tight aspect ratio of 2.8:1 made for very poor longitudinal stability. But she was in truth meant to be no more than a "flying scale model" for much larger Metalclad airships to be built later. There were plans for an MC.38 of 3.8 million and an MC.72 of 7.2 million cubic feet; but there never was any money for their development. The Navy felt that its first commitment had to be to the more conservative and proved Zeppelin-type airship. Charles P. Burgess, one of the most knowledgeable airship design engineers in the world, figured out to his satisfaction that a Metalclad represented the "ultimate airship." But the "ultimate" for any airship was <u>money</u>. No money was available for a second Metalclad. But the little <u>ZMC-2</u> flew on very successfully for more than a decade, until finally reduced to scrap in 1941.[30]

Meanwhile, in November 1929, the huge airship hanger in Akron, Ohio, was almost completed and airship construction was already proceeding under its roof. On 8 August 1931--- less than three years from date of contract---the <u>Akron</u>, the largest airship in the world at that time, made her first flight. Even before the <u>Akron</u> had flown, sub-assemblies for the <u>Macon</u> were already under fabrication, and she made her flight on 21 April 1933 after a construction period of 21 months.[31]

For all practical purposes the <u>Akron</u> and <u>Macon</u> can be treated as one airship. They were sister ships, duplicates of one another---although the <u>Macon</u> enjoyed certain minor refine- ments which provided a small margin of superior performance over her sister. More to the point, the <u>Akron</u> was lost in a violent storm over the Atlantic on 3 April 1933 before the <u>Macon</u> took to the air. So their careers in no way paralelled each other. And on a linear time/experience basis the <u>Macon</u> clearly picked up where the Akron left off.

Most of the <u>Akron</u>'s 18-month existence, which included 73 flights totalling 1,695 hours, was spent in working out minor technical bugs, generating performance data to determine the airship's flight characteristics, and training a cadre for the <u>Macon</u>. The <u>Akron</u> participated in only two minor naval exercises and for these she was ill-prepared. On the other hand, within six months of her first flight the <u>Macon</u> was hustled out to the West Coast and rather mindlessly tossed into a series of Fleet Exercises which culminated in the Caribbean in the spring of 1934. The <u>Macon</u>'s whole career of 21 months, which included 54 flights totalling 1,798 hours, was directed toward making her an operational naval airship: in today's jargon, a "weapons system."

The most unusual---indeed, truly unique---aspect of <u>Akron-Macon</u> was that within their 785-foot-long hulls each could carry four airplanes equipped with "skyhooks" which could be launched and retrieved by means of a "trapeze" lowered from the airship. Once swung aboard the airship, the airplanes were transferred to an overhead trolley to be rolled back to a stowage point in one of the four corners of the "hanger" area. If necessary, a fifth airplane could be carried by leaving it on the raised trapeze in the center of the hanger; this was done but rarely.

As "scout cruisers of the air" with a radius of action of 2,300 miles at 70 knots, <u>Akron-Macon</u> could launch their air-

THE MACON

Two of her F9C fighter planes climb up to the
USS Macon preparatory to hook onto airship's trapeze
and being "landed on board." (III-3 – U.S. Navy)

planes ahead on their flanks on over-the-horizon searches
which not only more than trebled their area of search but also
prevented the slow, conspicuous and vulnerable airship from
coming within sight of the object of search. By way of developing airship-airplane search tactics little was achieved with
Akron, except by way of "preaching" by her airplane pilots. A
great deal was achieved by the Macon, especially by way of
mathematically programmed search techniques, radio communications and radiocompass homing devices. But on 12 February 1935
the Macon experienced a minor structural failure which quickly
passed out of control and she crashed in the Pacific.

The loss of the Macon marked the end of an era: she was
not only the last rigid airship in the Navy but the last built
in the United States; and she was the last military rigid airship in the world.

Concurrent to the end of the Akron-Macon the great promise
of an era of American transoceanic commercial airships also
ended---before it could even begin. Although this effort
proved to be wholly abortive, the history of the airship in
America cannot really be understood without its treatment.

FATE OF COMMERCIAL AIRSHIPS

While Akron-Macon were under construction Goodyear revised their basic design with a 73-foot "stretch" to create a
commercial airliner capable of carrying 80 passengers and 12
tons of cargo. This was the stillborn GZ-3. Akron-Macon
were 785 ft. long and of 6,500,000 c.f.; the GZ-3 would have
been 858 ft. long and of 7,500,000 c.f.

In 1929 there was created the International Zeppelin
Transport Co. (IZT), a German-American consortium for transatlantic airship services; and there was a Pacific-Zeppelin
Transport Co., an all-American group for transpacific service.
Goodyear was an elementary constituent in both organizations,
but they were also supported by a formidable spectrum of American industrial firms and financial houses.

To be economically viable in an early stage of operations
such airship services required subsidies similar to commercial
airplane operations, namely air mail contracts. But because
of their phenomenal payloads and equally phenomenal building
costs, the airship's legal requirements were substantially
different from the airplane's. To establish these in law a
Merchant Marine Airship Bill was introduced into the Congress
in 1930. By 1933, it had zig-zagged its way through the maze
of House and Senate committees, had succeeded in passing the
House and there was every indication it would pass in the
Senate. But here the bill foundered which had nothing to do with
its merits. Two days later Congress adjourned. The Airship
Bill was lost---for at least that session of Congress. Or so

it seemed. A few days later, on 3 April 1933, the Akron crashed. Seventy-three persons died in the Akron, only three of her crew survived. And a multi-million dollar airship was wiped out. In the ensuing popular uproar the Merchant Airship Bill became a dead letter---duly sealed by the loss of the Macon two years later.[32]

After the loss of the Macon the Airship Question in America flew into its "years of confusion." Within the Navy the question had been posed and answered even while the Macon was flying when Admiral Joseph M. Reeves, Commander-in-Chief U.S. Fleet, remarked in secret testimony before the Navy's General Board: "For one dirigible at a cost of $4,000,000 you could have 26 of these patrol planes that you are talking about today, so in that comparison, as Commander-in-Chief of the Fleet, if you should ask me whether I would have one dirigible or 26 patrol planes, I would answer patrol planes."[33]

Reeves was speaking in the autumn of 1934. The "patrol plane" in question was the Consolidated PBY, contracted for in October 1933, whose prototype flew on 28 March 1935; and during 14-15 October 1935 it made a startling nonstop flight from Panama to San Francisco with, unknown to the world, plenty of range to spare. The PBY became an incredibly versatile airplane, a legend in its own time, retired only in 1957. During World War II literally thousands of PBYs were built. The same money that bought thousands of PBYs would have bought a few hundred rigid airships. How reliable, versatile and effective they would have been is debatable. It is clearly doubtful if any would have survived to 1957, much less 1976. Many PBYs are still flying today in civil services in far off corners of the world.

The commercial aspects of the Airship Question of the 1930s was answered in a study prepared for the Government in 1939. The study was sloppily done, studded with exaggerations on behalf of the airplane, and glossed over with too many cowardly equivocations; but in the end it finally came down against the airship.[34]

More to the point---which this study tended to skate around---is that the Martin M.130 flying boat which Pan American Airways had been using in transpacific services since 1935 cost only $350,000 each; and the new Boeing 314 flying boats which took to the air in 1938 and went into service in 1939 cost only $500,000 each. Thus for two "stretched" Akron-Macon airliners at a hypothetical price of $10 million an operator could buy 20 Boeing 314s; and instead of flying two transatlantic frequencies per week he could offer at least one a day, with airplanes---or cash---to spare. In 1928, C. G. Grey, the prickly but prescient editor of the British weekly, The Aeroplane, remarked: "Airships breed like elephants and aeroplanes like rabbits. Consequently the airship is many, many generations in the process of evolution behind the aeroplane."[35] This was never more clear than ten years later in 1938, by which time the British airship effort was eight years dead, the Akron gone for five years and the Macon at the bottom of the Pacific for three; a year had passed since the Hindenburg had burned at Lakehurst, the old Graf Zeppelin grounded never to fly again, and the new Graf Zeppelin's commercial future was dependent upon American helium.

Also in 1928, on the occasion of the Graf Zeppelin's first flight to America, after making the 18th flight ever across the North Atlantic, Charles Lindbergh remarked: "The airship has definitely established its present-day superiority over heavier-than-air craft for transoceanic travel. After four trips over the Atlantic the Zeppelin still holds a 100 per cent record, whereas such flights by airplane are at best hazardous undertakings."[36] Ten years later to the day, Lindbergh was visiting the Dornier aircraft factory at Friedrichshaven and made a point to call at the nearby Zeppelin works where the new Graf Zeppelin, sister ship of the ill-fated Hindenburg, rested tethered in her hanger. However beautiful her silvery form, Lindbergh was nevertheless depressed, remarking: "This airship represented the result of all the years of development of lighter-than-air. She seemed to me like a last member of a once proud and influential family. I can see no future for the airship. It is inherently too slow---about half the speed of a plane. There is not room for the dirigible between the steamship and the airplane. It may have a few more years of life, but then it will probably become even more extinct than the squarerigger and the tea clipper."[37]

Lindbergh had no idea of how few those "few more years" would be. Within two years, in May 1940, the Graf Zeppelin he had visited, and the old Graf Zeppelin he welcomed to America in 1928, were reduced to scrap. The rigid airship was rudely rendered extinct.[38]

BLIMPS

While the world was almost wholly absorbed by the awesome prospects of the large rigid airship, the non-rigid blimp experienced twenty years of relative neglect.

In 1918, the U.S. Navy had on its drawing boards a G-class blimp of 400,000 c.f., which was an extraordinarily large blimp for that day. But when it came time to let a contract for the G-ship's fabrication the war had ended; the stretched out and delayed plans for rigid airships made necessary "focus" on a diminishing number of dollars. The G-ship "giant blimp" was shelved for almost 20 years. At the same time, there developed a consensus that blimps, meant for training or short-range coastal patrol, should not exceed 200,000 c.f.; any logical "next step" would be to a "small" rigid airship of 2,000,000 c.f.

From 1919 to 1939 the Navy blimp development was negligible. What innovations that did occur were owed to Goodyear and, indirectly, to the Army. In 1923, Goodyear built a small single-engine blimp of its own, called the Pilgrim, of 47,700 c.f. The Pilgrim was striking to the eye; wholly different from existing Army and Navy blimps. Her control car was mounted up snug against her envelope, apparently an integral part of the hull. Technically, this was made possible by the car's suspensions being attached to a catenary system inside the envelope. This innovation was made practicable by the Pilgrim's use of helium. Aerodynamically the internal suspensions resulted in a phenomenal clean-up of the airship; and as a result of the car and the envelope approximating a single unit, the blimp became much easier to handle on the ground.[39]

In 1928 Goodyear added the Puritan to its airship advertising effort, but it was not until 1929 that the Goodyear blimp fleet was born. Suddenly, within five months, the Volunteer, Mayflower, Vigilant and Defender swarmed into the skies of America. The mission of this fleet was not merely to advertise rubber products, but to make Americans "airship conscious," and to train airship crews for the forthcoming--- but stillborn---fleet of transoceanic rigid airship airliners. Unwittingly, it also created a new Americanism, "the Goodyear blimp," whose usage seldom has anything to do with rubber tires or airships; and it made the work "blimp" synonomous with Goodyear.

After 1925 and all through the 1930s Goodyear developed a mechanical mooring system for its blimps so that its fleet could be serviced with minimum of ground crew, from a truck or the back of a bus. Whereas military blimps tended to be chained to their air stations where there were always large ground crews available, the Goodyear blimps migrated around the U.S., barnstorming as it were, and learned how to do it with minimum of ground facilities. Goodyear also put a castering pneumatic tire under the control car of its blimps. This was originally meant to make ground handling easier, and it did. But it was quickly discovered that it also allowed the airship to make a take off run like an airplane and exploit the dynamic lift created by its hullform to carry greater loads off the ground. In the early 1930s the Army was quick to exploit this "heavy take off" technique with its few blimps.

In 1931 the Navy procured its first new blimp in almost a decade. This was the K-1, which was unusual in that it was designed to burn a fuel gas (similar to propane), in its engines.[40] Inside the K-1s 319,000 c.f. envelope was a ballonet which enclosed 51,700 c.f. of fuel gas. What made this attractive is that the fuel gas had approximately the same density as air and thus weighed "next to nothing"---especially as compared to gasoline at six pounds per gallon. The K-1 represented an interesting experiment, and there tended to be a consensus among the airship pilots of that day that the K-1 was "too large" for a blimp.

In 1935 the Navy bought one of the Goodyear advertising blimps, the former Defender, "off-the-shelf," so to say; and she became the G-1, of no relation whatever to the aborted G-ship of 1918. The G-1 was the Navy's first truly "modern" blimp. But it was not until 1937 that the blimp began to experience a discernable renaissance in the Navy. When the Army terminated its airship operations in 1937, it turned over its leftovers to the Navy. Among this hodge-podge of curiousities were the TC-10 and TC-11, but also also the new TC-13 and TC-14, and these latter two were superior to all of the blimps the Navy had except, perhaps, the G-1. The Army's airship program was always starved for funds, but with respect to blimp development it was quite progressive.[41] Being "No. 2," they "tried harder."

Although the Army abandoned its airship operations in the name of "economy," if truth can ever be determined, it is likely that technological expediency will provide a more rational answer.[42] In 1934, the Army Air Corps started to receive its first Martin B-10s, which were procured in rather large numbers, but most significantly represented the first truly modern bomber in the history of the world. In 1934, the B-10's performance was no less than breathtaking. At almost the same time, in 1935, the Army bought its first autogiro, a rotary wing aircraft, which was smaller, relatively inconspicuous in battle conditions, cheaper, more rugged and easier to handle than any conceivable blimp. Thus it may be seen that by 1936 the Army airship was whipsawed between the modern bomber and the promise of the rotary wing aircraft.[43]

A quarter of a century later the Navy blimp would be caught in a similar technological whipsaw and go the same way as the Army blimp did in 1937. Meanwhile, the Navy was moving to catch up to where it had been with blimps twenty years before. And in 1938 the Navy received the new K-2 airship (of no relation whatever to the K-1), of 404,000 c.f. Thus after two decades the Navy had a blimp of approximately the same volume and performance as originally envisioned for the aborted G-ship of 1919.[44] The explanation of this is rather simple: in striving to achieve the "best," namely the big rigid airship, the tight budgets of the interwar years had made it necessary for the Navy to neglect the "good," i.e., the blimp.

WORLD WAR II

When the European War started on 3 September 1939 there were only eleven airships in the United States. Five were the Goodyear advertising blimps, small airships of varying performance. Seven belonged to the U.S. Navy, and this was a hodge-podge fleet, no two of which were remotely alike, and taken altogether represented a collection of 20 years of airship technology which required a museum to house.[45] There was the ancient J-4 which dated from the early 1920s, the "one-of" K-1 and the almost brand new K-2, the G-1 and L-1 training airships, the absolutely unique ZMC-2 (leaking helium badly), and the former Army TC-13. The Navy also had the Army's TC-14 control car since 1937, but never had been able to fund a new envelope. It is ironic that in this September of 1939, the United States blimp situation was only a little worse than the national four-engine airplane situation. There were eleven blimps and only a few more than two-dozen four-engine airplanes.[46]

As a result of the United States rearmament program of 1940 seven new K-type patrol airships and two L-type training airships were ordered. Less than half of these were in hand when Japan attacked Pearl Harbor. After the attack on Pearl Harbor the Navy commandeered the five available airships of the Goodyear fleet. However a mixed bag they represented, they served to practically double the Navy"s effective airship patrol force.[47]

Wartime expansion of the Navy's airship effort did not get under way until almost mid-1942. By 1943, Navy airship operations had expanded from its lone nest at Lakehurst to resume operations out of Moffett Field, California, and establish a chain of bases reaching from Massachusetts to Richmond, Florida, to Key West and into the Gulf of Mexico. By 1944 the system of airship bases facing the Atlantic reached across the Caribbean to South America and as far south as Rio de Janiero. Concurrently, unprecedented numbers of blimps were ordered. By the end of the war almost 200 had been taken into the inventory.[48]

The backbone of the Navy's anti-submarine warfare airship patrol fleet in World War II was the K-ship, an airship which varied in volume from an initial 416,000 c.f. to a final 456,000 c.f. Aside from an apparent difference, the increase in volume provided a nominal increase in lift of about 2,500 lbs., and concommitant increase in dynamic lift for heavy take-offs, which during the war tended to become the usual in Navy airship operations. Meanwhile, the G and L ships were retained as training airships.[49]

U.S. NAVY'S WORLD WAR II BLIMPS

Stable of the U.S. Navy's "blimps" of World
War II are shown in this composite: the L-ship,
123,000 c.f.; the G-ship, 196,700 c.f.; the K-
ship, 425,000 c.f.; and, the M-ship, 725,000 c.f.
(III-4 - U.S. Navy)

And there was attrition. The Navy's first airship losses of World War II proved to be quite extraordinary and rather mystifying. On the night of 8 June 1942 the airships G-1 and L-2 were groping around the Atlantic's night sky in the vicinity of Point Pleasant, N.J. They were making rendezvous with a Coast Guard cutter to test a "black box" for detecting submarines. While plodding around through the dark the the L-2 flew into the G-1. Both envelopes experienced catastrophic tears and the airships fell into the sea. Of the 13 persons on board the two blimps only one survived. Although there had been tales of collisions between airships, or near misses, all were apocraphyl.[50] This was the first mid-air collision between airships in the history of aeronautics. Sad to say, it was not the last. On the morning of 16 October 1943 the airship K-64 was returning to Lakehurst after an offshore patrol in poor visibility when, in the vicinity of Barnegat, N.J., the training ship K-7 popped out of the gloom and ran her down. The K-64 caught fire and fell into the sea with a loss of nine lives; the K-7 sustained only minor damaged.[51]

However extraordinary these accidents were, airship losses during the war were in no way disproportinate to airplane losses, and they increased in direct ratio to the number of airships being operated by hastily-trained wartime crews. A nominal 56 airships were "lost"---but most of these entailed ground handling accidents in which an envelope was torn, the blimp deflated, and there may have been minor damage to the control car. But a week or two later this same blimp, with repairs, would be flying again---after having become a "lost" statistic.[52]

The only blimp lost to enemy action was the K-74. On the night of 18 July 1943 she discovered the submarine U-134 on surface between Florida and Cuba and went in for an attack. As bad luck would have it, when the airship was over the U-boat her bombs failed to release. In the meantime the U-boat's flak gunners had riddled the blimp, and as the airship staggered away, the U-134 submerged and stole away---to be sunk weeks later by British bombers in the Bay of Biscay.[53] The K-74 landed at sea and finally sank; of the ten persons aboard the airship nine survived. Ironically, the K-74's pilot was almost awarded a court martial---for over-zealousness.

One of the most interesting airship operations of World War II occurred during 28 May-1 June 1944 when six airships of Squadron ZP-14 flew from the United States to Newfoundland and across the Atlantic to Port Lyautey in French Morocco, via a fuel and servicing stop in the Azores.[54] These were the first transatlantic flights made by a non-rigid airship.[55] Operating from near Port Lyautey these airships created a low altitude MAD (magnetic airborne detection) barrier across the Strait of Gibraltar to detect the German submarines which were known to be fleeing the Mediterranean at that time. After the Allied invasion of Southern France in August 1944 the blimps of ZP-14 followed the Fleet into the Mediterranean, operating from bases in Sardinia, Italy and from the old French airship base at Cuers near Toulon. And in these months they assisted in the sweeping of mines from Mediterranean ports and their offshore waters---a mission taken over many years later by the helicopter.[56]

Samuel Eliot Morison, the quasi-official historian of the U.S. Navy's operations during World War II, has written that the airship's anti-submarine capabilities "proved to be largely unfounded" and that "most naval officers regarded them as inferior to planes for area patrol and worse than useless in convoy coverage because they could be sighted by a U-boat even further away than the most smoke-careless freighter."[57]

In the mind of any historian who was interested in something more than writing up the Navy's operations in World War II as more than a Harvard-Yale game played in salt water combined with the scenario of High Noon, this might have raised a question about ASW air patrols. Was their primary mission to deter attacks upon the convoys, or was it to use the convoys--- their crews, bottoms and valuable cargos---as bait to lure submarines in for a possible kill, losing ships in the process? An important question. But Morison never thought to raise it, much less run down an answer. Morison went on to say that the presence of a blimp escort contributed greatly to the morale of the crews who manned the merchant ships---the U-boat target---in a convoy. And it is a matter of record that no merchant ships were sunk while under the escort of airships. As much as this can mean something, however, it can also mean nothing. It does not necessarily follow that U-boats were in the same area, sighted these convoys, and were deterred from attacking by the sight of the "rubber cloud."

Whatever interrogations Admiral Morison conducted of the former U-boat commanders (and they do not appear to be many, nor of any depth), one thing he failed to determine was the enemy's reaction to a Luftschiff upon the horizon. After the passage of 30 years we will probably never know. The blimp had few opportunities to "bite" and how nasty its bite could always be a hypothetical question. The great pity is that we will never know how good it might have been as a "barking dog."[58]

On the other hand, partisans of the airship love to point to statistics which show that the more blimp bases that were commissioned around the western rim of the Atlantic Basin and the more airships that were launched into the sky, the more the U-boat menace was beaten back.[59] This grossly overstates the case by ignoring the increasing numbers of escort ships available after 1942, the fleet of small but versatile escort carriers and their hunter-killer groups which came into being after 1943 which proved to be the most effective U-boat killers of the war; the hundreds of land-based patrol planes, the very long-range Liberators being the most effective, and the vitally important bases in the Azores created in 1944 which closed the dreadful "Atlantic gap."

The truth of the airship's contribution to naval operations in World War II---even a half-way muddled approximation of it---remains to be determined.

One of the most significant airship developments of the war was the M-ship, a relatively "huge" blimp of 625,000 c.f. In June 1942 the Navy ordered six and quickly increased the order to a total of 22; and almost as quickly it was inexplicably cut back to four. All of which suggests much disagreement on the subject within the Bureau of Aeronautics and the "too big" faction won the argument. Everyone would regret it after 1945 when they were stuck with stretching and "modifying" the ancient wartime Ks. The four M-ships were delivered in 1944 and from their original volume of 625,000 c.f. they were successively retailored with envelopes of 647,000 and 725,000 c.f., almost twice the volume of the K-ships. But in terms of time, technology and opportunity this is of less significance than the fact that a-way back in the "dark ages" of 1938 Goodyear had offered the Navy a blimp design of 800,700 c.f. It was rejected because in 1938 the Lighter-than-Air Section within the Bureau of Aeronautics thought it might yet get another rigid airship.[60] The "good" was to be sacrificed for the "better"; the possible for the desirable ---indeed, for the desired-most: the rigid airship.

During the war there was a small but senior and quite influential element within the Bureau of Aeronautics that continued to urge a revival of the rigid airship. Goodyear had the preliminary design of a 10,000,000 c.f. airship ready and in a variety of possible configurations. The question arises here is if elements within the Navy airship organization cut back the M-ship because they feared it would conflict with their hope---or dream---of reviving the rigid airship. It remains to be determined if there was an influential conviction, which, in its expectation of a revival of the rigid airship echoed the estimate of 1919 that a large rigid was the logical "next step," not the large blimp. The Navy ultimately procured a blimp of 1,500,000 c.f., the ZPG-3W of 1959, more than 15 years after a large O-ship of similar design was aborted in 1943.

Technology is by no means a simple matter of "nuts and bolts"; too much of its acceptance and ultimate success depends upon human emotions, old habits of mind, and the accidents of timing. The question here with respect to the very large blimp is if the "bird in hand" was sacrificed for the lure of faint warbling in the fogs of yesteryear.

AFTER WORLD WAR II

Cutbacks in Navy airship operations after the war seemed drastically greater that military cuts everywhere because of the relative smallness of the airship entity. Overseas bases were quickly rolled up; operations on the West Coast retreated to Moffett Field where they were finally terminated; while on the East Coast they retreated through the Gulf of Mexico, across Florida and up the East Coast to focus on Lakehurst. For a moment it appeared as if airship operations would be jammed back into the isolation of Lakehurst and be reduced to a New Jersey tourist attraction as they had on the eve of the war. But the onset of the Cold War and the ominous threat of the large Soviet submarine fleet served to breath new life into airship operations.

Meanwhile, in the immediate postwar era the Goodyear blimp fleet was revived with an initial fleet of five airships, four ex-Navy L-ships and one K-ship.[61] Goodyear no longer had the skies to itself. The New York advertising firm of Douglas Leigh & Co. bought several war surplus blimps, made arrangements to use Navy surplus base facilities and had no difficulty in finding ex-Navy airship crews to man its fleet of blimps. Leigh sold advertising on its blimps to anyone who would buy it. It appears to have been profitable as long as surplus Navy equipment and spares were available and the leasing of Navy ground facilities could be maintained. But surplus material could not last forever and the exigencies of the Cold War soon crowded Leigh & Co. out of Navy bases. That was the end of its operations.

The postwar era saw an organized effort to revive the rigid airship as a transoceanic airliner. The proposed airship could have been of 10,000,000 c.f. and almost a thousand feet long. There were three variants: a luxury version for 110 passengers in staterooms; a "mass transit" type for 300 passengers in reclining seats; and an all-cargo variant with 20,000 square feet of floor space for 180,000 lbs. of cargo. The airship proposals were rejected by President Truman's Air Policy Commission (Finletter Board), and although Congress subsequently passed an airship development act, it died as a result of Truman's pocket veto.[62]

If the rigid airship had been given a green light and they had cut metal on it in 1949, it is unlikely that the first article would have flown before 1951. Assuming that one could be produced at a rate of every 18 months thereafter, the fleet of four would not be operating before 1955. At least $64 million would have been spent. The same money would have bought 53 Douglas DC-6Bs or Lockheed Super Constellations. More to the point, when the first of four rigid airships came into service in 1955 the Boeing "Dash Eighty," prototype for the 707 airliner, would have already been flying for a year and be only two years away from airline service. In sum it can be said that 1948 was fifteen years too late for the rigid airship: it would never retrieve the position lost in 1933.

Of the Navy's post World War II airship operations little is known with any certainty because most of those years remain behind the wall of national security which, even when it can lowered, records tend to be of difficult access. During 1948-1958, the old K-ships of World War II were modernized to become 2Ks, 3Ks and even 4Ks, with larger envelopes and thus greater lift, and improved electronics, plus such new developments as the ability to take on ballast at sea, refuel in flight from the deck of an aircraft carrier, employ a towed sonar and later a variable depth sonar.[63]

Technologically, the Ks were a dead end. More significant for the postwar era were the M-ships. Although only four in number they were more versatile as squadron airships and priceless as prototypes for how large a non-rigid blimp could grow. Among other things developed with the M-ship was a tricycle landing gear to facilitate heavy take-offs and make ground handling easier; something a blimp never had before. To become more efficient the airship could only grow larger to increase its volume, because gas volume was its first factor of flight. First significant step in this direction after the M-ships was the ZPN of 875,000 c.f., which first flew in 1951 and was the prototype for the 'big bag' series of blimps which finally crossed the one million cubic foot "barrier" with the ZPG-2 series of 1953.

The ZPN was not only a big step toward volume but also it contained most of the innovations seen in all Navy airships thereafter. It had a well streamlined double-decked control car, the car's upper deck tucked away inside the envelope; both engines were inside the control car with the propeller on outriggers and the engines were capable of being cross-connected so that either engine could turn either propeller; and its empennage was quite unusual. Hitherto, an airship's tailgroup was afixed 90° to the vertical; the ZPN's were pitched at 45° in an "X" configuration. This not only eliminated the hazard of damaging the lower stabilizer during take-off runs, it is also said to have substantially increased the airship's maneuverability.

Concurrent to the "radical" ZPN's procurement during 1949-51, the Navy was also proceeding along more conservative lines with the ZS2G airship of 630,000 c.f. as an interim between the last "stretches" of the Ks and the new generaton represented by the ZPN. The ZS2G made its first flight in 1954 and 18 of them were ultimately procured between 1955 and 1958. They were distinctive to the eye as a result of their inverted "Y" tail structure. The ZS2Gs served well as a "backup" to the more advanced ZPG-2s which became available almost concurrently.

Meanwhile, the Navy had long since been concerned with an airborne early warning (AEW) mission relative to continental air defense and airplanes had already been procured for this mission. But whereas an airplane's endurance is measured in a few hours an airship's endurance can run to days. During March 1956 a ZPG-2 airship flew nonstop circumnavigation of the North Atlantic from South Weymouth, Mass., to the coast of Portugal, turning west off Morocco to the Virgin Islands, finally landing in Florida after flying a track of 9,740 miles and being in the air for 264 hours, 14 minutes and 18 seconds, a trifle more than ten days. This is an unrefueled endurance record which has remained unbroken from that day to this.[64] To exploit this endurance in terms of an early warning mission five ZPG-2 ASW blimps were procured as ZPG-2Ws, carrying a huge airborne radar installation. The 2W led almost immediately to the larger ZPG-3W of 1.5 million cubic feet, the largest blimp ever built. By the time the first four 3Ws entered service in 1959 lighter-than-air aeronautics as a whole was, ironically enough, almost at the end of its tether in the Navy.

The speed and reliability of other vehicles has always been the technological enemy of the airship. The speed and reliability that the modern airplane achieved quite suddenly during the 1930s literally transcended the utility of the rigid airship. Until the nuclear-powered submarine appeared in the late 1950s the airship had a distinct speed advantage. The nuclear-powered boat reduced this substantially, and combined with its capability to run at high speeds indefinitely, to dive deeper than diesel boats, and remain submerged indefinitely, rendered the blimp's ASW capability marginal. In 1958 the Navy created Task Group Alfa. It was a special Fleet organization with the specific mission of developing new ASW tactics. The blimp was not invited to join Alfa. The handwriting was on the wall. In a similar way the airship's early warning mission detecting the approach of relatively "slow" airplanes, was transcended by the ballistic missile. Assuming the Russian Sputnik demonstration of 1957 to mark the turning point, the threat against North America was less from manned bombers than ballistic missiles whose time-of-flight was measured in minutes. With each passing year there was a diminishing need of airships--airplanes, too, for that matter ---to provide an airborne early warning barrier.

Thus on 21 June 1960 the Secretary of the Navy approved the recommended phase-out of airship operations in the Navy. At this time Navy airship operations were already down to ten airships, as compared to about fifty only ten years before. On 31 October 1960 Fleet Airship Wing One and its two squad-

EARLY WARNING AIRSHIPS

Two ZPG-3W early warning airships at Akron, Ohio, in 1959. Displacing 1.5 million cubic feet the "3W" was not only the last airship procured by the Navy but the largest blimp-type ever made. (III-5 – U.S. Navy)

rons were formally decommissioned at Lakehurst. That was the end of the Navy's organized airship operations, and the last military airship operation in the world.

Two airships were kept flying for various research and development projects until 1962; but on 31 August 1962 the last of these airships made its final flight. This brought to an end the Navy's 45-year-old experiment with lighter-than-air aeronautics and terminating its longest military application in the history of flight.

During the airship's final years there were various proposals for applications other than those which were directly military. Both rigid and blimp types were many times proposed as the logical test bed for a nuclear engine---nothing ever came of these schemes, neither the aircraft nor the engine.[66] The blimp was seriously studied as an aerial command and control aircraft for SAC and the Air Defense Command; but the Air Force preferred to modify KC-135 jet tankers for this mission.[67] And it was proposed that blimps be used to airlift bulky stages of NASA's Saturn rockets directly from their factories on the West Coast to Cape Canaveral; but NASA preferred to use the "Pregnant Guppy" or stretched aircraft or ships and barges. In the end, everything came to nothing.

The Goodyear blimp was also in travail.[68] During the late 1950s television became a dramatically effective advertising medium and Goodyear began to channel ever more of its advertising budget into the ethereal medium. By 1959 the blimp fleet consisted of one airship, the Mayflower, and there were members of the Goodyear hierarchy who regarded her as "old fashioned," urging that the "blimp dollar" would yield more if it was invested in other media, especially television. Once again speed emerged as the airship's enemy; but in this case it was the speed of radio communications and the speed of light at that. At this point someone had the wit to make an extensive study of the "blimp situation" and it was discovered what the public had known for more than a quarter of a century: "blimp" had become synonomous with "Goodyear." What was more, it was finally recognized that the airship generated free TV time whenever it appeared over public events because cameramen could not resist turning their cameras skyward--- "and here comes the Goodyear blimp!" In turn, however, the TV nets found that the Goodyear blimps also made excellent camera stations when portable cameras had been developed.

And so the Goodyear blimp was saved. Today there is in America a fleet of three airships, based at Miami, Houston and in Los Angeles; once a year they usually fly back to Akron for an extensive inspection and overhaul. And there is a new blimp Europa based near Rome and which tours Western Europe during the summer. The Goodyear fleet has carried more than a half million passengers without injury and provide a measure of awe,

The Goodyear blimp Columbia, 192-ft. long, of 202,700 cubic feet, and powered by two 210-hp engines, cruises at about 35 mph, and is one of three similar airships operated in the United States, a fleet which flies more than 100,000 miles per year. What appears to be a grid on the blimp's lower hull is created by 3,780 electric light bulbs on each side, which, by means of a computer tape, can flash word messages and animated pictures for night advertising. (III-6 - Goodyear Photo)

good cheer and speculation wherever they appear. The younger generation is led to wonder what happened to the giant airships of years long gone while the older generation is often swept by a wave of nostalgia.

The Goodyear fleet has curiously served to bring the airship in America full circle to those days circa 1905 when the crude "home-built" airships of Thomas Scott Baldwin "barnstormed" state fairs. The airship's function then was advertising and entertainment and that is its only function now.

IN RETROSPECT

Over the years there have always been those who claimed that the airship was neglected, never fully exploited, and there were many missions that only the airship could perform. During September 1974, the Flight Transportation Laboratory of the Massachusetts Institute of Technology held a week-long symposium on lighter-than-air vehicles at Monterey, California. It was co-sponsored by NASA, the Navy, the FAA and the Department of Transportation, and more than 60 technical papers were given to more than 200 persons attending.[69] It was the first such symposium since the last formal meeting of the Guggenheim Airship Institute in Akron, Ohio, during the summer of 1935.[70] The only subject that this remarkable symposium in 1974 failed to consider was the source or sources of the hundreds of millions of dollars necessary to transform any of these possible projects into three dimensional reality. Money was always the problem of the airship in the 1920s, and 1930s; it appears even more so for the 1970s and 1980s.

If this paper had treated with the history of the airplane it would have to end on a positive note, summarizing the airplane's great services to society, its vital role in civilization and how it will continue to change the world. Even the humble balloon can be rendered similar honors. It can be pointed out that every day, thousands of times a day, the balloon is used by meteorologists all over the world, and more than a hundred times a year scientists use extraordinarily large balloons to probe the upper air.

Unfortunately the same cannot be said about the airship. The rigid airship stands in history as a marvelous engineering curiousity, a monument to early structural analysis, and a vehicle which will have everlasting attractions--until economists step into the picture. The romantic will be forever enamored of the rigid airship. But the brutal fact is that its military effectiveness was marginal at best and its social utility was zero. The blimp's military effectiveness was marginal at best and its only enduring social utility has been as a singularly effective advertising medium of great charm.

In spite of a recent revival of interest in the airship, and a rash of literature which asserts that the airship has a great and unexploited future, it nevertheless continues to appear that such a future was lost somewhere in an increasingly distant past.

REFERENCE NOTES

1. Richard K. Smith, First Across! The U.S. Navy's Transatlantic Flight of 1919. Annapolis: Naval Institute Press, 1973.

2. Graham Wallace, The Flight of Alcock and Brown. London: Putnam, 1955.

3. The New York Herald, 28 June 1919, p. 1.

4. Ibid.

5. Arthur Whitten Brown, Flying the Atlantic in Sixteen Hours. NY: Frederick A. Stokes, 1920, p. 109.

6. Patrick Abbott, Airship: The Story of the R.34 and the First East-West Crossing of the Atlantic by Air. NY: Scribner's, 1973.

7. New York Times, 2 July 1919, p. 12.

8. Jerome C. Hunsaker, "The Present Status of Airships in Europe," Journal of the Franklin Institute, vol. 177 (June 1914), pp. 597-639.

9. Jerome C. Hunsaker, "Naval Airships," Transactions, Society of Automotive Engineers, vol. 14, Part I (1919), pp. 578-89; and his "Airship Engineering Progress in the United States," Aviation, vol. 7 (15 August 1919), pp. 72-76; and (1 September 1919), pp. 123-28.

10. Douglas H. Robinson, "Dr. August Greth and the First Airship Flight in the United States," American Aviation Historical Society, Journal, vol. 21 (Summer 1976), pp. 89-91.

11. C. R. Roseberry, Glenn Curtiss: Pioneer of Flight. NY: Doubleday, 1972, pp. 35-58.

12. Charles DeForrest Chandler and Frank P. Lahm, How Our Army Grew Wings: Airmen and Aircraft before 1914. NY: Ronald Press, 1943, pp. 107-23.

13. The remains of the SC-1 were purchased by Mr. Gould Dietz of Omaha who realized their historic value---especially its Curtiss engine. He subsequently donated the engine to the Smithsonian Institution.

14. The Army was to have received all of the Navy's six D-ships but the D-1 and D-6 were destroyed by fire (the hydrogen hazard); and the C-2 and C-6 were substituted in their place. Meanwhile, in 1919, the Army initiated its own blimp procurement effort.

15. Archibald Turbull and Clifford L. Lord, A History of United States Naval Aviation. New Haven: Yale Univ. Press, 1949, pp. 63-66.

16. Most information in this paper re. Navy blimps is taken from Richard K. Smith, "An Inventory of U.S. Navy Airships, with Miscellaneous Characteristics, Performance and Contract Data, 1916-1961," Manuscript, 1964, 110 pp. This monograph exists only in typescript at the Office of Naval History, Washington, D.C.

17. Assuming the reader may wonder at the omission of E and F-type blimps, there was only one of each and they were essentially motorized kite balloons.

18. While in Germany Hensley was told (apparently by the braggart Ernst Lehmann who regarded most Americans with cynical contempt), about the L.72 being designed to bomb New York; he gullibly accepted it and brought this canard back to America where hack writers tend to resurrect it at least once a decade for the continuing misinformation of all. See Douglas H. Robinson, Giants in the Sky. London: Foulis, 1973, p. 139.

19. Charles L. Keller, "The Hensley Affair," American Aviation Historical Society, Journal, vol. 10 (Winter 1965), pp. 282-86.

20. Hensley's expedition was an amateurish affair as compared to some highly-organized missions put together by the Army and Navy in which engineers and scientists were quickly given commissions and uniforms so they could penetrate English and French research and industrial facilities to develop information that regular officers were incapable of perceiving. In contrast, before V-E day in 1945 Allied technical intelligence teams consisting of scientists and engineers in uniform but without rank moved into defeated Germany behind the armed forces. The 1918-1919 experience has so far been ignored by historians.

21. Best survey of the whole American rigid airship effort is Robinson, Giants in the Sky, Op. cit.

22. U.S. Department of State, _Papers Relating to the Foreign Relations of the U.S.: The Paris Peace Conference, 1919_ (Washington: GPO, 1946), vol. 8, pp. 443-446; and vol. 13, pp. 198-354.

23. _Papers Relating to the Foreign Relations of the U.S., 1921_, vol. 2, pp. 58-70; and _1924_, vol. 2, pp. 170-83. It is often remarked that the only "reparations" the U.S. got out of World War I was a "Zeppelin"; but the State Department was always at pains to make clear that the ZR-3 in no way constituted reparations.

24. Robinson, _Giants In The Sky, Op. cit._, pp. 186-206.

25. The importance of the Naval Aircraft Factory to U.S. Naval Aviation in World War I and the interwar years has been so disregarded (presumably because it did not fly!) that at this late date few even know it existed. A basic reference is F. G. Coburn, "Problems of the Naval Aircraft Factory During the War," Society of Automotive Engineers, _Transactions_, vol. 14, Part I (1919), pp. 304-332. Author was its wartime manager.

26. Clifford W. Seibel, _Helium, Child of the Sun_. Lawrence: University of Kansas Press, 1969, pp. 20 _ff_.

27. Hydrogen lifts 71 lbs. per thousand c.f.; helium 65.8 lbs. per thousand c.f. While this is a nominal 7% deficiency for helium, after all necessary design factors were included in an airship design for helium, the deficiency increased to at least 20% and could be as much as 30%.

28. The most informative discussion in the public record is "Technical Aspects of the Loss of the USS Shenandoah," _Journal of the American Society of Naval Engineers_, vol. 38 (August 1926), pp. 487-694.

29. U.S. Congress, Joint Committee, _Hearings, Investigation of Dirigible Disasters_, 73rd Cong., 3rd Sess., 1933, pp. 687-693. Here Mitchell's airship-bomber prophecies are in the record and, as usual, they are quite wild, if not absurd.

30. Carl B. Fritsche, "The Metalclad Airship," American Society of Mechanical Engineers, _Transactions_, vol. 50 (1929), pp. 245-66; and Richard K. Smith, "Ralph Upson: Career Sketch and Bibliography," American Aviation Historical Society, _Journal_, vol. 13 (Winter 1968), pp. 282-84, and vol. 14 (Summer 1969), pp. 142-43; and, Richard K. Smith, "C. P. Burgess and the Ultimate Airship," American Aviation Historical Society, _Journal_, vol. 14 (Spring 1969), pp. 30-36.

31. Richard K. Smith, The Airships AKRON And MACON: Flying Aircraft Carriers of the U.S. Navy. Annapolis: Naval Institute Press, 1965, pp. 31-44.

32. This whole political embroglio is related at some length in Richard K. Smith, "The Demise of the Rigid Airship," published in Defining Transportation Requirements. N.Y.: American Society of Mechanical Engineers, 1968, pp. 102-110.

33. U.S. Navy, General Board, Hearings (1934), p. 137; the only source of these documents is the Office of Naval History.

34. Grover Loening, Aircraft and the Merchant Marine. Washington: GPO, 1937. Airships are a coincidence in this "study"; it appears that its real intent was to make a case for the new Maritime Commission to take over transoceanic aviation and to create a competitor to Pan American Airways.

35. C. G. Grey, "On Airships and Things," The Aeroplane, vol. 34 (22 February 1928), p. 226.

36. The Chicago Tribune (21 October 1928), p. 6.

37. Charles A. Lindbergh, The Wartime Journals. N.Y.: Harcourt, Brace Jovanovich, 1970, p. 106.

38. Robinson, Giants In The Sky, Op. cit., pp. 295-96. The Graf Zeppelin II made her first flight with hydrogen on 14 September 1938, and was subsequently used to make electronic "spy" flights to feel out the British radar system.

39. Zenon Hansen, "The History of Goodyear Commercial Non-Rigid Airships," unpublished typescript, 41 pp. It was later serialized through several numbers of Bouyant Flight, journal of the Lighter-Than-Air Society and before the end of 1976, it will appear as an illustrated history of the Goodyear Blimp (to be published by Ronald Smith Printing Co., Bloomington, Illinois).

40. It is believed that the K-1 experiment was inspired by the Germans employing the same system in the Graf Zeppelin of 1928, which burned blaugas. The problem in using it with helium was that as the fuel gas diffused into the helium, as it inevitably would, thus diluting the helium and reducing its lift, the helium could not be reclaimed through purification (a high compression process), because the presence of the explosive fuel gas and had to be thrown away.

41. There is no monograph material available re Army blimp operations; but from what scrappy primary sources seen from time-to-time it appears that they did remarkably well with what little they had.

42. U.S. Congress, House Subcommittee of the Committee on Appropriations, Hearings, War Department Appropriations Bill for 1937, Part I, 74th Cong., 2nd Sess., 1936, pp. 350-51.

43. The autogiro proved to be uncompetitive with the Piper Cub-type "grasshopper" light plane as an Army cooperation and liaison aircraft; but in the late 1930s it had the appearance of a panacea.

44. Concurrent to the order for the K-2 in 1937 the Navy also ordered the L-1, which proved to be the prototype for the Navy's primary training airship of World War II.

45. In passing, it deserves note how relatively few airship artifacts of any significance have survived; and museum exhibits relating to airships usually appear to have put together during recovery from a fit of absent-mindedness. Even large national museums rarely, if any, have a curator of lighter-than-air technology.

46. In September 1939, the Navy had only two experimental four-engine flying boats; the Army had 13 B-17s and the one-and-only XB-15. All other four-engine aircraft, less than two dozen, were owned by Pan American Airways.

47. The Goodyear blimps were the Resolute, Enterprise, Reliance, Rainbow and Ranger, which became Navy L-ships, L-4 through L-8 respectively.

48. During the war it appears that the Navy procured a total of 154 airships by way of new construction: 127 K-types; 16 L-ships, 7 G-ships; and 4 M-ships. However, the figure of 165 is often used in public prints.

49. It appears that some of the K-ships never flew, their control cars were diverted to ground schools as training aids.

50. Douglas H. Robinson, The Zeppelin in Combat. London: Foulis, 1962, passim. Such "collisions" were usually reported by ground observers exercising their imaginations at night.

51. "Airship Losses During the War," 28 June 1946, 67 pp., a report obviously abstracted from accident reports and courts of inquiries but no source or authorship is given.

52. Ibid.

53. Samuel Eliot Morison, History of United States Naval Operations in World War II. Boston: Little, Brown, 1975, volume 10, p. 194. Hereafter abbreviated as NavOpsWW2.

54. These were the K-123, K-30, K-109, K-112 and K-101. The K-34 was subsequently lost at sea (10 Nov. 44), immediately offshore of Port Lyautey; the K-123 (15 Jan. 45) and K-109 (26 Mar.45) were lost as a result of freak accidents at Port Lyautey; and the K-89 was lost (23 Aug. 45) in an accident at Pisa, Italy.

55. In May 1919, the Navy had attempted a transatlantic flight with the blimp C-5 from Montauk, Long Island, to England via Newfoundland; it was destroyed by a gale during her servicing stop at Newfoundland. For details see R. K. Smith, First Across!, Op. cit.

56. Morison, NavOpsWW2, vol.11, p. 313.

57. Morison, NavOpsWW2, vol. 1, pp. 241-51.

58. Any careful reading of Morison's NavOpsWW2 will reveal that he was not at home and even uncomfortable with 20th century technology; that he loves his surface actions but comes close to resentment when airplanes intrude upon the picture; and that he would have been most pleased with World War II if its actions had been fought with square rigged ships on the model of the Saints, the Nile or Trafalgar.

59. Such is suggested in a charming little booklet entitled They Were Dependable: Airship Operations in World War II. Lakehurst, N.J.: Naval Air Station, 1956.

60. R. K. Smith, Airships AKRON & MACON, Op Cit, pp. 163-69.

61. Zenon Hansen, "Goodyear Commercial Non-Rigid Airships," Op cit.

62. Detailed in R. K. Smith, "Demise of the Rigid Airship," Op cit.

63. The rubrics of "national security" serve to make all airship information very vague after 1950, even in 1976.

64. "The Flight of the Snowbird," Office of Naval Research Review (June 1957), pp. 1-8.

65. New York Times (13 July 1961), p. 31; "Taps for Blimps," Time, vol. 79 (7 July 1961), p. 17. However, the Akron-Beacon Journal had sensed it all much earlier with the delivery of last 3W airship. See Hal Fry, "So Passeth an Era---Maybe," Akron-Beacon Journal (Sunday Section, 24 April 1960), pp. 19-21.

66. Only available reference is Edwin J. Kirschner, The Zeppelin in the Atomic Age. Urbana: Univ. of Illinois Press,

1957. It is in need of up-dating.

67. This study was prepared by L.S. Hill of the RAND Corp. in 1961, but it is not available for reasons unknown.

68. Hansen, "Commercial Non-Rigids," Op. cit.

69. Joseph F. Vittek, Jr. (ed.), Proceedings of the Inter-agency Workship on Lighter-Than-Air Vehicles. Cambridge, Mass.: M.I.T. Flight Transportation Laboratory, Report No. R75-2, January 1975.

69. Theodore von Karman and T. Troller (eds.), Report on Airship Forum, July 25-26, 1935. Akron, Ohio: The Daniel Guggenheim Airship Institute, Report No. 3, 1935, 133 pp.

PART II — AERONAUTICS
Donald S. Lopez, Chairman

ROBERT J. COLLIER TROPHY

109

I V

GENERAL AVIATION: THE SEARCH FOR A MARKET,
1910-1976

Tom D. Crouch *

    The term general aviation encompasses all civil aero-
    nautics with the exception of commercial airline ac-
    tivity. As early as 1925 this segment of the aviation
    industry had demonstrated the utility of the airplane
    in areas ranging from agriculture to city planning.
    The importance of the airplane to business was also
    well established by 1930. The initial development of
    pleasure and sport flying was largely the result of
    enthusiasm for aviation generated by spectacular air
    races and long distance flights. Since 1945 the di-
    verse elements that constitute the general aviation
    community have made impressive contributions to the
    growth of the American economy.

Traditionally, airplane manufacturers have sold their product to three
market areas: the military services, commercial air carriers, and all
other civil users of aircraft. This final category, covering everything
from crop dusting and skywriting to business and pleasure flying, is
general aviation. For many, the term general aviation calls forth
visions of light weight ragwings putting around a neighborhood airport.
The reality is much more complex and impressive.

In 1971, 97% of all civil aircraft registered with the Federal Aviation
Administration were classified as general aviation airplanes. By 1974,
the nation's fleet of general aviation aircraft numbered 153,000, as
opposed to 2,600 airliners and 34,000 military aircraft. Of this number,
72% saw business or commercial use. In agriculture, for example, 90% of
the 1974 U.S. rice crop was planted from the air. A total of 180,000,000
acres are seeded, fertilized, or sprayed by airplanes each year.[33,34,39,63]

The airplane has also become an indispensable tool of the businessman.
The approximately 40,000 business airplanes registered by the FAA in

---

*Curator, Astronautics, National Air and Space Museum, Smithsonian
 Institution. Dr. Crouch is the author of The Giant Leap (Columbus,
 Ohio, 1972) and a number of articles on the early development of
 aeronautics and astronautics in the United States.

1974 completed some 6,000,000 flights. Eighty-five of the top 100 firms on _Fortune_'s 500 in 1969 owned airplanes.

Some notion of the importance of American general aviation production can be gleaned from the fact that 90% of all general aviation airplanes in the world were built in the United States. One American general aviation manufacturer, the Piper Aircraft Corporation, claims to have built 25% of all the airplanes flying in the world today.[2,33,34,39,63]

Clearly, general aviation is a sleeping giant whose importance is often overlooked as the needs of military aeronautics and commercial air carriers capture public attention. This segment of the aviation industry has always faced a peculiar marketing problem. The requirements for military aircraft and airliners have long been well defined, with definite design and performance criteria that a product must meet if it is to be sold. General aviation, on the other hand, has been forced to explore a wide variety of potential uses for the airplane. The growth of general aviation can best be traced by investigating this process of market exploration.

The discovery of applications for the airplane was a problem faced by the first generation of aircraft manufacturers. While almost all aircraft companies based their hopes for eventual business success on military sales, exhibition flying proved the most important initial market. Both the Wright and Curtiss firms sponsored touring exhibition teams whose exploits they hoped would stimulate sales. With the advent of World War I, attention shifted to the production of aircraft for service on the Western Front. By the close of hostilities in 1918, the small military market for airplanes was well established. Pioneer experiments in the transportation of goods and passengers by air were being conducted in Europe and America and aeronautical enthusiasts assured the public that scheduled commercial air service would become a reality in the near future.

At the same time, airplanes were being put to work at tasks that would someday be subsumed under the term general aviation. The ready availability of war surplus aircraft encouraged businessmen and government officials to fully explore the potential of the airplane. As the "gypsy flyers" of the immediate post-war years began to seek a more settled existence, they established the first nonscheduled flying services. This group, willing to undertake any task that could be performed from the cockpit of an airplane, formed the core of early general aviation.[22,20]

A 1920 survey conducted by the Aeronautical Chamber of Commerce revealed that 87 such fixed base operations were already established in the United States. These firms operated some 425 airplanes from permanent air terminals scattered across the nation and claimed to have flown a total of 3,136,550 miles that year. Short passenger hops and flying instructions were the most common sources of revenue. A fee of $12.50 was typical for a 10 to 15 minute flight. Long distance air freight shipments were also becoming more common. A total of 41,390 pounds of freight was carried by air in 1920, at an average cost of 65 cents a pound mile.[20,22]

A similar survey conducted in 1922 revealed 129 flying services based at 107 airports in 31 states. By 1926, the number of fixed base operators had climbed to 357. In that year American flying services operated 710 airplanes over a distance of 8,471,517 miles.[20]

In addition to normal air taxi and freight activity these embryonic general aviation operators offered a wide assortment of aerial services during this early period. A partial list of the tasks undertaken as early as 1920 includes: political campaigning; skywriting; the transportation of payrolls, film and perishables; oil and timber surveys; herding sheep and cattle; the provision of emergency medical services; scouting for schools of fish; border patrols; police work; newspaper delivery; life saving patrols; the bombing of ice jams; and the preparation of real estate surveys. While many of these projects were undertaken solely for their publicity value, it gradually became apparent that there were tasks which the airplane could perform more efficiently that traditional methods.[20,22,44,49,72]

Agriculture was one of the first areas in which the airplane was employed with obvious success. As was often the case, early experiments in crop dusting and seeding were first undertaken by the Army Air Service. Once the value of the airplane had been demonstrated, commercial firms entered the field.

In August 1921, Lt. John Macready of McCook Field dusted an infested catalpa grove near Troy, Ohio with lead arsenate. This initial demonstration of the potential of crop dusting, undertaken at the request of the Ohio Department of Agriculture, was a complete success and led Dr. B.R. Coad, of the U.S. Department of Agriculture's Delta Laboratory at Tallulah, Louisiana, to conduct further tests in 1922. Two Curtiss JN-4 aircraft provided by the Air Service were used in a successful six-week effort to combat cotton leaf worm.

The Louisiana tests were continued on an expanded basis in 1923. DH-4B aircraft capable of carrying up to 250 pounds of dust were borrowed from the Army and improved dusting equipment based on the first year's experience was employed. Some 6,500 acres were successfully cleared of boll weevil and leaf worm during the 1923 season. The Air Service and the Department of Agriculture also cooperated to combat gypsy moths in New England and locusts in the Philippines in 1923. The utility of the airplane in seeding and conducting crop surveys was also demonstrated by Air Service pilots.[32,20,22,25,30,32,57,70,71]

The first of the agricultural aviation firms was formed by the Huff-Daland Manufacturing Company of Ogdensburg, New York, in 1924. Huff-Daland, which had earlier cooperated with the Delta Laboratory in developing a crop dusting airplane, formed the Huff-Daland Dusters, Incorporated, with headquarters in Macon, Georgia. The firm initially operated 18 airplanes from nine flying fields scattered across the South. Their services were sold to farmers on a contract basis at a price of $7.00 per acre for five applications. The operation proved so successful that the Aetna Insurance Company offered its first cotton

THE HUFF-DALAND DUSTER WAS THE FIRST AMERICAN AIRPLANE DESIGNED FOR CROP
DUSTING. (IV-1, COURTESY NATIONAL AIR AND SPACE MUSEUM)

THE STINSON RELIANT WAS A POPULAR BUSINESS AIRPLANE PRIOR TO WORLD WAR
II. (IV-2, COURTESY NATIONAL AIR AND SPACE MUSEUM)

insurance policy including boll weevil protection only to Huff-Daland customers. With the conclusion of the experimental period in agricultural aviation, local flying services in the south and midwest entered the field, finding it to be an excellant source of seasonal revenue.[20,22,25,32,30,57]

In the far west and Canada, general aviation operators found employment in forest fire detection. From 1919 to 1927 the Air Service conducted intermittent fire patrols for the U.S. Forest Service. In the absence of regular appropriations to fund the work, the patrols were often flown only during emergency periods, however. After 1927 the Forest Service contracted with commercial pilots who could maintain regular fire surveillance more economically than the Army.[1,3,20,22,45]

Aerial photography was yet another area opened to commercial flying services and aircraft manufacturers during the decade of the 1920's. As in the case of agriculture and forestry, government agencies pioneered aerial surveying and mapping operations. As early as 1919 the U.S. Coast and Geodetic Survey had mapped Atlantic City from the air. Other experiments in charting hard-to-reach areas like the Mississippi Delta were also conducted. A joint U.S. Army - Geological Survey project to map Schoolcraft, Michigan demonstrated the potential of aerial photography for city planners.[20,22]

The commercial exploitation of the field was largely the result of the activity of the Fairchild Aerial Camera Corporation. Originally founded in 1920 to produce aerial cameras and equipment, the company expanded in 1921 with the establishment of Fairchild Aerial Surveys Incorporated, a firm that planned and conducted the aerial mapping operations. A third corporate entity, the Fairchild Airplane Manufacturing Company, was founded in 1925 to produce an airplane that would function as a stable camera platform. The Fairchild cabin monoplanes produced by the firm became popular general purpose airplanes, particularly with bush pilots and others operating over difficult terrain.[20,4,6]

Fairchild's large scale operations began in 1923 with a commission to map New York City. Other localities, including Kansas City, Missouri; New Britain, Connecticut; and Wooster and Boston, Massachusetts followed suit. Other nationwide firms, notably Hamilton Maxwell, Incorporated, entered the field soon after Fairchild. Both companies provided contract work for scores of small flying operations. In 1923 pilots flying for Hamilton Maxwell covered 15,000 air miles, producing transmission line right of way studies for power companies in New York, Ohio, Pennsylvania, Michigan, and Maryland. Fairchild's application of aerial photography to tax assessment further expanded the utility of the service. In 1924, twenty-one of the sixty fixed base flying operations reporting to the Aeronautical Chamber of Commerce listed aerial photography as one of their principal services. By 1925 the large photo survey firms and their smaller contractors were doing an annual business approaching $1,000,000.[20,22,4,6,59]

As the barnstormers of 1919 were gradually transformed into the fixed base flying services of 1927, American businessmen were also considering

THE FAIRCHILD CABIN MONOPLANE WAS POPULAR AS AN EARLY BUSINESS AIRPLANE.
(IV-3 - COURTESY NATIONAL AIR AND SPACE MUSEUM)

THE TRAVEL AIR MYSTERY S, WINNER OF THE 1929 THOMPSON TROPHY RACE WITH A
TOP SPEED OF 235 MPH.   (IV-4 - BEECH AIRCRAFT CORPORATION)

the potential of the airplane in increasing efficiency and productivity. In 1927 at least 34 nonaeronautical business firms reported that they employed airplanes either for their own business purposes or for pleasure. Fifteen of these companies, obviously forming an early group of serious business aviators, had logged 197,858 miles of flying, carrying 560 passengers, most of whom were presumably company executives. The early growth of business aviation is not difficult to explain. Prior to the establishment of regularly scheduled airlines, large firms expanding into a national market found it necessary to transport executives from place to place with a minimum loss of business time. The airplane provided an obvious solution. The A.W. Shaw Company of Chicago, for example, purchased a six place Stinson cabin monoplane in 1926 to serve as an executive transport. During its first year of operation, the airplane logged over 12,000 miles. The Continental Motor Company's Ford Trimotor traveled over 10,000 miles shuttling personnel and parts between company facilities in Detroit and Muskegan, Michigan. Standard Oil of Indiana executives travelled 37,265 miles by air in 1926. A Travel Air owned by the Phillips Petroleum Company flew 37,000 miles on business during the same year. During 1928 Ford Company airplanes completed an astounding 1,009 flights, covering 278,949 air miles between various company facilities. Company freight carried on these flights totalled 1,663,120 pounds. The Richfield Oil Company operated Fokker, Stearman, and Waco aircraft as executive transports. These airplanes were also placed at the disposal of the governors of California, Washington, and Oregon for the entertainment of distinguished guests. Some 42 firms were listed as owning airplanes by 1928. Among these were some of the most familiar names in American industry, including B.F. Goodrich, Parker Pen, Anhaeuser-Busch, Continental Motors, Firestone Tire and Rubber, Jello, Pittsburgh Plate Glass, Remington, Royal Typewriter, Walgreen Drug Stores, The Cleveland Pneumatic Tool Company, and the National Lead Battery Company.[20,22,47,48,49,54,55,58]

During 1929 the number of business firms known to own at least one airplane climbed sharply to 148. One authoritative source claimed that one third of the airplanes built in America that year were sold for business use. The 1930 survey uncovered 300 business firms operating airplanes. Oil companies led the field, with large volume sales organizations, professional firms, lumber, paper, power and mining companies following close behind.[47,20]

Clearly, this boom in business flying represented a major market for aircraft manufacturers. In an effort to increase these sales, aircraft advertising emphasized factors such as safety, comfort and speed that were of particular interest to potential business flyers. Franchises and distributorships were established by companies like Mahoney-Ryan, Travel Air, Stearman, Fairchild, and Advance Aircraft. While many of these distributors also functioned as flying service operators, a substantial portion of their income resulted from aircraft sales to local businesses.[28]

The importance of business flying to aircraft manufacturers is apparent in the records of the Stinson Company. As early as 1929 this firm counted newspaper and magazine publishers, advertising agencies, banks, automobile manufacturers, a public utility company, contractors, engineering firms, radio manufacturers, the Yellow Cab Company, a hosiery manufacturer, roofing contractors, real estate brokers, and department stores among its customers. While the depression and the growth of the airlines slowed the initial boom in business aircraft sales, the market remained an important one. At least 38 of the 400 Beech Model 17 airplanes produced between 1932 and 1939 were sold as business airplanes. The twin engine Beech 18, which remained in production for 33 years, longer than any other airplane, became one of the most popular business aircraft ever produced.[47,43,60]

Air racing, exhibition, distance, and exploratory flying provided yet another market for airplanes following World War I. Air racing was initially dominated by military planes and pilots. After 1929, when Doug Davis won the 50 mile closed course race at Cleveland in the Travel Air Mystery S, the National Air Races became essentially civilian contests.[20,23,9]

The air races, and the series of spectacular distance flights that began with Richard Byrd's 1926 North Pole crossing and Charles Lindbergh's transatlantic solo, inaugurated a new era of public enthusiasm for aviation. The flyers of the period were portrayed as larger than life figures capable of performing feats far beyond the capabilities of normal human beings. A 1928 commentator speculated on the symbolic appeal of the aviator.

> Lindbergh himself is a symbol, more or less. It
> isn't Lindbergh as a person who inspires them so
> much as it is Lindbergh as an ideal. They recog-
> nize in him, qualities they would like to possess --
> courage, quiet confidence, modesty and spiritual
> freedom . . .[26]

The sense of flight as a liberating experience was particularly appealing to many who felt circumscribed by the complexities of modern life. Feminist Margery Brown, for example, commented on this point as it related to women.

> From conversations I have had with women I have come
> to the conclusion that flying, to them, is more
> symbolical than to men. To many men it is merely
> mechanical; to women it seems to signify rising
> above their environment in one way or another.
>   If anything bespeaks freedom from limitation,
> flying certainly does. I believe it symbolizes, to
> women, freedom from the irking limitations that have
> hedged them about for so many centuries.[26]

In view of the appeal that aeronautics exercised over the public imagination, it seemed logical for general aviation operators and manufacturers to consider the possibility of expanding their activities in the area of private flying.

There had always been a small number of pilots who flew for pleasure or personal transportation. For the most part, however, those who received flying lessons hoped to become commercial pilots. The cost of purchasing and maintaining an airplane was the most important factor retarding the growth of private flying. Consequently, the image of the private pilot was that of a wealthy man who could afford to pursue flying as a sport. The aerial country club movement, organized in 1929, suggested the construction of clubhouse facilities catering to the very rich, in which flying would replace golf, tennis, and polo, for example.[20]

Those few airplane manufacturers who did hope for private sales during the 1920's aimed their advertising at this group. In 1929 the editors of Country Life, in an effort to convince manufacturers to advertise their airplanes in the magazine, provided a "Portrait of a Prospect for a Private Plane." This hypothetical customer, naturally a reader of Country Life, was a great landowner, with a Park Avenue penthouse, a summer place in the Berkshires, and a ranch in Wyoming. He "goes South" after Christmas, slips off to his gun club on the Eastern Shore in the fall, and takes a party north of Rangely for the trout fishing every spring. His eldest son, now in his last year at Yale, is eager to purchase "a sport amphibian for the jolly crowd he travels with." This is the fellow, argued the editors, who would purchase a private plane to supplement his yacht and three cars. Obviously, the market for private airplanes would never be significant until it could be expanded to include less affluent purchasers.[13]

While the great depression dashed the hopes of many manufacturers who dreamed of an enormous post-Lindbergh market for expensive private aircraft, a number of firms continued to believe that a lightweight, easy to fly airplane could be sold to the general public. The Aeronautical Corporation of America opened the field with the Aeronca C-2, first marketed in 1929. Priced at $1,495, the C-2 was a single seat ultralight airplane powered by an Aeronca-built motor developing 26-29 horsepower. The new firm had built and sold 164 airplanes by the end of 1931. Encouraged by Aeronca's success, other firms began offering light planes selling for less than $2000 after 1930. American Eagle, Alexander, Curtiss-Wright, Welch, Rearwin, Porterfield, Taylor, Piper, and others all sought a share of the limited marked.[38,8,24,35,36,37,46,55]

By 1939, the Civil Aeronautics Administration listed 7,412 airplanes seating five persons or less being flown in the United States. Thirteen manufacturers had contributed to this total.

Table 1

NUMBER OF CERTIFIED PLANES OF FIVE-PLACE AND UNDER AS OF 1/1/39 *

Aeronca	853
Beech	163
Cessna	114
Stinson (Vulta)	779
Curtiss-Wright	741
Fairchild	567
Fleet	191
Luscombe	61
Piper	1,658
Rearwin	170
Taylorcraft	623
Monocoupe	293
Waco	1,050
Total	7,412

Moreover, CAA officials indicated that 80% of these airplanes were two-place, closed cabin, high wing monoplanes powered by a single engine producing from 50 to 100 horsepower. These figures indicate the enormous growth of that segment of the general aviation industry devoted to the production of light airplanes during the decade following the introduction of the Aeronca C-2.[38]

Due to common constraints in the areas of construction materials and techniques, available power plants, and price, the small private airplanes of the 1930's were remarkably similar. The typical light plane of the period featured a 35 foot wingspan and weighed from 1100 to 1300 pounds. It boasted a cruising speed of 50 to 80 miles per hour and a ceiling of from 12,000 to 16,000 feet. Almost all aircraft in this class were priced in the $1500 to $2500 range.[38,24]

The Piper Aircraft Company of Lock Haven, Pennsylvania had gained a remarkable lead over its competitors in the light plane field by 1939. William Piper, founder of the firm, was originally drawn into aircraft manufacturing by C. Gilbert Taylor in 1929. Taylor was at that time producing the E-2 "Cub." Dissatisfied with the arrangement, Piper dissolved the relationship and founded the Piper Aircraft Company in 1937. The fully developed Piper J-3 Cub, which first appeared in 1937, was to become one of the most popular airplanes ever produced. Like other manufacturers, Piper struggled through the lean years of the mid-30's, with sales to private pilots and flying schools. A major period of market expansion followed the establishment of the government Civilian Pilot Training Program in 1939. As early as 1937 Piper claimed to have

* John H. Geisse, Report to W.A.M. Burden on Postwar Outlook for Private Flying (Washington, 1944), 80.

THE AERONCA C-2 WAS ONE OF THE EARLIEST MODERATELY PRICED LIGHT PLANES
DESIGNED FOR SPORT PILOTS. (IV-5, COURTESY NATIONAL AIR AND SPACE MUSEUM)

THE PIPER J-3 CUB REMAINS THE BEST KNOWN GENERAL AVIATION AIRPLANE OF
ALL TIME. (IV-6, COURTESY NATIONAL AIR AND SPACE MUSEUM)

built 31.8% of all American commercial aircraft produced that year. Between 1939 and 1941, the firm constructed 8,020 airplanes, most of them Cub variants used to train fledgling military pilots. By the beginning of World War II, when the production of private aircraft was halted, the light plane industry could look back on a decade of growth and forward to the return of thousands of veterans eager to continue flying as civilians.[32,24,35,38]

In spite of the appearance of new light aircraft, flying remained an expensive enterprise for the private pilot. A $1500 price tag was still high even when compared to that of a yacht. Maintenance costs as high as $8.00 an hour for a Piper Cub flown 150 hours a year discouraged airplane ownership. A 1941 CAA survey revealed that 15,000 airplane owners had registered with the agency between 1931 and 1936, a period during which only 5000 new airplanes were produced. One third of those surveyed were forced to sell their airplanes within the first year of ownership and did not purchase another. Eighty-three per cent abandoned ownership within two and one half years.[38]

Throughout the 1930's such statistics led some aeronautical publicists and government officials to express dissatisfaction with the cost and performance of standard light aircraft. These men believed that airplanes could be mass-produced and marketed on a scale comparable to that of the automobile. They envisioned a very light, cheap, machine that could be flown with absolute safety after minimum instruction. Such a craft priced at current automobile levels of from $500 to $1000, would guarantee "an airplane in every garage." The potential of this market was not being realized, they argued, because established firms were satisfied with current sales subsidized by government flight training programs.

Eugene L. Vidal was the most vocal advocate of this point of view. Appointed Director of the Aeronautics Branch of the Department of Commerce in September 1933, Vidal proposed a "New Deal for Aviation" in which the Government would assist the recovery of the aviation industry by subsidizing the development of the "Poor Man's Airplane." The first step in this process was a demonstration of the fact that a market did exist. In November 1933 Vidal mailed questionnaires to 34,000 pilots, mechanics, and student flyers asking if they would be willing to purchase a hypothetical low wing metal monoplane with a maximum speed of 100 miles per hour, a landing speed of 25 miles per hour, retailing from $700 to $1000. At the same time he queried airplane manufacturers as to the possibility of producing such a machine given automotive style mass production techniques and a guaranteed market for 10,000 airplanes. Working with the White House, Vidal had received preliminary approval for a Public Works Administration grant of $500,000 to be used in assisting manufacturers to begin production. The idea became an immediate subject of discussion in aeronautical journals, where Vidal's proposed machine was immediately dubbed the "$700 airplane."[10,12,14,61,64,65,67,69]

Some 18,000 questionnaires were returned by February 1934, 13,000 of which indicated a willingness to purchase the airplane described. The industrial response was quite different, however. Most firms demonstrated either a complete lack of interest or open hostility toward the program. Aircraft manufacturers saw the Vidal plan as an attempt by inexperienced bureaucrats to circumvent the normal operation of the market. They realized that the "Poor Man's Airplane" was an impossible pipe dream. The craft envisioned by Vidal would require a means to lower the landing speed as well as to prevent stalls and spins in the hands of an inexperienced pilot. These requirements would price the airplane far beyond the $700 range. Moreover, manufacturers feared that talk of a $700 "dream ship" by federal officials would encourage prospective buyers of standard light planes to postpone their purchase until prices dropped. The resulting controversy convinced Harold Ickes to withdraw the $500,000 PWA grant in March 1934.[14,15,17]

Vidal remained determined to encourage the development of mass produced light planes. In July 1934 he announced a competition for the purchase of 25 new airplanes to be used by Bureau inspectors. Entries were to be two-place metal aircraft with a cruising speed of at least 110 miles per hour and a stalling speed no lower than 35 miles per hour. In order to qualify, a machine had to take off in 800 feet, land in 400, and demonstrate a range of 300 miles.[5,15,36,37,56,63]

Four machines were eventually purchased by the Bureau. The first, and most significant, of these was the W-1, designed and built by Fred E. Weick, senior aeronautical engineer with the NACA. In 1931 Weick and nine Langley Laboratory associates had inaugurated an informal private study aimed at developing a safe airplane for private pilots. The W-1, completed early in 1934, was the result. A high wing pusher monoplane, the W-1, featured tricycle landing gear for ease in landing and control on the ground. Fixed wing slats were included to increase stability and reduce the speed and distance required to take off and land.[67]

When Department of Commerce officials first learned of the W-1 in January 1934, they sought to encourage Weick's efforts by requesting the NACA to perform wind tunnel and flight tests with the craft. The 1934 competition requirements were partially based on the outcome of these tests. An engine failure during a W-1 flight test in 1934 led to a forced landing and some damage to the airplane. It was rebuilt under Weick's direction by the Fairchild Company. Renamed the W-1A, the craft was purchased by the Bureau and returned to the NACA for further testing. It was not entered in the competition because there were no plans for producing the aircraft for commercial sale.

The W-1A differed in some significant respects from its predecessor. The earlier wing slats were replaced by flaps and mid-wing slot lip ailerons. A two control system was also introduced to counter the tendency of student pilots to cross control the rudder and ailerons. In 1936 Weick resigned his NACA post and accepted a position with a firm willing to develop a production model based on the advantages demonstrated in the W-1A. The resulting Ercoupe, introduced in 1940, became an extremely popular airplane, a total of 6000 being produced before and after World War II.[67,68]

The Department of Commerce purchased three other aircraft as part of the safe airplane competition. The choice of these machines clearly demonstrated the continued desire to promote a revolutionary flying machine that might rival the automobile as a means of mass transportation. One of the new machines, the Waterman Arrowbile, was a tailless pusher monoplane with swept back wings, tricycle landing gear, and a two control system similar to that of the W-1A. Waldo Waterman, designer of the Arrowbile, intended the craft to serve as the first step toward a roadable airplane capable of being flown as a plane or driven as a car on the highway. The Department of Commerce paid $12,500 for its Arrowbile, but only flew it on special occasions because of its dangerous tendency to stall and spin.[16,73]

A roadable autogyro was also purchased under the terms of the competition. Delivered to the Department in 1937, the pilot landed in a park adjacent to the Commerce building, folded the rotors, disconnected the propellar, and drove to the main entrance. The craft was later driven to the Mall where it took off for a short flight to Bolling Field. Though under-powered, the roadable autogyro performed well as a one-man machine. When oil ran low during a flight to Charleston, South Carolina, the pilot was able to land on a highway and drive to a filling station.[73]

The third aircraft purchased was a more conventional Hammond-Stearman Model Y pusher featuring tricycle landing gear. As the winner of the competition, an original order was placed for 15 of these machines, although only 1 was ever delivered. A two-control airplane, the craft proved simple to fly. Its speed and rate of climb were so low, however, that Bureau officials demanded that it be reengineered before purchase.[73]

The Department of Commerce $700 airplane and competitive purchase programs had little impact on the general aviation industry, which continued to produce the standard types developed prior to 1935. By encouraging experimentation and publicizing new aircraft types, however, the Vidal plans did help shape the general public's view of the future of aeronautics.

Between 1937 and 1945 aeronautical journals and popular magazines featured stories suggesting that "fool proof" airplanes, autogyros, helicopters, and roadable airplanes might rival the automobile as family transportation in the near future. A 1944 Collier's survey of the post-war market for private aircraft revealed that 65% of the civilians who hoped to purchase airplanes after the war preferred roadable or helicopter types. Experienced general aviation manufacturers, on the other hand, realized that these experimental craft were totally unsuited for mass production and sale.[31]

Industrial leaders did believe that the post-war period would bring a significant increase in private flying, however. Government officials, journalists, and public opinion polls all predicted a post-war boom period for light airplane sales. William Burden, a Department of Commerce official, informed Congress that private plane sales represented the most logical field for post-war expansion of the aeronautical industry and suggested that production might eventually rise to 200,000 aircraft a year. S. Paul Johnston, a leading aviation authority, went even farther, predicting that as many as 500,000 light airplanes might be

THE BEECHCRAFT BONANZA, A FOUR PLACE ALL METAL AIRPLANE FIRST MARKETED IN
1947. (IV-7, COURTESY BEECH AIRCRAFT CORPORATION)

THE CESSNA AIRCRAFT COMPANY HAS CAPTURED A MAJOR SHARE OF THE POST-WAR
MARKET WITH OFFERINGS LIKE THE POPULAR CESSNA 150. (IV-8, COURTESY
NATIONAL AIR AND SPACE MUSEUM)

sold in the United States by 1950. Magazine articles with titles like "Your Family Plane of Tommorrow," "Wings for the Average Man," and "Plane for All," abounded. Surveys by Collier's and Ladies' Home Journal indicated that thousands of returning flyers would be unwilling to give up their wings, while other veterans would use G.I. Bill funds to learn to fly. Civilian war workers surveyed also indicated a desire to own a personal plane.[11,18,41,42,31,19,53]

The market seemed so promising that major aeronautical firms with no previous interest in light aircraft made plans to enter the field. Republic Aviation offered the amphibious Sea Bee, for example, while North American introduced the Navion.

Indeed, the 1946 sale of light planes rose to 35,000 from a pre-war high of 7700 in 1941. This level could not be sustained, however. The predicted post-war boom collapsed in 1947, as production fell to 15,764. By 1952 the annual production of general aviation aircraft had hit bottom at 3,058. By 1960 production had still not returned to 1941 levels. As late as 1964, 40% of the active general aviation aircraft were 15 years old or older, most of them remnants of the 1946-47 peak output. The most serious factor in the creation of this dismal statistical picture was the retarded growth of the light aircraft segment of the industry. The most impressive private planes produced following World War II, such as the Beech Bonanza and Cessna 150, were priced far beyond the range of the average automobile. As the dream of enormous sales was laid to rest, the industry began a slow climb back to stable levels.[21,33,34,38,43,50,35]

The number of home-built light aircraft grew rapidly following World War II. The construction of airplanes and gliders in home workshops was not a new phenomena in the United States, however. Simplified plans for machines like the Bleriot were sold to enthusiasts as early as 1910. These drawings could be supplemented by the wealth of technical detail available in contemporary aeronautical journals.

With the disappearance of inexpensive war surplus aircraft by 1925, home-builts returned to popularity. Plans and kits for airplanes that could be powered by converted automobile or motorcycle engines were offered for sale. By 1930 scores of amateur-built Heath Parasols (the original Heathkit), Swallow Sports, and Pietenpol Air Campers were being flown from small airports across the nation.

Often based very loosely on the original drawings, many of these home-built airplanes were dangerous and very difficult to fly. A case in point is the Pou-du-Ciel, or Flying Flea, a design imported from France in 1935. Hailed by its promoters as a "fool proof" airplane, simple to build and easy to fly, the Flea was actually a poorly engineered craft that carried many novice pilots in England and America to their deaths.

The home built movement gathered momentum once again after 1945. The foundation of the Experimental Aircraft Association in January 1953 and the appearance of the first "fly-ins" were major factors in creating a new generation of home enthusiasts.[73]

Soaring has also become an increasingly popular sport flying activity since World War II. Americans could boast a long tradition of success in gliding dating from 1885, when Californian John Montgomery made the first true glide in a heavier-than-air craft in modern times. Gliders had also played a major role in the development of the first successful Wright airplane.

Modern American enthusiasm for soaring, however, dates not from these early efforts, but from accounts of German sport gliding following World War I. Paul Hesselbach's 1928 Massachusetts flights and Wolfram Hirth's 1930 U.S. tour introduced Americans to the pleasures of soaring. The Bowlus and Franklin firms were producing American-made gliders prior to 1935. The Schweizer Aircraft Corporation of Elmira, New York, also established during this period, remains the most significant American glider firm. The Soaring Society of America, founded in 1932, continues to coordinate soaring activity in the United States.[58]

Significant growth continued in business aviation almost unabated following World War II. In recent years, the sale of multi-engine aircraft and airplanes seating four or more persons suitable for business use has been the most important factor in the increase in the number of registered general aviation aircraft. By 1968, business aviation accounted for 38% of total general aviation air mileage. An additional 48% was claimed by flying service operators, leaving only 23% for all personal flying.[33,34,62]

Unlike the private pilot whose insistance on a moderate price tag has discouraged rapid technical advance, the business owner has been willing to pay for increased speed, comfort, and carrying capacity. The introduction of turboprop and turbojet engines is an example of this demand for innovation in business aircraft. Gates Learjet, Beech, Fairchild Hiller, North American Rockwell, Grumman, Piper, and Cessna have all entered the business market with turbine aircraft. By 1968 a total of 1,833 turbine powered airplanes were at work in general aviation, almost three-quarters of them serving as business transports. All of the top ten firms on Fortune's 500 in 1969 maintained fleets of these aircraft.[33,34,50,62]

In the 57 years since 1919 general aviation has grown from gypsy pilots willing to undertake any task that would enable them to remain in the air, to a major segment of the nation's aeronautical industry. While the commercial air carriers have enjoyed enormous success in speeding the transport of passengers and goods, general aviation has played a major, though less spectacular, role in the growth of the American economy.

THE TWIN ENGINE BEECH 18 REMAINED IN PRODUCTION FOR 35 YEARS.   (IV-9, COURTESY BEECH AIRCRAFT CORPORATION)

THE LEAR JET REVOLUTIONIZED BUSINESS FLYING.   (IV-10, COURTESY NATIONAL AIR AND SPACE MUSEUM)

Table 2

PRIVATE AIRPLANES REGISTERED WITH THE C.A.A. AS OF JANUARY 1, 1939 *

Year of Manufacture	Single Engine	Multiple Engine	Total	Open Cockpit	Closed Cockpit	Total
1926	40	1	41	39	2	41
1927	117	--	117	98	19	117
1928	603	17	620	421	199	620
1929	1420	34	1454	944	510	1454
1930	811	15	826	524	302	826
1931	888	22	610	371	239	610
1932	235	6	241	92	149	241
1933	268	43	311	57	254	311
1934	409	47	456	67	389	456
1935	544	53	597	28	569	597
1936	1028	77	1105	24	1081	1105
1937	1684	100	1784	69	1715	1784
1938	1444	29	1473	7	1466	1473
Total	9191	444	9635	2741	6894	9635

---

*   John H. Geisse and Samuel Williams, Report ... On Postwar Outlook for Private Flying, Washington, 1944.

Table 3

ACTIVE U.S. REGISTERED GENERAL AVIATION AIRCRAFT ON RECORD WITH F.A.A.[+]
DECEMBER 31, 1971 AND 1966

Type of Aircraft	1971		1966		Percent Increase
	Number	Percent of Total	Number	Percent of Total	
Total, all aircraft	131,149	100.0	104,706	100.0	25.3
Total, fixed-wing	127,112	96.9	102,207	97.6	24.4
Piston aircraft, total	124,629	95.0	101,292	96.7	23.0
Single-engine, total	109,100	83.2	88,621	84.6	23.1
1-3 place	44,637	34.0	35,681	34.1	25.1
4 places and over	64,463	49.2	52,940	50.6	21.8
Multiengine	15,529	11.8	12,671	12.1	22.6
Turbine, total	2,483	1.9	915	0.9	171.4
Turboprop, total	1,492	1.1	498	0.5	199.6
Single-engine	140	0.1	32	*	**
Multiengine	1,352	1.0	466	0.5	190.1
Turbojet, total	991	0.8	417	0.4	137.6
Single-engine	17	*	6	*	183.3
Multiengine	974	0.8	411	0.4	137.0
Total, rotary-wing	2,352	1.8	1,622	1.5	45.0
Turbine	670	0.5	70	0.1	**
Piston	1,682	1.3	1,552	1.4	8.4
Total, all other aircraft	1,685	1.3	877	0.8	92.1
Gliders	1,607	1.2	841	0.8	91.1
Balloons	74	*	34	*	117.6
Blimps	4	*	2	*	100.0

* Less than 0.05 percent.
**More than 200 percent.
+ F.A.A. Statistical Handbook of Aviation, Washington, 1972.

REFERENCES

1. _____, "Airplane Patrol for the Forest," <u>Air Service Journal</u>, vol. 4, No. 5, Feb. 1919 p. 12

2. _____, "Airscene," <u>Air International</u>, vol. 11, No. 1, July 1976

3. _____, "The California Aerial Forest Fire Patrols," <u>Aircraft Journal</u>, vol. 5, Nov. 1919 p. 12

4. _____, "Commercial Aerial Photography," <u>Aircraft Journal</u>, vol. 6, No. 13 Mar. 27, 1920 p. 9

5. _____, "The Department of Commerce Light Plane Specifications," <u>Aviation</u>, vol. 33, No. 7 July 1934 p. 208

6. _____, "The Fairchild Aviation Corporation," <u>Aero Digest</u>, vol. 24, No. 1, Jan. 1934 p. 25

7. _____, "Flying Equipment," <u>Aviation</u>, vol. 35, No. 17, Nov. 1936 pp. 27-29

8. _____, "The Light Plane Situation," <u>Aviation</u>, vol. 30, No. 2, Feb. 1931 pp. 80-84

9. _____, "Lindbergh's Feat to Fill the Sky with Flyers," <u>Literary Digest</u>, vol. 93, June 11, 1927

10. _____, "Low Priced Airplane," <u>Aviation</u>, vol. 33, No. 2, Feb. 1934 pp. 40-42

11. _____, "Planes For All," <u>Business Week</u>, No. 719, June 12, 1943 pp. 105-106.

12. _____, "The Poor Man's Airplane," <u>Western Flying</u>, vol. 14, No. 2, Feb. 1934 p. 9

13. _____, "Portrait of a Prospect for a Private Plane," <u>Sportsman Pilot</u>, vol. 11, No. 3, Oct. 1929 p. 11

14. _____, "The Status of the Vidal Plane," <u>Western Flying</u>, vol. 14, No. 3, Mar. 1934 p. 19

15. _____, "Wanted--25 Planes," <u>Western Flying</u>, vol. 14, No. 6, June 1934 pp. 8-10

16. _____, "Waterman Arrowbile," <u>Historical Aviation Album</u>, vol. 3, Temple City, Colo., 1965

17. _____, "What the Industry Thinks," <u>Western Flying</u>, vol. 14, No. 2, Feb. 1934 p. 11

18. _____, "Wings for the Average Man," American Exporter, vol. 132, No. 5, May 1973 p. 32

19. _____, "Your Family Plane of Tomorrow," Better Homes and Gardens, vol. 22, No. 9, Sept. 1942

20. Aeronautical Chamber of Commerce, Aircraft Yearbook, New York, 1919-1941. See text for a citation as to year.

21. Ball, Larry, Those Incomparable Bonanzas, Wichita, 1971

22. Bilstein, R.E., Prelude to the Air Age: Civil Aviation in the United States, 1919-1929, Ph.D. Dissertation, The Ohio State University, 1965

23. Bowen, R. Sidney, "Ten Years of Air Race Programs," Aviation, vol. 29, No. 3, Sept. 1930 pp. 130-134

24. Boyne, Walter J., "Those Anonymous Cubs," Aviation Quarterly, vol. 1, No. 4, Winter 1975

25. Britton, Rey, "Crop Dusting as a Business," Western Flying, vol. 11, No. 6, June 1932 p. 20

26. Brown, Margery, "Women and Flying," Popular Aviation, vol. 4, No. 11, Aug. 1929 pp. 32-34

27. Burtt, Robert M., "Preparing For the Private Market," Aviation, vol. 29, No. 6, Dec. 1930 pp. 343-346

28. Clary, Robert S., "Why Not Retail Airplanes," Popular Aviation, vol. 4, No. 1, Jan. 1929 pp. 18-22

29. Cleveland, Reginald and Leslie Neville, The Coming Air Age, New York, 1944

30. Coad, B.R., "Dusting Cotton from Airplanes," U.S. Department of Agriculture Bulletin, No. 1204, Jan. 1924

31. Crowell-Collier, Tomorrow's Customers for Aviation, New York, 1944

32. Downs, Eldon W. and George Lemmer "Origins of Aerial Crop Dusting," Agricultural History, vol. 39, No. 3, July 1965.

33. FAA, Federal Aviation Agency Historical Fact Book, Washington, 1966

34. FAA, FAA Statistical Handbook of Aviation, Washington, 1972

35. Francis, Devon, Mr. Piper and His Cubs, Ames, Iowa, 1973

36. Geisse, John H., "Airplanes for Private Owners," National Aeronautical Magazine, vol. 13, No. 8, Sept. 1935 pp. 5-7

37. Geisse, John H., "The Private Owner Airplane," U.S. Air Services, vol. 2, No. 4, Apr. 1935 pp. 21-24

38. Geisse, John H. and Sam C. Williams, Report to W.A.M. Burden on Postwar Outlook for Private Flying, Washington, 1944

39. General Aviation Manufacturers Association, The General Aviation Story, Washington, 1974

40. Hoyt, Kendall, General Aviation: A Future Mass Industry, Washington, 1964

41. Johnston, S. Paul, Horizons Unlimited, New York, 1941

42. Johnston, S. Paul, Wings After War, New York, 1944

43. McDaniel, William H., The History of Beech, Wichita, Kansas, 1971

44. Mackey, Joe C., "Money in Smoke," Aviation, vol. 36, No. 6, June 1937 pp. 22-23

45. Mark, Frederick, "Airplanes Aid the Forester," Popular Aviation, vol. 12, No. 4, Apr. 1933 pp. 217-219

46. Matt, Paul R., "Aeronca: It's Formation and First Aircraft," Historical Aviation Album, vol. 10, Temple City, Cal., 1972

47. Miller, A.A., "Business On the Wing," Sportsman Pilot, vol. 2, No. 3, Sept. 1929 p. 24

48. Muller, Charles G., "Business Speaks Up Almost Flying," National Aeronautical Magazine, vol. 9, No. 11, Nov. 1931 p. 23-25

49. Muller, Charles G., "Uses of Aircraft in Industry," National Aeronautical Magazine, vol. 9, No. 6, June 1931 pp. 25-29

50. Munson, Kenneth, Private Aircraft, New York, 1967

51. Nevill, John T., "The Story of Wichita," Aviation, vol. 20. Nos. 4, 5, 6, Oct.-Dec. 1930

52. Nicholson, Norman, ed., Readings On Post War Personal Aircraft, Fort Worth, 1944

53. Ogburn, William Stewart, The Social Effect of Aviation, New York, 1946

54. Pritchard, Robert J., "Airplanes for Business Use," Western Flying, vol. 15, No. 3, Mar. 1935 p. 8

55. Pritchard, Robert J., "The Business Plane Market," Western Flying, vol. 16, No. 1, Jan. 1936 pp. 16-19

56. Pritchard, Robert J., "The Small Plane Develops," Western Flying, vol. 15, No. 5, May 1935 pp. 10-12

57. Riis, Roger William, "Commercial Crop Dusting," Aviation, vol. 18, No. 21, Mar. 25, 1925 p. 573

58. Ross, Malcom, Sailing the Skies: Gliding and Soaring, New York, 1931

59. Sagendorph, Kent, "Aerial Tax Assessing," Popular Aviation, vol. 4, No. 3, Mar. 1929 pp. 11-15

60. Smith, Robert T., Staggerwing: Story of the Classic Beech Biplane, Media, Pa., 1967

61. Vidal, Eugene, "The Poor Man's Airplane," Western Flying, vol. 14, No. 2, Feb. 1934 pp. 9-11

62. Warford, Jeremy J., Public Policy Toward General Aviation, Washington, 1971

63. Warner, Edward P., "The Aeronautics Branch Writes a Specification," Aviation, vol. 33, No. 7, Jul. 1934 p. 218

64. Warner, Edward P., "$700--And How?," Aviation, vol. 32, No. 12, Dec. 1933 p. 382

65. Warner, Edward P., "$700 Private Plane," Aviation, vol. 32, No. 12, Dec. 1933 p. 382

67. Weick, Fred E., "The W-1 Airplane," Aviation, vol. 33, No. 7, Jul. 1934 pp. 209-211

68. Weick, Fred E., "The W-1A Airplane," Aviation, vol. 35, No. 1, Jan. 1936 pp. 17-20

69. Whitnah, Donald R., Safer Skyways: Federal Control of Aviation, 1926-1966, Ames, Iowa, 1966

70. Winters, S.R., "Crop Survey by Airplane," Popular Aviation, vol. 3, No. 3, Sept. 1928 pp. 11-15

71. Winters, S.R., "Plant Protection by Airplane," Popular Aviation, vol. 4, No. 2, Feb. 1929 pp. 11-15

72. Woodhouse, Henry, "How the World Found One Hundred Uses for Aeroplanes," Flying, vol. 9, Nos. 8-9, Sept.-Oct. 1920

73. Bowers, Peter M., Guide to Homebuilts, New York, 1967

74. Federal Aviation Administration Central Office Records, National Archives and Records Service, R.G. 237

75. R. T. Jones, "Recollections From an Earlier Period in
     American Aeronautics," <u>American Review of Fluid Mechan-
     ics</u>, vol. 9 (1977), 1-11

V

TRENDS IN MILITARY AERONAUTICS, 1908-1976

Robert Perry

Aviation historians have tended to emphasize the
achievements and singularities of military aeronautics,
but an overview of trends and tendencies may provide
a better perspective. The considerable pre-1945 debt
of the military to civil aircraft designers, the
abandonment of incremental design evolution for
technological leaps after 1945, and the extreme
interdependence of airframe and engine development
over sixty years of advancement are three of several
major trends, rather more significant than "records
and spectacles."

One of the numerous publications that catalogs U.S. military aircraft
credits the United States with having originated and put into service some
160 basic airframe designs in the years between 1914 and 1969, counting
only those that carried weapons and actually went into operation. Twice
as many were rejected by one service or another following preliminary
evaluation, and at least 300 "non combat" types of aircraft entered the
inventory in those years. Some of the basic designs in each category had
more than 10 variants--the P-40, P-47, and P-51, for example. More than
50 different manufacturers delivered aircraft to the U.S. military and
naval services between 1908 and 1976. And aeronautics trends extended
well past airframes, of course; engines, armament, and avionics developments were at least as important. Merely to list records set and broken,
technologies brought to heel, barriers perceived and thrown down, would
take many, many pages. Thick volumes have been written on single aircraft
models; a comprehensive bibliography of publications on U.S. military
aeronautics would capture thousands of books and tens of thousands of
articles, journals, and specialized publications.

If, then, it is futile to attempt in brief compass to capture even
the highlights of 68 years of military aircraft development, what may be
done? The response here will be to propose several broad theses and
general trends that characterized different parts of the entire period
and to attempt to illustrate tendencies by example or attribution.
Occasional lingering over one aircraft or another is unavoidable, but that
seems reasonable if only because the National Air and Space Museum houses
so many examples of many of the marvelous, ingenious, and ultimately
beautiful creations to which the structure, and this session, are alike
dedicated.

FIRST MILITARY AIRPLANE

Orville Wright successfully demonstrated over Ft.
Myer, Virginia, in 1908, and the aircraft also met the
specification of the Signal Corps that it be transport-
able in Army wagons. (V-1 - Courtesy NASM)

If the topic is six decades of aeronautical progress by the U.S.
military services, it becomes necessary to trundle casually and quickly
through the first of those with eyes mostly averted, and to avoid as
artfully as possible discussion of the preceding five years (1903-1908)
during which the United States armed forces refused steadfastly to con-
cede that the ungainly creations of Orville and Wilbut Wright could have
any conceivable military utility. The Wright Flyer of 1908, the first
aircraft purchased by the United States, was one among 381 airplanes
that came into military hands before April 1917--when 55 were service-
able--notwithstanding that by then the major European powers had repeatedly demonstrated not merely the military utility, but the absolute
essentiality of an air arm.

To say that the military and naval establishments of the United
States entered the air age with great caution is no exaggeration. Not
until January 1919 did the first single-seat fighter of American design
fly, rather too late for World War I, and another two and one-half years

passed before the Navy acquired a similar fighter, although the basic type had been operating over the Western Front years previously.

That the first bomber designed and built in the United States flew in 1918 rather than in 1920 is a compliment to the stubbornness of its creator, Glenn Martin, rather than to any foresight on the part of American defense officials; he completed the basic work on the MB-1 well before funding was authorized or contracts were drawn.

There was, of course, no market for military aircraft in pre-1917 America. "Too proud to fight" also meant "too proud to prepare" for a nation which still honored the myth of the Minuteman. Nor was the default limited to aircraft. Submarines and tanks found few advocates among generals and admirals before the mid-1920s.

Nevertheless, a few aircraft of American design participated honorably in, and to some extent influenced the course of World War I. Curtiss flying boats patterned after the pre-war *America*, which had been designed for transatlantic flight and with some good luck might actually have achieved that goal, were operational with the Royal Navy Air Service as early as 1914, and in May 1917 a Curtiss H-12 flying boat (a monster for the time, having a wingspan of nearly 93 feet) became the first American-built, American-designed aircraft to destroy an enemy air vehicle--a Zepplin. Another H-12 was the first aircraft in history to kill a submarine. The quality of the Curtiss design may perhaps be judged in the circumstance that as late as 1945 the British were still using flying boats (not built by Curtiss, of course) of a design derived in most respects from that 1913 concept. Or perhaps that is a better commentary on the reluctance of some military and naval authorities to be greatly impressed by advances in technology between the wars.

Whatever the interpretations, and they have been many and varied in the intervening years, between the Kittyhawk flight of 1903 and the end of World War I neither the Army nor the Navy air services of the United States made any important contribution to military aeronautics. They did little to generate requirements, sponsor research, or reward enterprise. Excepting a few heretics, many of whom had been encouraged to leave the service by 1925, no influential American spokesman for air power emerged from World War I and certainly there was no widespread appreciation by American tacticians that the outcome of a great land battle could be seriously influenced by the quality and quantity of military aircraft possessed by one of the combattants. With a few notable exceptions, one of them the MB-1, which for a time in the early 1920s was at least the equal of other aircraft of its type elsewhere in the world, the tardy and mostly abortive effort of American developers and manufacturers to provide American aircraft for Americans to use in the First World War had few lasting consequences.

There was, inevitably, one important exception to that generality. The Liberty engine--or perhaps more precisely, the *legend* of the Liberty engine--established a tradition that was to prove invaluable to American aviation in decades to come. Whether fact or legend, it assumed the

successful application of American concepts of design efficiency to the
major challenge of pre-1920 military aeronautics: powerful, reliable
aircraft engines. But it must also be conceded that the Liberty engine
was not the marvel that myth alleged, and that between the two wars the
British and the Germans did much more to advance the technology of
liquid-cooled aircraft engines than did Americans. It was the air-cooled
radial engine that gave later generations of American aircraft their
performance edge, when one existed, during the 1930s and the early 1940s,
and it is chiefly to the technical specialists of the U.S. Navy and the
astuteness of civil aircraft manufacturers that credit must go. The aircraft manufacturers and the emergent civil airlines of the United States
arranged the post-1938 reconvergence of high-performance engines with
military airframes capable of extracting their performance potential.

Somehow during the 1920s, notwithstanding scrimped budgets, the
services managed to buy a few aircraft now and again. That they did so
was owing more to institutionalism than to any national appreciation of
the need to provide modern aircraft for the Army and Navy. In time the
two air services grew their own advocates, variously eloquent, as was
also the case with submariners, and those converted cavalrymen who came
to see that it was either tanks or walking. But given a choice between
exploiting newly available technology and buying aircraft that could go
immediately into squadron service, aviators (and tank specialists and
submariners, for that matter) usually elected to buy what was offered in
the market place rather than to strive for greater modernity or higher
performance. As has often been the case when budgets are slender and
needs are great, the amounts spent on aircraft tended to be decided in
intra-service bargaining sessions, infantry competing with artillery,
battleships with carriers, and aircraft, submarines, and tanks making the
best of the scrapings.

During the starveling years between 1925 and 1935, virtually all
major advances in American military aeronautics stemmed from the
initiatives of private companies, and very often from the inspiration of
some single designer or design team. With occasional and not very
remarkable exceptions, performance and structural specifications--
requirements--originated by the services fostered pedestrian, uninspired
aircraft designs. Indeed, given the frequently brilliant conceptions of
private designers and manufacturers, it is difficult not to conclude that
the persistent conservatism of military and naval authorities actually
impeded the natural evolution of military aircraft technology.[*]

Quite the reverse trend characterized the 20 years after 1945.
Instead of being a long step behind civil and private aircraft design,

---

[*] That was true of British military aeronautics through at least 1935,
and of French aircraft technology through its death rattle in 1940. Even
the Germans invested heavily in designs reminiscent of World War I during
the early years of their rearmament. The vital relationship of innovative
technology and military requirements has been little examined; it is an
area that some future analyst or historian may yet fruitfully mine.

military aircraft design became so adventuresome that the civil aircraft
industry seemed timid by comparison, and when timidity was overcome, most
notably in the case of the British Comet, the Anglo-French Concorde, and
the aborted Boeing SST, the consequence most generally was massive and
costly technical difficulty or economic calamity--or both. Only very
recently have requirements for affordable development costs, economical
operation, and operational reliability been fitted into a military agenda
of wants that emphasized performance and new technology, and ignored risk.
But the memory of participants tends to dwell on the pleasant and the
glorious, and to depreciate or ignore the mundane or the unpleasant.
Perhaps for that reason, the main trends in American military aeronautics
between 1925 and the late 1930s have been largely ignored by aviation
historians and a few exceptional events or developments have been high-
lighted.

A case worth examining is the transition from the classic biplane
fighter (epitomized by the Fokker D-VII and the Spad XIII of 1918) to the
superb conception, epitomized by the Mustang, Corsair, Spitfire, and
Messerschmitt Bf.109 of 1945. The United States Army Air Corps accepted
its last "classic" biplane fighter in 1932--the lovely but antiquarian
P-6E. The Navy did not remove the last of its Grumman biplane fighters
from American carriers until 1940. (The Japanese, who presented the only
credible threat to American naval power, abandoned the biplane three
years sooner.) Between 1935 and 1937 the Germans manufactured a few
"classic" biplane fighter designs, but by the latter year were entirely
committed to Heinkel and Messerschmitt monoplanes. The British, Italians,
and Russians were more persistent, each continuing to produce and use
fighter biplanes in front-line service into World War II.

The transition was more difficult than straightforward chronology
suggests. For all practical purposes, the U.S. Navy was unable to obtain
a satisfactory monoplane fighter until Grumman made the large but still
evolutionary step from the superb but outdated F-3F (one example of which,
in commercial guise, hangs in the National Air and Space Museum) to the
marginally adequate F-4F (also on display). In the interim the Navy
bought biplanes with retractable landing gear (in one ludicrous case, as
a means of further extending the life of the vintage-1922-design Curtiss
naval fighter family) and enclosed cockpits, the hallmark of the F-3F.
Indeed, the F-3F and its contemporary, the Polikarpov I-15 (which continued in front-line Russian service until 1942 and operated in Finnish
colors through 1945), represented the very summit of efforts to preserve
the dogfight traditions of 1918. In their early years both were superior
in most combat attributes to the monoplane fighters that nominally
replaced them in service--Polikarpov's I-16 and Brewster's F-2A Buffalo
of unlamented memory.

But what is striking about the transition, in the United States, is
that all of the essential ingredients of the "classic" World War II
fighter were available 10 or 12 years before they were adopted by the
services. The XPS-1 Dayton-Wright fighter prototype of 1921 incorporated
retractable landing gear of the general type later favored by Grumman,
Curtiss, and other carrier-fighter designers. Cantilever wings, entirely

unbraced, appeared in the Fokker PW-5 in 1922, the first U.S. military aircraft so built, but had been featured in Junkers designs as early as 1915 and became relatively common among civil-design monoplanes of the late 1920s. (As early as 1920, the NACA characterized the cantilever monoplace as "the airplane of the future.") But wing flutter problems encountered with the few military monoplanes of cantilever construction built during the early 1920s seem to have induced military buyers to retreat to the biplane, leaving monoplane development mostly to American civil aircraft builders and foreign designers. One consequence was that the Lockheed Orion of 1931, a low-wing version of the older Vega, but with retractable gear, was roughly 50 MPH faster (at 225 mph top speed) than any fighter then in service anywhere in the world! But it was the Boeing Monomail of 1930 that set the patterns of the next 15 years: an all metal cantilever monoplane with retractable landing gear and (on one model) an enclosed pilot compartment--and which also was faster than any fighter in service. So was Boeing's B-9, which appeared in 1932--but with open cockpits for the crew, a concession to the persistent military preference for that arrangement.

Martin built a very similar aircraft, the B-10, and somehow induced the Air Corps to accept the notion of enclosed crew stations, which gave the Martin aircraft a 15-mph speed advantage over the B-9 and put Martin back in the bomber business. (The B-10 soldiered on, in various guises, into World War II; the B-9 quickly passed from the scene). But the lesson was not lost on Boeing. When the Air Corps in 1934 asked for proposals for a new multi-engined bomber, Boeing responded with the Model 299, a highly integrated, thoroughly modern prototype with two more engines than the Army had indicated interest in. The eventual production aircraft carried the designation B-17.

But all this occurred in the regime of "big" aircraft. It has little to do with fighters, although it was obvious to virtually all American aircraft designers that the advances first foregathered in the Boeing Monomail and applied thereafter to a succession of highly successful bombers and civil transports could readily be incorporated in fighters, with considerable advantage to the breed.

With one important exception (discussed below), by 1932 only the Americans had designed and built efficient, integrated aircraft embracing all of the major advances in aircraft technology achieved between 1915 and 1929.[*] Big and small, military and civil, the aircraft of France, Britain, Russian, and the several smaller states which maintained design and manufacturing capabilities tended to be ungainly, externally braced,

_____

[*] Variable-pitch propellers and increasingly efficient air-cooled engines were essential ingredients of the 1929-1932 "revolution" in aircraft design. By the early 1930s slotted wings were frequently encountered, and by 1932 Boeing, Lockheed, and Northrop had begun to use flaps to improve the low-speed handling characteristics of their monoplane designs. All of those innovations were first applied successfully to commercial rather than military aircraft in the period 1925-1932.

MARTIN B-10
(V-2 - NASM)

BOEING B-17E
(V-3 - NASM)

BOEING P-26
(V-5)

BOEING XP-940
(V-6)

protuberance encrusted machines closely related to those in operation by 1920.

In 1931, after the principal ingredients of the design revolution (except variable pitch propellers) had been successfully applied to several American civil aircraft, Boeing proposed and built (almost entirely with its own funds) a "Model 248" fighter prototype. As with the B-9 design (concurrently in development), Boeing incorporated as many recent aeronautical advances as company officials believed would be acceptable to the Army Air Corps. Thus the aircraft was an all-metal, low-wing cantilever construction monoplane with a high-performance radial engine--but it also featured wire bracing for the wing, an open cockpit, and fixed landing gear. At 234 mph, the P-26 (as it was numbered when it entered service) was marginally faster than the in-production Lockheed Orion and had appreciably better performance than any other military aircraft then in use--but that was to be a transient circumstance. Perhaps more interesting, Boeing was interested in building a slightly different fighter aircraft that provided an enclosed cockpit, an unbraced cantilever wing, and retractable landing gear. By the time the first production P-26 had entered Air Corps service in 1933, an XP-29[*] with those features was under construction in Boeing shops. Weighing about 10 percent more than the P-26, but otherwise similar in dimensions and power, the XP-29 had a small speed advantage over its predecessor. The Air Corps decided against investing in so radical an aircraft because benefits seemed slight, so the might-have-been archetype of the standard World War II fighter vanished from history.

On the other side of the world, the prototype Polikarpov I-16, conceived later than the P-26, made its first flight on the last day of 1933. It did not go into production for another 18 months, but it nonetheless captured the distinction of being the first low-wing single-seat fighter monoplane with retractable undercarriage to enter operational service with any air force.[**] Inferior in several respects, including top speed, to the P-26, the I-16 nonetheless was subjected to continual development over the next five years and in its ultimate form achieved a high speed in excess of 325 mph. That performance was mostly chargeable to more powerful engines, although the final version (Type 24, vintage 1939) had only about 900 horsepower--a power rating provided by the Pratt and Whitney R-1830 engine installed in some American aircraft as early as 1934. In 1936, Seversy and Curtiss offered their P-35 and P-36 designs to the Air Corps. Although neither was competitive with the contemporary

_____
[*]The YP-24 (YIP-24/YP-25/YIA-11...), a two-place enclosed cockpit fighter prototype of 1933 vintage, having fully retractable gear and an in-line engine, had comparable performance.
[**]In early and late versions it had an enclosed cockpit but was most commonly built without the sliding canopy initially featured.

Supermarine Spitfire and Hawker Hurricane, they were not inferior to the early Messerschmitt Bf.109 (which then was handicapped by a grossly inferior engine, whereas the British fighters benefitted enormously from the performance conferred by their Rolls-Royce Merlins).[*]

Considering the handicaps under which American designers were obliged to function through much of the 1930s, it is perhaps anticlimactic that two American fighters were judged after the fact to be the best to serve in large numbers in World War II; North American's P-51 Mustang and Vought's F-4U Corsair claimed that distinction, (although patrons of other models continue to dispute the judgement). Less surprisingly, Boeing's progression from the B-9 through the B-17 to the B-29 kept American's supreme in heavy bombers, while Martin, North American, and Douglas carried the earlier advances of civil aircraft designers through the highly successful B-26, B-25, and A-26 respectively. Least surprising of all, the radial engine that first demonstrated its potential in American civil transports of the early 1930s provided the edge that made most of those aircraft so capable. The exception, of course was the P-51, which was conceived late enough to take advantage of another major aerodynamic advancement--the laminar flow wing--but which did not demonstrate its full potential until a British-designed Merlin engine was substituted for the less satisfactory American-built Allison that originally equipped it.

Before leaving the piston-engine era, it is useful to consider the implications and consequences of the trends that marked its final two decades. As remarked here and there, but without special emphasis, essentially all of the significant advances in military aeronautics adopted by the U.S. air services before 1938-1939 were proposed by private developers, often without rousing any service enthusiasm and frequently in the face of opposition. If 1935-1936 was the year of ultimate transition from the classic wire and fabric biplane fighter to the high performance monoplane of World War II, it remains that Boeing had an earlier vision--earlier than those epitomized by Mitchell's Spitfire, Camm's Hurricane, or even Polikarpov's "Rata" (I-16). But the Army Air Corps preferred a more conservative course, and to Polikarpov went the honors of innovation. Even later, Seversky and Curtiss built their P-35 and P-36 prototypes with little or no service support (as did Mitchell and Camm, for that matter). As suggested by the several examples noted previously, until World War II had all but begun, the U.S. air services tended not to encourage major design innovations in new aircraft. Nor did most foreign air forces, of course. But in America the ingredients were available, had been commercially demonstrated, and and were repeatedly offered. It is not at all inconceivable that in a

---

[*]It is an interesting commentary on the convergence of aeronautical trends in fighters that the Curtiss, Seversky , Supermarine, Hawker, and Messerschmitt fighters, as well as the still better but politically unacceptable Heinkel He.112, all made their first flights in a period spanned by the summer of 1935 and the spring of 1936.

more favorable climate Boeing could have incrementally improved the
XP-29 design of 1933, exploiting that concept in much the fashion of
contemporary bomber concepts. Messerschmitt did as much, as did Mitchell's
successors with the Spitfire.

Three trends in American military aeronautics appear to have held
constant between 1920 and 1940. First, with occasional and not usually
important exceptions, most superior military aircraft to enter service
with the Army and the Navy originated outside the main stream of the
military requirements process. They began, in the British vernacular, as
private ventures. Second, service aircraft designs changed slowly; innovation, even if it implied little more than exploiting such proven
devices as cantilever wings or retractable landing gear, met resistance.
Third, it was not aircraft design as such, but isolated examples of design brilliance combined with the fortunate availability of high-
performance radial engines that proved the salvation of U.S. military
aeronautics during World War II.[*] No American aircraft equipped with
in-line liquid-cooled engines of American design except the P-38 was
able to cope, on a one-for-one basis, with the fighter aircraft of
Germany and Japan--which suggests that Lockheed's P-38 was a highly
inspired design in its own right.

What did wartime experience, or perceptions, do to those trends? It
in most respects reversed two of them and--with allowances for the emergence of jet rather than reciprocating engines--generally reinforced the
third.

No post-1945 American combat aircraft was carried to the prototype
stage, or farther, by a private concern. All were funded by the services.
Some, it is true, were proposed and carried through initial design by
private initiative, the F-100, F-104, F-5, and still embryonic F-16/F-18
being prominent examples. But the enormous cost of creating the complex
systems that are modern jet aircraft has all but precluded any possibility
that the "private ventures" which resulted in the P-26, XP-29, P-35, or
P-51 will again be supported. With partial exceptions, and those rare,
formal military requirements or service-funded studies of prospective
designs have fomented postwar American military aircraft.[**]

Second, risk aversion was notably absent in most military aircraft
developments of 1945-1965 and only since 1965 has a tendency to weigh
the potential ill consequences of excessive enthusiasm for attractive
new technology gradually begun to reassert itself. Some ambitious post-
war development efforts have had such long gestation periods that service
operations have lagged six to ten years behind design start. The B-70
was obsolete before its design concept could be successfully proven,

---

*Again, with the singular but important exception of the P-51.
**Obviously that generalization does not include the several military
variants of civil aircraft which have been adapted to service needs, although of relatively large and costly jet aircraft so employed only the
Boeing 747 and the Douglas DC-9 have almost pure civil-airline origins.

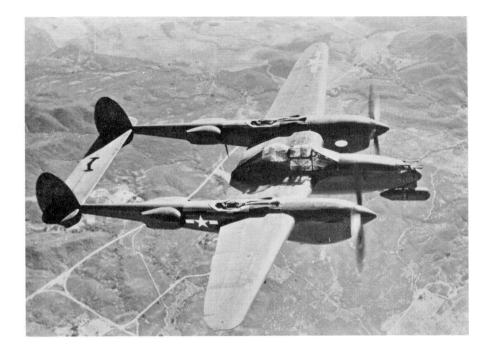

LOCKHEED P-38

(V-7 - Courtesy of Lockheed-California Co.)

NORTH AMERICAN P-51

(V-8 - NASM)

NORTH AMERICAN F-86
(V-9 - NASM)

LOCKHEED F-104C
(V-9a - Courtesy of Lockheed-California Co.)

whereas aircraft such as the F-106, F-111, and B-1 have spent far longer in development than their sponsors anticipated. A considerable number of attempted developments were aborted when technology proved intractable, requirements being essentially unsatisfiable. But where once military aeronautics lagged well behind civil aircraft development, the reverse has become the case.

Trends in engine development showed the least variance from prewar patterns--again because the costs of conceiving, designing, testing, demonstrating, and manufacturing large aircraft power plants were too great for private enterprise. As in the past, it has been a combination of successful engines with skillful airframe design that has distinguished American military aircraft of recent decades. Indeed, the chief problem of foreign aircraft designers (excepting in the Soviet Union) has been the necessity of working with available engines, virtually all of American origin.

The most striking difference between American military design practices in prewar and postwar aeronautics has been the general abandonment of incremental model improvement as a policy. It is true that changes of a modest sort have characterized the successive production versions of many military aircraft, but the sort of continuing transition that marked pre-1940 fighters and bombers has all but vanished. To some extent that difference may be attributed to the considerable difficulty of incorporating markedly more powerful engines or strikingly different wing or fuselage designs in highly integrated aircraft systems of the post 1945 era.* Another obvious contributor to the general tendency was the very rapid progression of airframe and engine technology between 1945 and 1955: however refined, however carefully modified, an F-84 or F-100 became essentially unable to compete on even terms with its opposition and had to be replaced with a more modern aircraft.

If in the pre-1945 era the tendency of the services was to limit their R&D support of the aircraft industry chiefly to engines, aeronautical equipment, and partial subsidy of a few prototypes, since 1945 the trend has been completely reversed. The introduction of "X-series" designators immediately after the war signaled a major change; aeronautical research could make the progress essential to advances in the military arts only if the military fully supported the enterprise. Before 1939 one small laboratory complex at Wright Field provided the principal support of Army Air Corps aircraft development; by 1965, an 80,000

---

*The singular exception in the western world of military aeronautics has been Dassault, who over a period of nearly 20 years continually invested in incremental design changes to the Mirage fighter series and kept his products competitive with those of other nations notwithstanding. It should go almost without saying that the continuing production of such as the A-4, B-52, and the F-4 has not been without design change and improvement, but the basic configuration and equipment of the aircraft were little altered over the years.

CONSOLIDATED B-36, "PEACEMAKER"
Initially designed in 1941 for intercontinental operations it appeared after World War II. B-36D had ten engines (2 jet engines in each wing pod for dash speeds). It was augmented in SAC by B-47's and replaced by B-52's. (V-10- NASM)

MCDONNELL FH-1, "PHANTOM"
First Navy jet fighter Carrier Qualification, a FH-1 landing on the U.S.S. Saipan, May 3, 1948. (V-11- U.S. Navy Photo)

man establishment extended over much of the nation was performing that function. Nevertheless, the contributions of small groups of highly capable designers in private firms remained vital: Ed Heineman's A-4, C. L. Johnson's F-104, U-2, and SR-71 (among several others), McDonnell's F-4, and Boeings B-52 must certainly be rated as among the most important military aircraft of the past three decades, and all were privately conceived.

And something must be said, at the end, about the special institutional attributes of military aeronautics which have developed during those decades. Military aeronautics has finally acquired an effective constituency. One of the universally accepted perceptions of World War II was that aeronautical doctrine, strategy, training, and tactics were of small consequence to the outcomes of campaigns and wars unless superior technology was also thrown into the balance. Questions of quality versus quantity in military aircraft have been argued for nearly 30 years. They still remain unresolved. But whether by design or happenstance, the United States depended upon a quantitative edge in aircraft in World War II and has since chosen to repose confidence in the superiority of machines, and to a lesser extent of men, rather than numbers. While that marked technological advantage is maintained, there seems no reason to challenge such a judgement. But from time to time in history, there occur technological plateaus. Scientists and engineers reach the limits of readily exploitable technology. The miscalled sound barrier was one, which was vastly over rated. The Mach 2.5 heat barrier is another. A breakthrough, when it comes, has tended in the past vastly to increase the cost of whatever is being bought. Performance improvements, when achieved, have not always been proportional. In constant dollars, fighter aircraft of the Korean War era cost rather more than ten times as much as the fighter aircraft in production in the midst of World War II; today the F-14 costs about ten times as much as its Korean War predecessor, and the variety of machines required to support the needs of military aeronautics today has increased enormously. When once planners thought in terms of fighters and bombers, and perhaps of transports, now they must include in their calculations helicopters and a host of spacecraft and incredible numbers of land and air and sea-based missiles which, had they arrived a generation earlier, might have made the sphere of military aeronautics uninhabitable and its principle function irrelevant.

The adequacy of advances in military aeronautics is never fully tested except in combat. Most Americans hope that there will not again occur the need to put to the test once more the assumed advantages of American military aeronautics over those of other nations. American military aviators have for practical purposes flown through the envelope of the atmosphere that supports winged aircraft. They have flown so fast that the materials of yesterday would soften and bend under the heat of air friction alone. They depend wholly on mechanical and electronic sensors and on calculating devices to augment the limited ability of man to cope with the enormous rate at which critical flight information accumulates. Yes, unless what always happened in the past does not again happen in the future, coming decades will see military aeronautics move

BOEING B-52B, "STRATOFORTRESS"

(V-12 - NASM)

forward again, reducing the spectacular achievements of today to the
status of minor entries in a chronology mostly of interest to historians
and other gadflys of this technological age. They will learn, again,
that developing military aircraft is a very risky business, that the
temptation to herald remarkable achievement and to overlook persistent
advance is compelling, and that what is most remarkable is the frequency
of man's success in subduing the harsh uncertainties of military
aeronautics.

BIBLIOGRAPHICAL NOTE

The literature on American military aviation is enormous in quantity--but it is of most uneven quality. Perhaps the most useful source is the *Journal of the American Aviation Historical Society,* periodically indexed and generally reliable. The occasional oversights of contributors are often remarked by readers, so it is advisable to consult the "letters" section for several months following the publication of any particular article in order to ensure against oversight. Robin Higham's *Air Power, A Concise History* (New York, St. Martins, 1972) is a thoughtful overview, more concerned with policy, tactics, and strategy than machinery. Although some 17 years old, and therefore lacking any coverage of critical policy questions of the 1960s and 1970s, *The Impact of Air Power,* E. M. Emme (editor), Princeton, Van Nostrand, 1959, remains the basic source book. Ronald Miller and David Sawers, *The Technical Development of Modern Aviation* (London, Praeger, 1970) and Robert Schlaifer and S. D. Heron, *Development of Aircraft Engines and Fuels* (Cambridge, Harvard, 1950) are considerably superior to any other general treatments of basic technology. Schlaifer is outdated and Miller and Sawers are far more concerned with civil than military aviation, but they remain models of the genre.

For information about aircraft development there are almost too many sources and, unhappily, many of the more "popular" volumes are thoroughly unreliable. Legend and misinformation abound, and they are self perpetuating; few aviation enthusiasts are trained historians, and fewer historians apply their critical talents to aviation. Of the encyclopaedic volumes, J.W.R. Taylor's *Combat Aircraft of the World from 1909 to the Present* (New York, Putnam, 1969), is still the most comprehensive and reliable. Taylor and Kenneth Munson, *History of Aviation, Aircraft Identification Guide* (London, New English Library, 1973), and F. K. Manson and Martin Windrow, *Know Aviation* (London, G. Philip and Son, 1973) are useful data books. J. C. Fahey's *U.S. Army Aircraft 1908-1946* and *USAF Aircraft 1947-1956* are invaluable references for the early periods. C. H. Gibbs-Smith, *The Aeroplane: An Historical Survey of its Origins and Development* (London, H.M.S.O., 1960), is an excellent if somewhat dated account with emphasis on the pioneering period.

Serious researchers will tread with great caution through most of the periodical literature on aviation history. Over the years one of the most consistently respectable journals has been William Green's *Air International*--and its predecessors (difficult to locate in this country), *Flying Review International* and *RAF Flying Review.* Although of somewhat limited use to researchers because of a consistent policy of avoiding source citations, they nonetheless have provided details of aircraft development obtainable elsewhere only with great labor. Bibliographical notes in Green's publications and in the *Journal of the American Aviation Historical Society* provide comprehensive, if sometimes uncritical, reviews of the multitudes of specialized publications that continue to appear.

V I

COMMERCIAL AVIATION: FROM THE BENOIST AIRBOAT
TO THE SST, 1914 - 1976

Richard P. Hallion[*]

American air transportation has experienced rapid
growth since 1914. Much of this is due to the inter-
relationships that developed within the aircraft
industry, federal regulatory agencies, and the airlines themselves. Exploitation of key technical advances has led to American domination of the airliner
market since 1934. Current transports such as the wide
bodies and SST pose serious economic and social questions that must be resolved if the air transport system
is to remain healthy.

"{The} conquest of the air will prove, ultimately, to be man's greatest
and most glorious triumph. What railways have done for nations, airways
will do for the world."
                    Claude Graham-White and Harry Harper, 1914

"The airplane gives to man a new freedom, eliminating the geographical
barriers of river, sea, mountain and desert between him and his kind,
and thus eliminating those prejudices and misunderstandings which have
jeopardised human relations in the past."
                              Harry F. Guggenheim, 1930

The history of American air transport is a saga of chances taken or ignored,
profits gained and lost, technical developments introduced or passed
up. It has its own peculiar galaxy of pioneers, ranging from engineers
and entrepreneurs to pilots and administrators. In a little less than a
half-century from the Wright's pioneering flight, American airliners flew
a greater number of annual air passenger miles than annual railroad passenger miles covered by Pullman cars. The airplane, in just a half-
century, swept past the accumulated accomplishment of over a century of
railroad expansion. Another measure of American commercial aviation
growth is in the employment figures and appropriations of aviation

[*]Curator, Science and Technology, National Air and Space Museum, Smith-
sonian Institution. Dr. Hallion is the author of Supersonic Flight
(New York, 1972), and won the 1975 AIAA History Manuscript Award for
Legacy of Flight: The Daniel Guggenheim Fund for the Promotion of
Aeronautics and the Formative Era of American Aviation.

155

regulatory agencies. In 1927, the Department of Commerce's Aeronautics Branch, the Federal Aviation Administration's (FAA) ancestor, employed 234 and had a budget of $550 thousand. In 1971, the FAA had an employment of 54,515, and a budget of over $737 million.[1]

The aircraft themselves changed dramatically. The trimotor Fokker F.VIIb-3m of 1926 cruised at 95 mph with eight passengers. The Lockheed L-049 Constellation of 1946 flew 47 passengers at 280 mph. Then came the jets. The Boeing 707-120 of 1960 cruises at 535 mph with 111 passengers; the Boeing 747-200B of 1970 carries 374 passengers at 589 mph. And now, with the Anglo-French Concorde, cruising speeds have jumped over a whole Mach number, to 1,410 mph. In its phenomenal technical development, the airliner is unmatched by any other form of transporation.

American air transport had its birth on New Year's Day, 1914, at Tampa Bay, Florida. Pilot Tony Jannus flew paying passenger A.C. Thiel in a Benoist XIV flying boat from St. Petersburg to Tampa, the first "airline" passenger service in the U.S. The "St. Petersburg-Tampa Airboat Line," lasted three profitless months, during which time it carried 1,204 passengers.[2,3] In September 1911, Earl L. Ovington flew a small amount of mail between Nassau and Mineola, New York, during the International Aviation Meet. Despite the success of this experiment, the Post Office could not obtain Congressional approval for airmail service until 1916, the war then delaying airmail operations for two years. The "Father of Airmail," Assistant Postmaster General Otto Praeger, received permission for trial service between Washington, D. C., and New York via Philadelphia. On May 15, 1918, the first official U.S. airmail operations began, with modified Curtiss JN-4H "Jenny" biplanes flown by Army pilots. One pilot became lost after takeoff from Washington's Polo Grounds (his mail eventually arriving in New York by train), but two others successfully delivered the southbound mail from New York to the Nation's Capital. On August 10, 1918, this experimental service came to an end. Two days later, Post Office pilot Max Miller inaugurated the world's first permanent mail service, flying 222 lbs. of mail from Washington to Philadelphia in a 150 h.p. Standard Aero-mail plane. The "Aerial Mail Service" grew quickly. During 1920, the Post Office initiated transcontinental mail service from New York to San Francisco via Cleveland, Chicago, and Omaha, using a combination of day flights and night mail trains, shaving 22 hours off the quickest train-only service. The next year, the Post Office started plane-only transcontinental service, finally eliminating all rail transportation in connection with the airmail on July 1, 1924.[3,4,5,6,7,8,9]

The Post Office had little desire to continue federal operation of what officials believed should be a private-sector activity. As a result, Congress passed the Air Mail Act (43 Stat. L., 805), popularly known as the Kelly Act, in February 1925. The Kelly Act approved federal subsidy of air mail service; the government paid private companies to haul the mail. The Kelly Act was of crucial importance to the subsequent growth of American air transport, inasmuch as it encouraged private companies to enter the air commerce field. When these firms carried passengers as well, the United States had the makings of its modern airline industry. By 1926, several companies had received airmail contracts. The first to

FOKKER F-10 TRIMOTOR
(VI-1, National Air and Space Museum)

DOUGLAS DC-3
(VI-2, Sherman Fairchild Collection, National Air and Space Museum)

operate, Ford Air Transport, managed a Detroit-Chicago-Cleveland network starting on February 15, 1926. The Post Office finally discontinued its own government air mail service on September 1, 1927. During government operations, the Post Office had flown 10 million miles and carried 7 million pounds of mail at a total cost of $15 million.[3,4,5,7,10,11]

While the air mail existed on firmly established ground, the same could not be said of passenger operations. Much as conditions after World War II combined to thwart acquisition of proposed new airliners, conditions after World War I, with the large numbers of surplus aircraft, worked against the development of specialized air transports. Aeromarine West Indies Airways operated a 105 mile passenger route from Key West, Florida, to Havana, starting on November 1, 1919, using twin-engine Aeromarine Model 75 flying boats, originally developed for naval use.[3]

That same year, Alfred Lawson developed the first multi-engine passenger airplane designed in America, the Lawson C-2. This aircraft, a twin-engine biplane with a completely enclosed cabin, spanned 91 feet, and could carry 16 passengers for 400 miles. In August and September 1919, the C-2 flew from Milwaukee to Washington and back, receiving favorable press reviews. Lawson embarked on an even more ambitious project, the three-engine L-4 "Midnight Liner," but due to pilot error and Lawson's own bad judgment, it crashed on takeoff. Financially ruined, Lawson left the aircraft industry entirely. The C-2 and L-4, antecedents of such aircraft as the Curtiss Condor, were simply built at the wrong time, for American air transportation had not advanced far enough to take advantage of their full potential. Surplus D.H. 4's and Jennies adequately filled existing air commerce needs.[12,13,14,15,16]

On May 20, 1926, President Calvin Coolidge signed the Air Commerce Act of 1926 (44 Stat. L., 568) into law, the first federal attempt to regulate civil aeronautics. Chaotic, unsafe, and unregulated aircraft ownership and operation, together with growing recognition that the U.S. lagged behind Europe in established passenger air services all contributed to passage of this regulatory legislation. The Joint Committee of Civil Aviation of the Department of Commerce and the American Engineering Council, and the President's Aircraft Board, chaired by financier Dwight Morrow, had recommended creating a civil aviation regulatory body within the Department of Commerce. The Air Commerce Act created an Aeronautics Branch charged with promotion and regulation of air commerce, including registration and rating of pilots and planes, creation of civil airways, and establishing aids to air navigation, such as the four-course radio range. This milestone act marked the beginning of civil aviation regulation in the U.S.[1,7,17,18,19,20,21]

One critical event enabling American air transport to match and then surpass that of Europe, was philanthropists Daniel and Harry Guggenheim's establishing The Daniel Guggenheim Fund for the Promotion of Aeronautics. This fund, in operation from 1926 to 1930, laid the foundations for organized nationwide aeronautical education programs, conducted basic research on "blind" flying and S.T.O.L. aircraft, and established a "Model Air Line" on the West Coast using Fokker trimotors.[22,23]

Low engine reliability had generated the trimotor configuration, since existing twin-engine aircraft (often having inherently high-drag and hence poor single-engine performance) offered little improvement over single-engine types. The trimotor airliner first appeared in Europe in 1924 with the Handley Page W/8E. The monoplane Junkers G23 trimotor followed a year later. The next year, Anthony Fokker developed the monoplane cantilever wooden-winged F.VIIa-3m, a Wright Whirlwind-powered trimotor development of the single engine F.VIIa, for the first Ford Airplane Reliability Tour. This aircraft, the first Fokker trimotor, easily won the 1925 Ford tour, inspiring Ford's own William B. Stout and his engineers to adopt a similar trimotor configuration, using Hugo Junkers' metal construction techniques, the genesis of the famous Ford Tri-Motor. The age of the trimotor transport had arrived.[24,25,26,27,28,29]

On May 27, 1927, Harry Guggenheim, president of the Guggenheim fund, proposed creating an experimental passenger air route with radio communications and using the latest transports. Most airmail operators rejected his plan, but Harris M. "Pop" Hanshue of Western Air Express enthusiastically agreed. WAE had begun the nation's first scheduled passenger service on May 23, 1923, using single-engine Douglas mailplanes. Now, Guggenheim and his advisors selected a Pratt & Whitney "Wasp" version of the Fokker trimotor for the "Model Air Line" experiment. This new plane, developed especially for the Guggenheim Fund, was the Fokker F-10. The first of three for WAE flew on March 21, 1928. The Guggenehim-funded Model Air Line began operations in May 1928, between Los Angeles and San Francisco. The route included a complete weather-reporting network of 22 stations connected by telephone. Later, the service expanded to 40 stations with telephone and teletype interstation communications. This system, under the direction of meteorologist Carl Gustaf Rossby, served as the prototype for future federal airways reporting networks, just as the Model Air Line served as an example for future airways management.[3,22,30]

The Guggenheim Fund contributed to air transportation in four other ways as well. It sponsored "town marking" as a aid to cross-country navigation, promoted the use of airmail, sent Lindbergh and Richard Byrd's Josephine Ford on "airmindedness" publicity tours around the country, and developed "blind flying" techniques. At its Full Flight Laboratory at Mitchel Field, Guggenheim Fund test pilot James H. Doolittle successfully demonstrated three critically important instruments specially developed for the fund, the Sperry artificial horizon, Sperry gyrocompass, and the Kollsman precision altimeter, by making the world's first successful "blind" flight, from takeoff through landing, in a modified Consolidated NY-2, on September 24, 1929. Together with the popular impact of Lindbergh's flight, the Guggenheim Fund can be numbered among the catalytic factors that boosted future air passenger services. In 1927, 18,679 persons travelled by air. In 1930, this had jumped to 385,000, rising to over 200 million annually by 1975.[21,22,31,32]

The trimotor dominated American air transportation until March 31, 1931, when a Fokker F-10 shed its wing in flight and crashed, killing all on board, including famed football coach Knute Rockne. In the ensuing publicity, the wooden-wing Fokkers came in for a full measure of criticism. Passengers and crews already disliked the noisy, drafty trimotors, while airline operators regarded their operating costs--roughly 7 cents per seat mile--as too high. Aerodynamicists and structural theorists preaching the gospel of streamlining and stressed-skin construction scorned the awkward trimotors. Now, a wave of technological innovation combined with a belief that air travel required faster, more powerful, and comfortable transports, spawning the modern piston-powered transport.

The 1920's had witnessed many technical innovations. The ones of subsequent major importance were the rise of the radial engine, the emphasis on streamlining and drag reduction, the adaptation of the cantilever monoplane configuration, and the development of semi-monocoque stressed-skin construction. The highly-reliable Wright Whirlwind and Pratt & Whitney Wasp engines (their reliability due in no small measure to the sodium-cooled exhaust valve developed by S. D. Heron), initiated the dominance of the radial piston engine over the more cumbersome and complex inline engine for air transport duties, making possible the practical and safe twin-engine transport. The first Wasp had a horsepower-to-weight ratio of .66; by 1945, later P&W R-2800's boasted a .995 hp/lb ratio.[2,26]

From 1926, until the advent of the jet, the radial piston engine dominated air transport propulsion. Bulky radials were anathema to the gospel of streamlining, first eloquently pronounced by B.M. Jones in 1929. By that time, however, the drag-reducing Townend ring and the much more efficient long-chord NACA cowling (which won the 1928 Collier Trophy for Fred E. Weick and NACA) had made their appearance. Aerodynamics-conscious engineers incorporated cowled radials on new designs, the first being the streamlined Lockheed Vega of 1927, (which re-introduced the European monocoque tradition) and the trend-setting streamlined Northrop Alpha of 1929, (which pioneered aluminum monocoque structure and introduced John K. Northrop's stressed-skin multicellular wing construction). Further, designers now mounted the engines on the leading edge of the wings (but farther ahead of the wing than Hugo Junkers' practice so that propeller efficiency increased), avoiding the inherent high drag characteristics of the Ford and Fokker trimotors with their "afterthought" below-the-wing engine installations.[2,6,27,28,33,34]

Completing the propulsion picture was the controllable-pitch propeller, dating to early studies by Seth Hart and R. I. Eustis, though primarily from the work of Frank W. Caldwell with Hamilton-Standard in 1929-1930. The controllable-pitch prop maximized efficient usage of available engine power throughout the range of aircraft operation, from takeoff to landing. Additional refinements, such as sound-proof cabins, the wing flap (to reduce landing speeds and increase lift, permitting higher wing loadings and hence, more payload), the retractable landing gear (first appearing in practical form on the Dayton-Wright Racer of 1920), the adaptation of the cantilever monoplane configuration, and the appearance of American all-metal stressed-skin structures (advancing beyond the pioneer work of Adolf Rohrbach in this field) all made the imminent appearance of the first "modern" air transports inevitable.[25,26,27,28,33,34,35]

So it was that on February 8, 1933, the revolutionary Boeing 247 twin-engine all-metal monoplane transport took to the air, starting airline service with United less than two months later. At once the trimotors, the Curtiss Condors, the Bellancas, and their ilk were obsolete. American air transport technology had come of age, sweeping ahead of the rest of the world. But already Boeing had a rival. Douglas, in partnership with Transcontinental and Western Air (TWA) determined to better even the 247. A huge cutaway drawing of the 247 hung in the Douglas plant at Santa Monica with the admonition, "Don't copy it! Do it better!" And Douglas did. The DC-1, which first flew on July 1, 1933, had wing flaps (which the 247 did not), twelve rather than the 247's ten passengers, an unobstructed cabin with the wing carrythrough under the cabin (unlike the constricted mid-wing 247), and refined aerodynamics.[27,28,36,37,38,39]

Though the 247 had just entered production, the DC-1 rendered it already obsolescent. Douglas engineers did not stop here. Rather than place the DC-1 in production, they enlarged it into the DC-2, with 14 passengers and more powerful engines. When Cyrus R. Smith, the hard-driving chieftan of American Airlines, prodded Douglas to develop a "sleeper" transport, the result was the DC-3, a natural outgrowth of the earlier DC-2. With 21 passengers, its seat-mile costs were a third less than the DC-2, and much less than the 247. It was the first airplane that could turn a profit simply by carrying passengers. The DC-3, which entered service with American Airlines in 1936, had operating costs of 1.27 cents per available seat-mile, compared to 2.11 for the Boeing 247. Nor was this revolution in air transport design limited only to Boeing and Douglas. Lockheed joined up in 1934, a year after the 247 and DC-1, with the twin-tail L-10 Electra, a 10-passenger twin-engine transport having all the technical advances of its larger cousins, but particularly suited for shorter routes and smaller traffic loads.[27,28,37,39]

The 1934 MacRobertson England-to-Australia air race rudely awakened a biplane dominated Europe to the American ascendency. A specially built two-man De Havilland D.H. 88 high-performance racer came in first, but a KLM DC-2 was a close second, followed by a United Boeing 247D. No European transport could have matched the feat, and orders for Douglas DC-2's and DC-3's flooded Santa Monica. By 1938, Douglas had orders for 803 DC-3's, and DC-3's carried 95% of America's civil air commerce.[27,28,37,39]

Until 1934, economic regulation of the nation's airways consisted primarily of Post Office-awarded air mail contracts. A major political scandal alleging airline-Post Office collusion in contract award practices erupted in 1933, culminating in President Franklin Roosevelt's executive order transferring responsibility for hauling the mail from the airlines to the Army. Appalling casualties reflected the woeful state of American military aviation, so much so that F.D.R. cancelled Army mail operations, and Postmaster General James Farley authorized renegotiated airmail contracts. Congressional pressure generated the Black-McKellar Air Mail Act of June 1934, which replaced the McNary-Watres Airmail Act of 1930. The 1930 Act, inspired by then-Postmaster General Walter Brown, attempted to unify the airline industry into three large transcontinental companies, to encourage passenger service (the Post Office awarded contract bonuses if mail operators carried passengers), and eventually avoid the need for wholesale mail subsidy. The 1934 Act emphasized competition between carriers (critics alleged "cutthroat bidding"). and divested companies of interests in both air transportation and aircraft manufacturing. The act transferred airmail regulatory functions to the Interstate Commerce Commission. As a result of this furor, and the need for a clean new image, the old Aeronautics Branch became the Bureau of Air Commerce, largely just a change in title.[1,4,7,17]

Four years later, because of some well-publicized accidents, especially the death of Sen. Bronson M. Cutting (R-New Mexico) in the crash of a DC-2 on May 6, 1935, and allegations of Commerce Department laxity and mismanagement of the airways (charges generally without foundation), Congress passed the Civil Aeronautics Act of June 1938. The 1938 Act created an independent Civil Aeronautics Authority responsible for air safety (via an independent Air Safety Board), economic regulation, and airways management, effectively combining the functions of the old Bureau of Air Commerce and ICC. F.D.R., unhappy with having an independent aviation regulatory agency, used the powers afforded by the Reorganization Act of 1939 to abolish the Air Safety Board and reconstitute it as the Civil Aeronautics Board (CAB), reshuffling the Civil Aeronautics Authority around as the reorganized Civil Aeronautics Administration (CAA). Both the CAA and CAB went back to at least nominal control by the Commerce Department. This arrangement continued until creation of the Federal Aviation Agency in 1958.[1,4,7,40,42]

While these administrative changes occurred, appropriations for the CAA and its predecessors increased from $6,416,620 in 1930 to $25,768,000 in 1940. Airline passengers carried rose from 384,506 in 1930 to 3,038,619 in 1940. "Controlled" civil airways mileage on the Federal Airways System went from 2,041 miles in 1926, to 15,258 in 1930, to 32,100 in 1940. The beacon range light total jumped from 719 in 1927 to 2,304 in 1940. The number of four-course radio range stations grew from 9 in 1929 to 292 in 1940. The first three Air Route Traffic Control Centers (ARTCC), at Chicago, Cleveland, and New York, began service on July 6, 1936. By the end of 1940, a further eleven had entered service. The next year, the CAA commissioned the first six airport Instrument Landing Systems (ILS). American airliners could now fly in complete safety amid weather conditions that would have grounded them a decade earlier.[1,4,7,41,42]

The 1930's saw the emergence of the first four-engine transoceanic and transcontinental transports. On May 20, 1939, twenty years after the NC-4 and twelve years to the day since Lindbergh's departure from Roosevelt Field, Pan American Airways launched the first American commercial operations to Europe when its Boeing Model 314 Yankee Clipper flying boat left Port Washington for Marseilles, via the Azores and Lisbon. The 314 Atlantic service marked the culmination of Juan Trippe's plans for Pan Am's pre-war oceanic conquests. Trippe started his flying boat operations in 1928, with a series of Sikorsky designs furnishing service around the Caribbean. He expanded into the Pacific in 1935 with Martin Model 130 service from California to China, and then tackled the Atlantic. The flying boat, however, was not a completely satisfactory concept, despite

BOEING 314
(VI-3, C.G.B. Stuart Collection,
National Air and Space Museum)

DOUGLAS DC-4
(VI-4, National Air and Space Museum)

its superiority to the airship. (Airships could carry large numbers of passengers but a great cost. LZ-129 <u>Hindenburg</u> could carry 72 passengers, but seat-mile costs were on the order of 29 cents.) The necessarily restricted configuration layout--boat hull, high wing, drag-producing floats or sponsons--contributed to high costs. The flying boat simply lacked the flexibility of the long-range landplane. Debris in water proved a great safety hazard. So did weather; in the winter of 1940, for example, Pan Am had to move its flying boat operations from Long Island to Baltimore, then to Norfolk, then Charleston, and eventually to Miami, all because of ice! When the successful long-range landplane became available, the flying boat swiftly passed from the transoceanic air transport scene, despite anachronistic British attempts to revive it, even with turbojet propulsion.[27,39,43,44,45,46,47,48]

The four-engine landplane transport had appeared as early as 1913, with the Sikorsky <u>Bolshoi</u>. In 1920, Adolf Rohrbach had created the four-engine Zeppelin-Staaken E.4250 monoplane, the ancestor of all future all-metal stressed-skin airliners. The ungainly Junkers G38ce followed in 1929. In the 1930's, Boeing developed the Model 299, prototype for the famous B-17 and the first modern four-engine low-wing monoplane, and the large and underpowered XB-15. Douglas followed these efforts with its DC-4E transport, a large and overly complex airliner that first flew on June 7, 1938. The DC-4E, designed with NACA stability and control criteria in mind, incorporated a number of noteworthy features, including tricycle retractable landing gear, power-boosted controls, slotted flaps, and a flush-riveted skin. Douglas began the DC-4E in 1935 at the request of the five largest U.S. airlines (TWA, Pan Am, American, Eastern, and United) as a plane able to cross the country with only one fueling stop (as compared with three needed by the DC-3's). Too ambitious, costly, and complex, the DC-4E failed to win airline acceptance.[26,27,28,39]

Disappointed, Douglas turned to developing a much smaller and less complex aircraft--the four-engine low-wing DC-4 now so familiar to airline operators around the world. Boeing, on the other hand, chose to adopt its bomber design technology, using the XB-15's wings as the basis of those on the Model 314 flying boat, and the B-17's wing and tail configuration for the Boeing Model 307 four-engine airliner. The 307 Stratoliner made its first flight on December 31, 1938, and entered service with TWA in April 1940. It enjoyed the distinction of being the first pressurized airliner, coming on the heels of the experimental Lockheed XC-35 testbed of 1937. The 307 had only limited success (just ten were built), for Boeing soon devoted its production activities to producing B-17's and later B-29's for wartime needs. Further, its tailwheel undercarriage placed the 307 at a distinct disadvantage with respect to later designs, as typified by that tricycle classic, the DC-4.[26,27,28,39]

With the DC-4, which began service in 1943, air transport technology hit a configuration stagnation point. Future piston engine or turboprop-powered transports, from the DC-4 to the Ilyushin Il-18, all tended to look the same, fulfilling Peter Brooks' generic term, "DC-4 Generation."[27] The DC-4 directly spawned the DC-6, DC-6A, DC-6B, DC-7, DC-7B, and the DC-7C "Seven Seas." Lockheed, rejecting Douglas' pragmatic parallel-section fuselage design, developed the sinuous but cramped Constellation. Like the DC-4, the graceful triple-tail "Connie" evolved stretched developments, culminating in the L-1049G "Super Constellation" (1954), and the L-1649A Starliner (1956). Boeing, as usual drawing on their bomber work, combined the aerodynamics of the B-29/B-50 to produce the C-97 and its civilian counterpart, the Model 377 Stratocruiser.

The "DC's," "Connies," and 377's reigned supreme over the postwar air transport market. In 1951, 80% of the world's airliners were U.S. built, and of these, 56% came from Douglas. Exotic projections, such as the Republic RC-2 Rainbow, could not compete with these established vehicles, though they drew some airline interest. Large capacity aircraft, such as the Convair XC-99 and Lockheed Constitution, held little appeal, for the existing traffic loads simply did not warrant these early "wide-bodies." Seat-mile costs in 1948 were down to 1.57 cents for the DC-6, compared to the trimotors' 7 cents per mile. Between the heyday of the trimotor and the post-war DC-4 generation, airliner speeds had jumped 150%, while operating costs had been better than halved.[27,28,49]

By 1945, 175 supply flights crossed the Atlantic daily, the fruits of wartime expansion. The war's end saw virtually immediate commercial exploitation. American Overseas Airlines, using DC-4's, began the first scheduled landplane service between America and Europe on October 23, 1945. At the end of the year, a TWA Constellation had set a crossing record of 12 hours and 57 minutes between Washington and Paris. On February 11, 1946, the United States and Great Britain signed the Air Service Agreement, popularly known as the Bermuda Agreement, which established the pattern for future bilateral civil aviation agreements. (The Bermuda Agreement, in force since 1946, is currently under attack by many nations, including Great Britain itself, as various international carriers vie for more favorable route negotiation). The postwar CAA continued its support of domestic airways development. Airport construction and expansion, especially on a local level, mushroomed as a result of the Federal Airport Act. On October 15, 1950, the CAA placed the first vertical omnirange (VOR--the predecessor to the VORTAC civilian-military navigation system) controlled airways into operation, beginning a program of decommissioning the older four-course radio ranges two years later.[1,7,44,50]

A tragic mid-air disaster highlighting weaknesses in the air route traffic control system occurred in 1956 with a collision between a United DC-7 and a TWA Constellation over the Grand Canyon, killing 128. The CAA reeled under a swift succession of other airliner collisions before moving to broaden radar coverage and reserved airspace. But this was not enough. Congressional outcry, combined with the report of Edward P. Curtis, President Eisenhower's Special Assistant for Aviation Facilities Planning, led to the complete restructuring of federal civil aviation regulation under the Federal Aviation Act of August 23, 1958, which created an independent Federal Aviation Agency (FAA) separate from the Department of Commerce. The FAA inherited all CAA functions, adding much of the CAB's authority in air safety. Most importantly, it had sole responsibility for controlling the airspace. Eight years later, on April 1, 1967, the FAA reorganized as the Federal Aviation Administration (the new FAA),

LOCKHEED L-049 CONSTELLATION
(VI-5, National Air and Space Museum)

BOEING 707-120B
(VI-6, National Air and Space Museum)

losing its independence and becoming a part of the Department of Transportation (DOT), The Secretary of Transportation now held all the functions, duties, and powers of the old FAA, except for those of air safety, which the new FAA Administrator held. The old CAB's air safety functions transferred to the DOT's National Transportation Safety Board (NTSB), which could act independently of the DOT Secretary. This is the present DOT/FAA/CAB/NTSB system.[1,7,44,50]

The major revolution that occurred in air transportation after the Second World War was the introduction of the jet transport. Using gas turbine technology derived from the prewar work of Hans von Ohain and Frank Whittle, designers conceived airliners capable of efficient operation above 450 mph. The jet promised and delivered greater power, greater speed, and greater operating economy.

Great Britain became the first nation to exploit gas turbine propulsion for air transports, starting with the turboprop Vickers-Armstrong V.630 Viscount of 1948, and the pure-jet De Havilland D.H. 106 Comet I of 1949, both developed at the recommendation of the two wartime Brabazon Committees. America lagged behind England in jet transport development, much as it had in the race for the first jet engine. American airline executives preferred clinging to the tried and proven radial piston engine. BOAC put the Comet I into service on May 2, 1952. The effect upon American airlines was immediate, and Pan Am even placed an order for three Comets for delivery in 1956. At the end of 1952, William Littlewood, American Airlines' vice president for engineering, warned the Institute of the Aeronautical Sciences that Britain led the United States in high-speed transport development, cautioning that America's only gas turbine transport to date was an experimental Convair 240 with Allison T-38 turboprops. For a brief while, it appeared that Britain might capture and hold a large portion of the air transport market. Yet all this changed rapidly, from circumstances fortuitous to American industry and tragic for Britain. Two Comets, "Yoke Peter" and "Yoke Yoke," mysteriously crashed. Subsequent analysis placed the cause as fatigue-induced explosive decompression. The crashes almost bankrupted De Havilland--Pan Am, among others, cancelled its Comet order--and put the jet transport market once more up for grabs.[26,27,28,51]

The Comet I acted as a catalyst for American jet airliner development, and the accidents gave American industry a chance to catch up. In 1948, Boeing engineer Robert Hage had written glowingly of jet propulsion for medium-range airliners. Boeing already had unique experience it could apply: the XB-47 Stratojet bomber program, which joined the jet engine to a large six-engine transport-size plane having the latest German-American aerodynamic innovation, a sharply sweptback wing. In May 1952, after examining many different configurations, Boeing embarked on a jet tanker and transport development program, using a low sweptwing and four pod-mounted engines. The prototype of this aircraft, the Boeing Model 367-80, completed its first flight on July 14, 1954, scant months after the last Comet crash. As hoped, the Air Force ordered a batch of Boeing jet tanker aircraft (the first of the KC-135 series), and this enabled the company to offer the aerodynamically-similar Model 707 to the airlines. Not to be outdone, Douglas started work on a similar-looking rival, the Model 1881, the prototype DC-8, and Convair initiated design studies for what eventually became the disappointing 880. To the casual observer, the 707, DC-8, and 880 all had the same appearance, with low sweptwings and swept tail surfaces, and four podded engines under the wings.[27,28,36,44,52]

The airlines' rush to Boeing and Douglas began when Pan Am ordered 707's and DC-8's on October 13, 1955. As with the earlier piston-engine transport market, American products continue to dominate the jetliner market. The first 707 flew on December 12, 1957, and the first DC-8 on May 30, 1958. Meanwhile, De Havilland had solved the Comet's problems and placed a longer-range model, the 79-passenger Comet IV, in service. The honor of inaugurating the first transatlantic jet service fell to BOAC, on October 4, 1958. But it was also the Comet's swansong. Pan Am followed with the faster 111-passenger 707-120 on October 26, 1958, introducing the larger 140-passenger 707-320 a year later. The slower, smaller Comet, costing twice as much as a 707 to operate, quickly disappeared from transatlantic service. Over a million passengers flew the Atlantic in 1958, surpassing the total of Atlantic steamship passengers for the first time. The airplane was now more dominant as a "people mover" than either the train or ship; within a decade, from 1958 to 1968, Atlantic air passenger traffic totals rose from 1 to 6 million annually.[27,28,36,44,52]

By the 1960's, the jet revolution was firmly established, with both pure jet and turboprop aircraft on routine airline duty. The U.S. had outpaced its European rivals with the 707 and DC-8, while the Lockheed L-188 Electra four-engine turboprop was a match for any foreign aircraft of comparable type. Only in the area of a turboprop-powered "DC-3 replacement" did the United States lag behind the other nations, having to adopt the Dutch Fokker F-27 Friendship and the French Nord 262, both twin-engine aircraft. Of the two, the F-27 proved more popular and, indeed, this aircraft is the world's most successful civil turboprop airliner. Occasionally, accidents once more pointed the need for careful design, greater regulation, or stimulated new technical developments. The tragic Electra crashes in 1959-1960, induced by propeller autoprecession, reaffirmed the need for absolutely complete design analysis and testing; the accidents occurred in spite of the Electra's reputation of being the most thoroughly tested airliner in service to that date. The new jets, especially the fanjets, offered 25% lower fuel costs than piston engine types, and had a longer engine time between overhaul, 8,000 hours vs. 2,000 hours. The 1966 operating costs for a 707 were 1.318 cents/mile, compared to 1.763 for an Electra, and 4.1 for a piston-engine DC-7C. Between 1964 and 1969, the number of piston-engine airliners still in service dropped precipitously. At the same time, the number of multi-engine jet transports in use rose from about 600 to 1,300.[28,53,54]

The 1960's also witnessed the rapid expansion of local service airlines. In 1944, the CAB had announced an experimental program supporting "feeder lines" to encourage regional and local air services. The first of these feeder carriers to start operation was Essair, flying twin-engine Lockheed L-10's. Essair started service on August 1, 1945, flying between Houston and Amarillo, Texas. By 1970, there were nine feeder airlines,

including such large carriers as Allegheny, flying modern turboprop and
turbojet aircraft such as the Douglas DC-9-30 (seat cost/mile of 1.17
cents) over extensive networks. In 1970, these carriers flew 27 million
passengers to 453 cities. Yet another 'sixties phenomenon, the scheduled
air taxi, a third level carrier flying light aircraft such as the Beech
99 and the De Havilland Twin Otter, also appeared. In 1964, only twelve
such carriers existed, but by 1969, the total had risen to 200 air taxi
operators. While economic analysts differed in their interpretation of
the CAB's local service experiment and the local service growth phenomenon,
industry spokesmen considered it a "monumental success." As the needs for
local services grew, the aircraft industry furnished more economical,
larger capacity, and faster airplanes. Thus, the DC-3's and Convair 240's
of the 1950's gave way to the Fairchild/Fokker F-27's and Douglas DC-9's
of the 1960's. Here, too, the jet airplane had proven more economical
and efficient than its piston-powered rivals.[28,55]

The costly purchasing of jet transports in large numbers caused the airlines and the International Air Transport Association (IATA) much concern
until widespread marketing, an increase in international tourism, and the
airlines' own promotion of economy-class service combined to generate
increasing load factors. The net profit (in percentage of domestic airline
revenue) rose from .5% in 1963 to about 6.5% in 1966. Indeed, the 707
and its rival, the DC-8, proved the most successful money makers in air
transport history.[27,54] This pleasant situation encouraged the airlines
and the industry to proceed with medium range jets (the private-venture
trijet Boeing 727 of 1963 proving the most successful), the narrow-body
"stretch" DC-8 Super Sixty series, the wide-body large capacity (300-500
passengers) "jumbo" or "superjets," and the supersonic transport (SST).

Domestic airline profit margins and passenger load factors began a steady
descent in the late 1960's, while airliner operating costs rose. The profit margin plummeted to zero in 1970, staggering back up to 2.4% in 1972.
The United States had captured the world air transport market so completely
that the sagging American economy, which caused many people to have second
thoughts about spending on travel, immediately hurt the world's airline
profit picture, as reflected by IATA statistics. This immediately affected
the economic outlook for "jumbo" wide-body and SST service. The descent
began gradually, catching the airlines virtually unawares. Pan Am and
Boeing agreed to a joint superjet wide-body venture in December 1965, and
Pan Am placed a $525 million contract for twenty-five four-engine Boeing
747's (the first wide-body superjet) on April 13, 1966. United followed
a year later, and other American and international carriers soon jumped
on the jumbo bandwagon. The first 747 flew on February 9, 1969. Pan Am
placed the Boeing superjet in scheduled operations on January 22,
1970.[1,5,54,55]

Reflecting a traditional pattern in American air transport development,
other manufacturers followed with their own wide-body jets, but on a scale
smaller than the gigantic 747. McDonnell-Douglas flew the 380-passenger
DC-10 trijet on August 29, 1970, and Lockheed followed with its own
slightly smaller widebody trijet, the L-1011, on November 16, 1970.
Through an international consortium, Europe produced its own equivalent,

BOEING 747
(VI-7, National Air and Space Museum)

BAC-AEROSPATIALE CONCORDE SST
(VI-8, BAC-USA)

the twin-engine Airbus A300B. All these aircraft use 47 to 51 thousand lb. thrust high bypass ratio turbofan engines, reflecting the tremendous pace of postwar jet engine development.

Wide-body superjets pose a special set of economic problems. If operating near maximum capacity, their seat costs per mile are minimal. Yet, they must carry a higher passenger load than their narrow-body ancestors if they are to turn a profit. The 747 has seat-mile costs of less than 1.3 cents for maximum capacity. Most, however, are flying at less than half their available capacity, and in this situation, with load factors of about 45%, seat costs/mile can rise above an unhealthy 4 cents, well over the operating costs of an earlier narrow-body jetliner. The present airline situation and aviation fuel costs (a critical issue in an era of politically inspired oil embargoes) have combined to ruin predicted economic gains from the superjets, though freighter versions for all-cargo operations continue to hold great appeal and potential. Six hundred wide-bodies are in service, but American airlines have not placed new production orders since 1973. Costs of the 747 rose from a predicted $18 million per aircraft in 1965 to about $35 million per aircraft a decade later. The smaller DC-10's and L-1011's have proven more economical, but none of the superjets, the 747 included, are returning on their development costs—an estimated $4 billion total, requiring 1,200 aircraft sales just to break even. Indeed, the world's airlines have only placed firm orders for 700 superjets. Consumer advocates suggest airline "deregulation" as one potential means of enabling the wide-bodies to make a profit. Meanwhile, the aircraft companies continue to experience work force reductions. Boeing relies on smaller narrow-body aircraft sales—the 707, 737, and, especially, the highly successful 727—to help offset the lagging 747. Viewed from this perspective, no matter how much passengers may like them, the wide-body superjets must be regarded as a bitter disappointment—an advanced idea in search of a market. In 1973, Laurence S. Kuter, a former Pan Am executive vice-president, wrote that the joint Pan Am-Boeing 747 venture was the "great air transport gamble of the seventies," and that by the mid 1970's, both Pan Am and Boeing might achieve a big win or an enormous loss. With more than $2 billion tied up in development costs, Boeing hoped to sell between 800 and 1,000 747's by 1980. This is clearly impossible, and Pan Am is fighting desperately to survive. It is evident that Boeing and Pan Am gambled and lost. One can only hope that future conditions will enable the belated realization of the superjet's bright promise.[54,55,56,57,58,59,60]

The most controversial air transport venture yet undertaken is the much-publicized supersonic transport (SST), which entered service in 1975 with Aeroflot, the Soviet state airline, and in 1976 with British Airways and Air France. The American government deliberately decided in 1971 not to undertake development of an American competitor. American SST thinking stemmed from technopolitical goals, including appeals to national pride, and drew on results from the highly successful postwar supersonic research program begun by John Stack and the NACA during the Second World War. The first major advocacy of an American SST came in 1959, with SST proponents encouraged by the Convair B-58 supersonic bomber experience and the proposed XB-70 looming on the horizon. The FAA set up an SST Advisory Group in November 1961, and on January 16, 1963, this body recommended SST development as a top priority federal project, following with a request for industry proposals on August 15, 1963. NASA's Langley Research Center undertook a series of SST wind tunnel studies in support of the FAA's efforts, the SCAT (Supersonic Commercial Air Transport) configurations. On January 15, 1964, Boeing, Lockheed, and North American submitted design proposals. Boeing's reflected the company's interest in variable-sweep wings (an outgrowth of company participation in the TFX competition), while North American's clearly drew on that company's work with the XB-70. Lockheed incorporated a very clean double delta arrangement, with obvious reference to its work on the A-11/YF-12A program. On December 31, 1966, the FAA declared Boeing's Mach 2.7 Model 2707 four-engine variable-sweep design the winner. Such direct FAA management was a necessity, for initial cost estimates placed the SST beyond the economic capability of the traditional airline-airframe industry partnership. Like its European and Soviet competitors, the American SST was almost entirely a government funded project.[1,61,62]

France and Great Britain had examined SST feasibility as early as 1956, signing a joint SST development agreement on November 29, 1962. Subsequent Anglo-French efforts concentrated on developing an aluminum Mach 2 four-engine 140-seat slender delta, the BAC-Aérospatiale Concorde. The Soviet Union adopted a similar planform while developing its own Mach 2 counterpart, the Tupolev Tu-144. The U.S., with experience in high-temperature flight structures, elected to pursue a technologically more complex four-engine Mach 2.7 design, recognizing that the American aircraft would emerge well after Concorde and the Tu-144. The Tu-144, the first SST to fly, completed its maiden flight on December 31, 1968. Concorde followed on March 2, 1969, when the French-built 001 prototype flew at Toulouse. In contrast, the Boeing design was, by this time, embroiled in rising costs, design changes (including a major switch from a variable-sweep wing to a fixed delta), and growing criticism. Critics ranged from thoughtful spokesmen who questioned its economic utility and environmental impact to neo-Luddites exercising an antitechnological prejudice stemming, at least in part, from a reaction against American involvement in Vietnam and the peculiarities of domestic urban politics.[1,28,63,64,65]

In early 1971, pro- and anti-SST partisans applied intense pressure on Congress, which had authority to approve or deny development of two Boeing SST prototypes. Despite strong Administration support, the SST went down to defeat on March 24, 1971, when the Senate voted against appropriating $289 million for prototype fabrication.[1] The United States consciously withdrew from the SST race, leaving the field to the Concorde and Tu-144. The result was economic devastation for Seattle, and a sharp drop in aerospace industry morale. No one could deny, however, that the United States stood little chance of recouping its SST investment even had the Boeing SST entered service.

Without question, the SST represents a tremendous technological achievement. Concorde, with its sustained Mach 2 cruise speed, reduces the seven-hour London-New York flight time to three and a half hours. Though a civil aircraft, the Concorde defies the tradition that civil aircraft are less technologically advanced than comtemporary military aircraft. It is faster than most, and can, for example, outturn the McDonnell-Douglas F-4 Phantom II fighter at Mach 2 and 60,000 feet. Yet serious economic and environmental questions remain. The Arab oil embargo of 1973 had an immediate adverse effect on aircraft fuel **costs,** to the detriment of the wide-body "jumbos," (some of which carry more than 50 thousand gallons of fuel) and the SST. In today's fuel-conscious economy, the petroleum-fueled SST looks increasingly like a liability. Concorde, for example, requires as much as 2½ times the amount of fuel per passenger as a 747, if both aircraft are full.[65] Its seat-mile operating costs are currently estimated by Air France at 11.76 cents (12.07 cents for British Airways), well over the 4.5 cents optimistically projected in 1972.[66,67]

What does the future hold? Observers can look to such developments as synchronous navigation satellite aids, the supercritical wing, liquid hydrogen fuel, increased use of wide-body cargo aircraft, second and third generation SST's, special crude petroleum carriers, advanced turbo-props, V/STOL city center services, advanced air route and terminal approach control systems, and continued debate over such questions as the Bermuda Agreement and airline regulation. Should current growth figures remain applicable, it can be expected that the number of passengers carried on American airlines will double by 1990. There are even studies underway on liquid hydrogen-fueled hypersonic transports, perhaps flying from off-shore airport facilities. Indeed, an "HST" could well enter commercial service by the year 2000, a half century after its first conception by H.S. Tsien in 1950. If it does, the twentieth century will have witnessed the growth of aircraft speed from 40 mph in 1903 to 4,000 mph by 2000. Put more vividly, from 1903 to 1925, airplane speeds went from 40 to 100 mph; from 1925 to 1950, 100 to 300 mph; from 1950 to 1975, 300 to 1,400 mph; from 1975 to 2000, 1,400 to a possible 4,000 mph! If previous history serves as any guide at all, one can only say that the engineering resources for an HST are available. Whether or not they will be utilized to produce such a vehicle is an economic question that cannot yet be answered. Whether they should be utilized is a philosophical question involving the values humanity places on speed, technology, and other needs.[66,67,68,69,70,71,72]

So stands American air transportation in the Bicentennial of the nation. Assuredly the predictions of Claude Graham-White and Harry Harper have come true, for airways _have_ done for the world what railroads did for nations in an earlier age. And if the hopeful vision of international harmony that Harry Guggenheim dispensed has not yet attained fulfillment, at least the airplane has reduced traditional geographic barriers to meaningless map lines. As always, an unpredictable future lies ahead. But the past is secure, and Americans can take justifiable pride in the role they have played in bringing the air transportation revolution to pass.

TABLE I

TRANSPORT AIRCRAFT COMPARISON, 1914-1976

Year	Type	No. of Passengers	Range (miles)	Speed (mph)
1914	Benoist XIV	1	--	64
1919	Lawson C-2	26	400	90
1922	D.H. 4A	2	250	110
1926	Fokker F.VIIa-3m	8	550	95
1930	Northrop Alpha	6	600	145
1934	Boeing 247D	10	745	160
1936	Douglas DC-3	21	1,500	185
1940	Boeing 307	33	1,675	222
1942	Douglas DC-4	42	2,140	227
1946	Lockheed L-049	47	3,050	280
1952	D.H. Comet I	36	1,759	490
1955	Douglas DC-7C	105	4,250	360
1958	Boeing 707-120	111	3,380	535
1967	Douglas DC-8-62	189	6,000	600
1970	Boeing 747B	374	7,080	589
1976	Concorde SST	100	4,000	1,410

TABLE II

OPERATING COSTS PER AVAILABLE SEAT-MILE, BY TYPE, 1937-1976

Type	No. of Passengers	Cost in Cents
LZ 129 Hindenburg	72	29.05
Boeing 247D	10	2.11
Douglas DC-3	21	1.27
Boeing 307	33	2.34
Boeing 314	40	4.80
Douglas DC-4	42	1.47
Lockheed L-049	47	1.86
Douglas DC-6	68	1.57
Boeing 377	89	1.78
Lockheed L-1049G	95	1.47
Douglas DC-7C	105	1.63
Boeing 707	140	1.22
Douglas DC-8	189	1.15
Boeing 747	362	2.17
Concorde SST	100	11.76[+]

[+] Air France estimate for transatlantic service. British Airways estimate is 12.07 cents.

REFERENCES

1. Arnold E. Briddon, Ellmore A. Champie, and Peter A. Marraine, <u>FAA Historical Fact Book: A Chronology, 1926-1971</u>, (Washington: 1974).

2. Charles H. Gibbs-Smith, <u>Aviation: An Historical Survey From its Origins to the End of World War II</u>, (London, 1970).

3. R.E.G. Davies, <u>A History of the World's Airlines</u>, (New York, 1964).

4. Hugh Knowlton, <u>Air Transportation: Its Growth as Business</u>, (Chicago: 1941).

5. Robert Kane and Allen D. Vose, <u>Air Transportation</u>, (Dubuque, Iowa: 1974).

6. Carroll V. Glines, <u>The Saga of the Air Mail</u>, (Princeton, 1968).

7. Donald R. Whitnah, <u>Safer Skyways: Federal Control of Aviation, 1926-1966</u>, (Ames, Iowa, 1966).

8. Benjamin B. Lipsner and Leonard Finley Hilts, <u>The Airmail: Jennies to Jets</u> (New York, 1951).

9. Rudolf Tuma, "Golden Anniversary--Air Mail Service," <u>Journal of the American Aviation Historical Society</u>, Vol. 13, No. 2 (Summer 1968).

10. Elsbeth E. Freudenthal, <u>The Aviation Business: From Kitty Hawk to Wall Street</u>, (New York, 1940).

11. Lester D. Gardner, "The Development of Civil Aeronautics in America," 4th International Congress on Aerial Navigation, October 1, 1927.

12. Frank J. Clifford, "Ham & Eggs Lawson," <u>FAA Aviation News</u>, Vol. 9, No. 3, (July 1970).

13. Robert F. Brooks, "The Airliner and Its Inventor: Alfred W. Lawson," Paper 69-1041, Annual Meeting of the AIAA, October 20, 1969, Anaheim, California.

14. George Hardie, Jr., "The Airline That Might Have Been," <u>Historical Messenger of the Milwaukee County Historical Society</u>, Vol. 27, No. 1 (March 1971).

15. Alfred W. Lawson, Lawson: Aircraft Industry Builder, (Detroit: 1943).

16. "Lawson Air Liner Makes History," Aerial Age Weekly, Vol. 10, No. 2 (September 22, 1919).

17. Laurence F. Schmeckebier, The Aeronautics Branch, Department of Commerce,(Washington, D. C.: Institute for Government Research, The Brookings Institution, 1930).

18. Joint Committee on Civil Aviation of the U.S. Department of Commerce, Civil Aviation: A Report (New York, 1926).

19. Herbert Hoover, The Memoirs of Herbert Hoover: The Cabinet and the Presidency, 1920-1933, (New York, 1952).

20. Harold Nicolson, Dwight Morrow,(New York, 1935).

21. C.V. Glines, "A Look at the Past," Air Line Pilot, Vol. 45, No. 6 (June 1976).

22. Richard P. Hallion, Legacy of Flight: The Daniel Guggenheim Fund for the Promotion of Aeronautics and the Formative Era of American Aviation (Ph.D. dissertation, University of Maryland, 1975), and the earlier "official history" by Cleveland. See note 23.

23. Reginald M. Cleveland, America Fledges Wings: The History of the Daniel Guggenheim Fund for the Promotion of Aeronautics,(New York, 1942).

24. Jerome C. Hunsaker, "A Survey of Air Transport and Its Communication's Problem," (Bell Telephone Laboratories, July 1, 1927).

25. Edward P. Warner, Technical Development and Its Effect on Air Transportation, (Norwich University, 1938).

26. William Littlewood, "Technical Trends in Air Transport," The Sixteenth Wright Brothers Lecture, Institute of the Aeronautical Sciences, Washington, D. C., December 17, 1952.

27. Peter Brooks, The Modern Airliner: Its Origins and Development, (London, 1961).

28. Ronald Miller and David Sawers, The Technical Development of Modern Aviation, (New York: 1970).

29. Leslie Forden, The Ford Air Tours, 1925-1931, (Alameda, California, 1973).

30. Donald R. Whitnah, A History of the United States Weather Bureau, (Urbana, Ill., 1961).

31. Daniel Guggenheim Fund, Solving the Problem of Fog Flying, (New York, 1929).

32. Grover Loening, Takeoff Into Greatness, (New York, 1968).

33. C. R. Smith, "Safety in Air Transportation Over the Years," 8th Wings Club "Sight" Lecture, The Wings Club, New York, N.Y., May 19, 1971.

34. George W. Gray, Frontiers of Flight: The Story of NACA Research, (New York: 1948).

35. Nicholas J. Hoff, "Thin Shells in Aerospace Structures," 4th von Kármán lecture, 3rd Annual Meeting, AIAA, Boston, Mass., November 29 1966.

36. Harold Mansfield, Vision: The Story of Boeing (New York, 1966).

37. Douglas J. Ingalls, The Plane That Changed the World, (Fallbrook, Calif., 1966).

38. Douglas Aircraft Company, Engineering Department Technical Data Report SW-157A, "Development of the Douglas Transport."

39. John B. Rae, Climb to Greatness: The American Aircraft Industry, 1920-1960,(Cambridge, Mass., 1968).

40. Nick A. Komons, The Cutting Air Crash: A Case Study in Early Federal Aviation Policy, (Washington, D. C., 1973).

41. John H. Frederick, Commercial Air Transportation, (Chicago, 1951)

42. Jerome Lederer, Safety in the Operation of Air Transportation, (Norwich University, 1939).

43. J. T. Trippe, "Ocean Air Transport," Twenty-ninth Wilbur Wright Memorial Lecture, Royal Aeronautical Society, June 17, 1941, London.

44. Richard K. Smith, "Fifty Years of Transatlantic Flight," Paper 69-1044, Annual Meeting of the AIAA October 20, 1969, Anaheim, California.

45. Peter W. Brooks, "Why the Airship Failed," The Aeronautical Journal, Vol. 79, No. 778 (October 1975).

46. Aeronautical Chamber of Commerce of America, Inc., "Superiority of Flying Boats in Transocean Service: A Report to the U. S. Maritime Commission," (August 18, 1937).

47. Matthew Josephson, Empire of the Air: Juan Trippe and the Struggle for World Airways, (New York, 1944).

48. Igor I. Sikorsky, The Story of the Winged-S, (London, 1939).

49. The Aircraft Industries Association of America, Ind., The Aircraft Year Book, 1951, (Washington, D. C. 1951).

50. Clayton and K. S. Knight, Plane Crash: The Mysteries of Major Air Disasters and How They Were Solved, (New York, 1958).

51. Derek D. Dempter, The Tale of the Comet (New York, 1958).

52. Robert E. Hage, Jet Propulsion in Commercial Air Transportation, (Princeton, N.J., 1948).

53. Robert J. Serling, The Electra Story, (Garden City, N.Y., 1963).

54. Alan H. Stratford, Air Transport Economics in the Supersonic Era, (London, 1973).

55. George C. Eads, The Local Service Airline Experiment, (Washington, D. C., The Brookings Institution, 1972).

56. Roy J. Harris, "Early Revival Unlikely as Jumbo-Plane Sales Continue to Languish," The Wall Street Journal, August 10, 1976.

57. "Operating and Cost Data, 747, DC-10, L-1011," Aviation Week & Space Technology, Vol. 104, No. 25, (June 21, 1976).

58. Michael E. Levine, "Does Airline Regulation Benefit the Consumer?" Engineering and Science, Vol. 39, No. 3, (March-April 1976).

59. Civil Aeronautics Board, Aircraft Operating Cost and Performance Report, 1973 and 1974, Vol. 9, (Washington, D. C., July 1975).

60. Civil Aeronautics Board, Wide-Bodied Jet Aircraft Operating Cost and Performance Report, U. S. Certificated Air Carriers, 1970-73, Vol. 16, (Washington, D. C., May 1974).

61. NASA LRC, Fifty Years of Flight Research, (Washington, 1968).

62. George N. Chatham and Franklin P. Huddle, The Supersonic Transport: A Look at the Key Issues, (Washington, D. C., Library of Congress, 1971).

63. Norman Barfield, Aérospatiale/BAC Concorde, (London, 1973).

64. Kenneth Munson, Airliners Since 1946, (New York, 1972).

65. BAC/Aérospatiale, "Concorde Background Brief."

66. "Concorde Breakeven Load Factor Set at 60%," Aviation Week & Space Technology, Vol. 104, No. 23, (June 7, 1976).

67. Rosalind K. Ellingsworth, "Concorde Economics Keyed to Utilization," Aviation Week & Space Technology, Vol. 105, No. 8, (August 23, 1976).

68. Gerald G. Kayten, "2001: An Aeronautics Odyssey," _Aerospace_, Vol. 14, No. 1, (February 1976).

69. Paul R. Ignatius, "Air Transportation: Accomplishments, Challenges, Opportunities," _Aerospace_, Vol. 13, No. 12, (December 1975).

70. Andrew M. de Voursney," ...And to the Future," _Air Line Pilot_, Vol. 45, No. 6, (June 1976).

71. Hsue-shen Tsien, "Instruction and Research at the Daniel and Florence Guggenheim Jet Propulsion Center," _Journal of the American Rocket Society_, June 1950.

72. Thomas Love, "In Focus: NASA Takes Optimistic Look at Future of Aviation," _The Washington Star_, August 25, 1976.

PART III — ASTRONAUTICS, 1957-1976
Frederick C. Durant III, Chairman

VII - INSTRUMENTED EXPLORATION AND UTILIZATION OF SPACE:

THE AMERICAN EXPERIENCE

R. Cargill Hall

VIII - THE HEROIC ERA OF MANNED SPACE FLIGHT

Edward C. Ezell

The Smithsonian's Langley Medal

VII

INSTRUMENTED EXPLORATION AND UTILIZATION OF SPACE,

THE AMERICAN EXPERIENCE

R. Cargill Hall[*]

> This paper considers the principal forces and
> conditions that shaped the growth and development of
> the unmanned space program of the United States after
> World War II.

Early in the twentieth century a few individuals proved the
theoretical feasibility of spaceflight. They sought the mastery of
space to (1) increase man's store of fundamental knowledge and (2) help
meet some of his physical needs. The coupling of the physical and engineering sciences, industrial advances, and state support produced awesome progress in rocketry and astronautics. Within living memory these
twin goals became a reality. As goals, the exploration and utilization
of space remain essentially unaltered;[1] for the most part, they have
been realized with automated devices, unmanned machines directed and
controlled from the Earth.

Once begun, this enterprise proceeded rapidly. The practical
space applications achieved and new knowledge acquired have appeared one
after another, pell-mell; we now share the benefaction of improved communications, meteorological forecasting, cartography, navigation, reconnaissance, and land and water resource surveys; we read of scientific
findings about the Sun and stars, the planets, and interplanetary medium;
we view closeup objects that astronomers for years only dreamed of seeing. For most of us this has created something of a sensory over-
load. Like Winnie the Pooh bumping downstairs on the back of his head
behind Christopher Robin, one would like to know why he advances this
way and how it came to pass--"if only he could stop bumping for a
moment and think of it." Instrumented space exploration and utilization
is a very large subject, one not easily handled in the few pages here.
Focussing on the principal forces and conditions that shaped the growth
and development of the United States unmanned space program, the author
hopes to minimize the bumping and maximize understanding.

THE BEGINNING

If you could see it, the taproot of practical astronautics in
the United States might appear like a three-tined fork composed of

[*]Jet Propulsion Laboratory, California Institute of Technology. Any views expressed in this paper are those of the author.

183

military, scientific, and industrial interests. The tines materialized soon after World War II in military studies of Earth satellites, in scientific activity organized for the purpose of exploring directly the Earth's upper atmosphere and the near space medium, and, contributing to this work, in the collective efforts of space flight proponents in industry and university laboratories who advanced satellite proposals of their own and cross-pollinated ideas in professional organizations they shared in common, such as the American Rocket Society. By the end of the 1940s these groups had firmly established--and a government panel had officially acknowledged--the technical feasibility of space flight.[2]

The tines of the fork converged between January and September 1955 in what was perhaps the most momentous period for the inchoate American space program. During this time the Army Ballistic Missile Agency and the Naval Research Laboratory submitted proposals for separate scientific satellite projects to the Department of Defense. In addition, the Air Force issued a General Operational Requirement for its own strategic system of reconnaissance satellites and shortly thereafter contracted with industry for design studies of that system. A few months later President Eisenhower endorsed a scientific satellite project as part of the nation's contribution to the International Geophysical Year, known as the IGY. Finally, in August, a special government committee selected the Naval Research Laboratory Vanguard scientific satellite proposal for development in the IGY.[3]

Thus, two years before Sputnik, the United States possessed a modest space program divided between instrumented applications and scientific satellites. Both of these efforts moved slowly, staying within funding prescriptions and avoiding unwanted interference with the development of the nation's long-range ballistic missiles just underway. They shared a low priority among other high technology programs, and the administration discouraged government officials from public discussions of space flight.[4] This condition changed dramatically in October-November 1957, after the Soviet Union launched Sputniks 1 and 2. Despite Presidential assurances, the Russian space accomplishments fueled a national debate over American defense and science policies; what had begun as an evenly if slowly spaced research and development program was to be spurred forward at a gallop.[5]

The Sputniks, with their "Pearl Harbor" effect on informed opinion, signalled the beginning of a second important period for the space program. As indices of technical competence, they also introduced another goal into space affairs: national pride and international prestige. The United States government moved immediately to restore public confidence at home and prestige abroad. In short order the Army was authorized to begin preparations to launch a scientific satellite as a backup to the Navy's Vanguard Project, and the Department of Defense created the Advanced Research Project Agency, assigning to it temporary responsibility for directing all United States space research projects. In January 1958 the Air Force started the Discoverer Project--a test-bed variant of the reconnaissance satellite that could be placed in orbit more quickly with a smaller launch vehicle. And in March the Secretary of Defense ordered the Advanced Research Projects Agency to launch space vehicles "to provide a close look at the moon."[6]

The popular demand to get on as rapidly as possible with the exploration and utilization of space was undeniable. To guide these developments, the President declared on April 2, 1958, a unified national space agency had to be established.[7] Few disagreed, least of all a number of prominent American scientists who had also begun to consider seriously the future of research in space, the prospects for obtaining more federal funds for this activity, and the ways of organizing it within the government that met their expectations of scientific independence, integrity, and excellence.[8]

During the dialogue and in the legislative action of 1958, the nation's leaders favored civilian control of expanded United States air and space activities. Aside from national defense and military operations, for which the Department of Defense remained responsible, the National Aeronautics and Space Act declared that all aeronautical and space activity sponsored by the United States would be directed by a civilian agency guided by eight objectives. First among them was basic scientific research, defined as "the expansion of human knowledge of phenomena in the atmosphere and space . . . ." Signed into law by President Eisenhower on July 29, the act wrote a broad and comprehensive mandate for the peaceful pursuit of new knowledge and accompanying technology in space. But scientists still had to harness if they could the National Aeronautics and Space Administration, or NASA, to their own special desires for space exploration.

SCIENCE IN SPACE

Space science, that is, scientific research conducted in outer space, had in 1958-1959 coalesced about two primary areas of interest: planetary science and sky science.[9] Sky scientists sought to understand the mysteries of the upper atmosphere and the fields and charged particles surrounding the Earth. They emphasized meteoritics, solar and cosmic ray physics, plasma dynamics, and the interaction of solar and terrestrial electromagnetic fields. Planetary scientists, on the other hand, were occupied with the origin, composition, and evolution of planetary bodies in our solar system, including the Moon. They hoped, for example, that new data would provide important clues concerning the formation of the Earth and its Moon.

When NASA began operating in late 1958, planetary scientists had just begun to meet and make plans; they depended upon a technology and, more important, a complex interplanetary flight capability, yet to be created. Sky scientists were already a cohesive group, well organized and reasonably well publicized. Active in on-going government sponsored upper air and satellite research projects, they sat together on various official and semi-official panels which counseled federal agencies on prospective projects, judged experiment proposals, and allocated space for the experiments on rocket sondes and IGY satellites. It was largely individuals with such sky science backgrounds, linked organizationally, familiar with each other, and experienced in sounding rocket research, who first came to occupy space science positions in NASA. It was largely a sky science program, both in practice and in a final recommendatory report that NASA inherited from its predecessor agency, the National Advisory Committee for Aeronautics. And it was thus no surprise that sky science dominated the nation's first space projects--including the initial lunar flights.

The pre-NASA IGY scientific satellites were instrumented by sky scientists to explore the near-space medium, and they made important contributions to fundamental knowledge. The experiment of James Van Allen launched in early 1958 on the Explorer and Vanguard satellites discovered a belt or shell of trapped radiation surrounding the Earth. That proved to be one of the most significant findings of the International Geophysical Year program, and it stimulated more scientific interest in the physical processes at work in the interplanetary medium. It also affected directly the Pioneer lunar probes ordered by the Advanced Research Projects Agency. Although the first two lunar spacecraft carried a small television camera to provide a "close look at the moon" for planetary science, the cameras were removed from the last three flights in favor of experiments to measure the fields and particles between the Earth and the Moon. These flights offered strong evidence, confirmed by later Pioneer and Mariner missions, of the presence of the solar wind. In 1959 NASA officials also altered the scientific objectives of their first series of lunar flights, the Atlas-Able series, in a similar manner. The aberrant behavior of the launch vehicles, the transportation systems needed to position scientific instruments in space, precluded any scientific return from these television-equipped lunar flights. In fact, none of the Atlas-Ables even left the Earth's atmosphere. (Figure 1)

Sky scientists could nevertheless proceed without the large launch vehicles, precise guidance, and spacecraft capability required for planetary research, and they made good use of the opportunities and the technology available. For example, employing the smaller Thor-Able launch vehicle, in March 1960 NASA placed the spheriodal, spin-stabilized Pioneer 5 machine on a space trajectory carrying it and a number of experiments to measure the interplanetary medium successfully into solar orbit between the Earth and Venus. But if sky science claimed the attention and laurels in the nation's early space missions, by 1959 planetary science, aided by events in the international arena, was on the march.

Homer E. Newell, a physicist-sky scientist from the Naval Research Laboratory who had transferred to NASA to head its space sciences division, was alert to the aspirations of planetary science. He contracted with the Space Science Board of the National Academy of Sciences for advice on space science objectives that embraced planetary research. When in January 1959 he created scientific working groups, he also established a Working Group on Lunar Exploration. Made up largely of scientists from the academic community, the lunar working group operated as a forum for the exchange of views and it had charge of

Figure 1

Atlas-Able Launch Vehicle
at Cape Canaveral, 1960
(Courtesy TRW)

evaluating and recommending to NASA the experiments to be placed in orbit around the Moon or landed on its surface. Planetary science--lunar enthusiasts in particular--now had a voice at NASA Headquarters.

That voice was amplified by the growing competition in space affairs between the United States and the Soviet Union. In January 1959, the Russian Luna 1 flew past the Moon--the first man-made object generally recognized to have escaped the Earth's gravitational field. At NASA Headquarters, Newell's assistant Robert Jastrow informed his boss that "the national space program will be open to strong criticism if a very early and vigorous effort is not made in . . . lunar exploration . . . . The criticism will be especially strong if it turns out that a slow-paced U.S. lunar program must be contrasted with early Soviet achievements in this field." Jastrow's opinion was shared by many NASA officials, including the agency's Administrator T. Keith Glennan. An electrical engineer and former President of the Case Institute of Technology, Glennan met with officials of the Eisenhower Administration in July and argued that the nation should defer flights to the more distant inner planets and concentrate its instrumented deep space efforts instead on flights to the Moon.

Glennan's proposal was approved; scientific findings about the origin and nature of the Moon would not be consigned by default to the Russians. By the end of 1959 NASA had begun work on the Ranger and Surveyor projects. The Ranger spacecraft, with experiments selected by the Working Group on Lunar Exploration, were to hard-land operating seismometers on the Moon, take closeup pictures before crashing, and assay the surface material with gamma ray spectrometers during 1962. The Surveyor machines, planned to follow Ranger in 1963-1964, would soft land a variety of similar experiments. Plans also called for Prospector, a soft-landed lunar roving vehicle in the mid-1960s, capable of moving about on the Moon's surface and, in later missions, of returning surface samples to Earth. Flights to Venus and Mars, known as Mariner, were postponed to 1962 and 1964.

In early 1960 Homer Newell put the finishing touches on NASA's science policy. He had elected to employ small contingents of qualified scientists at Headquarters and the NASA field centers. Following the precedent of the IGY and sounding rocket programs of the 1950s, he had chosen to delegate the bulk of NASA's basic research to university scientists. NASA would tap the best scientific talent available in the nation. But Headquarters would exercise the right of final approval for the scientific experiments as well as choose the mission objectives. In April 1960 Administrator Glennan signed a management instruction to this effect. Developed by Newell, the instruction created a Space Sciences Steering Committee composed only of Headquarters personnel that replaced the working groups. Subcommittees, arranged by discipline, with membership drawn from among NASA and academic scientists, would evaluate proposals for authorized flights and recommend for approval preferred experiments to the Steering Committee. These arrangements established the framework and set the procedures for instrumented space science at NASA in the years that followed.

Two additional disciplines had by now joined sky and planetary science as the third and fourth branches of NASA's space sciences tree. The first of these, astronomy and astrophysics, was concerned primarily with the vast areas of the universe outside the solar system, the history and nature of this universe, and the basic physical laws that regulate it. The second, life sciences, involved the entry of man into space and the physiological, psychological, and behaviorial effects that the space environment has on living organisms of all kinds. Life science also embraced the quest for extraterrestrial life forms, an area of inquiry that tied this segment of the discipline closely with planetary science.

The nation's instrumented space sciences program had grown rapidly and diversified by the end of 1960 into the principal components that still characterize the endeavor. It possessed firm commitments in the years just ahead to explore the Moon and inner planets, the space medium, the Sun and stars, and the physiology and behavior of living organisms in space. Indeed, in May 1961 Lloyd V. Berkner, Chairman of the Space Science Board of the National Academy of Sciences speaking before the first national Conference on the Peaceful Uses of Outer Space, could proudly laud the high water mark attained by American space science. Virtually every NASA space mission to date, he enthused, had been directed to scientific pursuits.[10]

APOLLO'S PRIORITY

The successes of space science in early 1961 were impressive, but its implications of still more handsome opportunities to follow were illusory on two counts. First, NASA had inherited most of the early space science missions, missions that used the technology of the day. The lunar, planetary, and astronomy missions that NASA planned would employ larger launch vehicles and complex second generation spacecraft stabilized on three axes. Some delays in development and flight failures of these costly and unproven launch and space systems could be expected. Second, the space race, as it came to be called, supported other powerful interests in NASA besides space science. These interests claimed missions of their own, especially missions involving manned space flight

Most of NASA's leaders were engineers, and most of them had come from the National Advisory Committee for Aeronautics--an agency that formed the nucleus around which the space agency was fashioned, and one that had been involved historically with research into the problems of manned flight. Indeed, NASA had been in operation but a few days when its leadership approved Project Mercury, a plan for placing a man in space. Just to fly a man into Earth orbit, keep him alive, and return him safely called for remarkable feats of engineering--from complex life support systems to atmospheric reentry and recovery systems. Compared to the effort that went into satisfying these engineering demands, pure science was virtually invisible in Mercury.[11]

Not to be outdone, on April 12, 1961, the Soviet Union launched Major Yuri Gagarin on a one-orbit flight around the world, eclipsing the

Mercury project much as Sputnik 1 had overshadowed Project Vanguard in 1957. In the United States, demands intensified to expand and accelerate the nation's space program. The response of the newly elected President was a bold challenge. On May 25, John F. Kennedy requested of Congress a program to land a man on the Moon and return him safely to Earth before the decade ended. The President's call struck a responsive chord among a majority of legislators and the public--by now more than ever eager to beat the Soviet Union in a major space endeavor. The decision was made; Congress appropriated funds to begin what eventually became known as Project Apollo. James E. Webb, a lawyer, financier, and former Director of the Bureau of the Budget, whom President Kennedy had nominated as the new NASA Administrator, reorganized the space agency accordingly. Manned space flight was separated from space science and applications and elevated to a major office. By the end of 1961, only a few months after Lloyd Berkner had taken obvious pleasure in the fortunes of instrumented space sciences, the space program entered another significant period, that of manned flight to the Moon.[12]

The actions for a large manned effort affected the space science program directly and adversely. Project Apollo grew like a baby Paul Bunyan, and within two years consumed more than 50 percent of the entire NASA research and development budget. Homer Newell found himself unable to obtain funds for many deserving space science projects. Complicating the situation even further, launch vehicle and spacecraft malfunctions caused all three of the scientific Moon Rangers to fail in 1962, and technical difficulties delayed the lunar Surveyor and the Orbiting Solar Observatory projects. NASA's science managers now possessed too many scientific clients and too few instrumented flight opportunities to accommodate them. In 1963 many scientists began to complain bitterly about the diminishing flight opportunities, unfulfilled expectations, and what they viewed as an inordinate emphasis upon manned space flight at NASA. That emphasis, some critics snapped, favored space spectaculars over quality space science.[13]

Nevertheless, for the next ten years Apollo would remain the cynosure of NASA and the nation. Every resource available to NASA would be bent to this task, and that included especially the instrumented lunar flights. Apollo needed immediately data about the Moon's surface so that smooth landing sites could be selected and the landing vehicle designed with confidence.

In late 1962 the unmanned lunar program was redirected to meet these needs. The Lunar Orbiter Project replaced Prospector in 1963 to photograph the lunar surface in fine detail. More Ranger flights, carrying television cameras only, would provide closeup photographs before crashing on the surface. The experiments planned for the Surveyor machines, with one exception, were likewise altered to furnish more data on touchdown dynamics and the bearing characteristics of the surface. These missions, launched between 1963 and 1969 served Apollo well; they also returned valuable scientific information about the

Moon's shape, center of mass, gravitational anomalies, and surface
features. The manned missions of Apollo would conduct detailed scientific investigations of the Moon after 1969.[14]   (Figures 2 and 3)

What about the other portions of the space science program?
Planetary flights continued exclusively in the name of science, but,
as was the case for all instrumented space science missions, felt
severely the funding constraints that followed Apollo, the war in
Vietnam, inflation, and later in the 1970s, the investment in the manned
space shuttle. Nonetheless, progressing in fits and starts, sometimes
using refurbished, spare spacecraft, between 1962 and 1976 instrumented
vehicles explored the inner planets, Venus, Mars, and Mercury, and one
outer planet, Jupiter. (Figures 4 through 7)   Sky scientists surveyed
the interplanetary medium during the same period primarily with
Explorer, Pioneer, and Orbiting Geophysical Observatory satellites.
These machines measured extensively the fields and particles generated
within the Solar System, and the cosmic rays that penetrate it from
without. Astronomers employed three small astronomical satellites,
a like number of large Orbiting Astronomical Observatories, and seven
Orbiting Solar Observatories to observe and catalogue astronomical
sources at non-visual wavelengths, obtain valuable ultraviolet photographs of the stars, and photograph in detail the Sun and its corona.
In the mid- to late 1960s, life scientists used three biosatellites
to study the effects of weightlessness and radiation on plants and
other organisms. The manned Gemini, Apollo, and later Spacelab projects furnished them a more extensive program of biological research.
(For a synopsis of the instrumented space science missions, see Appendix A).

Seeking to maximize the return available to space science,
between 1967 and 1969 Homer Newell's successors modified the procedures
for planning and implementing space science missions. First, short-
lived ad hoc panels replaced the standing subcommittees of the Space
Sciences Steering Committee to evaluate and recommend experiments for
each new flight project. These panels were selected to provide competence in all disciplines relevant to the project, while at the same
time minimizing the conflict of interest problem--where experimenters
sometimes sat in judgment on the proposals of others. Second, faced
with a shrinking budget, the Office of Space Science and Applications
created special missions boards, such as the Astronomy Missions Board
and the Lunar and Planetary Missions Board, composed primarily of
individuals drawn from the academic community. These boards considered
broader issues than was possible with the old discipline subcommittees
of the Space Sciences Steering Committee, and recommended missions--
or mission options that might be realized with reduced funds--preferred
in the next ten or fifteen years for submittal to NASA's leaders and
the Congress. In addition, the Space Science Board of the National
Academy of Sciences, besides its customary counsel on research goals
and objectives, also supplied NASA more detailed recommendations on
mission planning and mechanization.

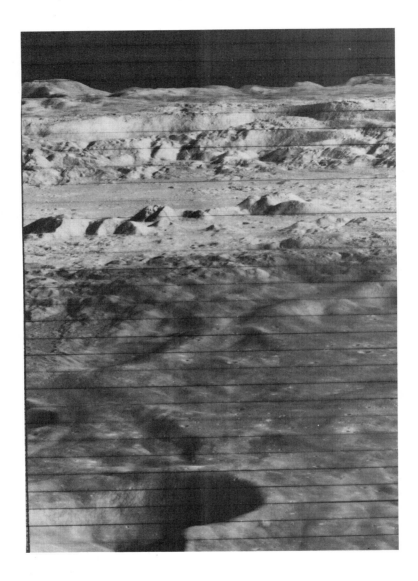

Figure 2

Lunar Orbiter Oblique
View of the Crater Copernicus

Figure 3

Apollo 12 Astronaut
Examining an Instrumented
Surveyor Spacecraft on the Moon, 1969

Figure 4

<u>Mariner 10</u> Picture of
Venus and its Atmosphere
From a Distance of 720,000
kilometers, 1974

Figure 5

The Surface of Mars
Photographed From Viking
Lander 1, 1976

Figure 6

Mariner 10 Picture of Mercury
From a Distance of 200,000 kilometers,
1974

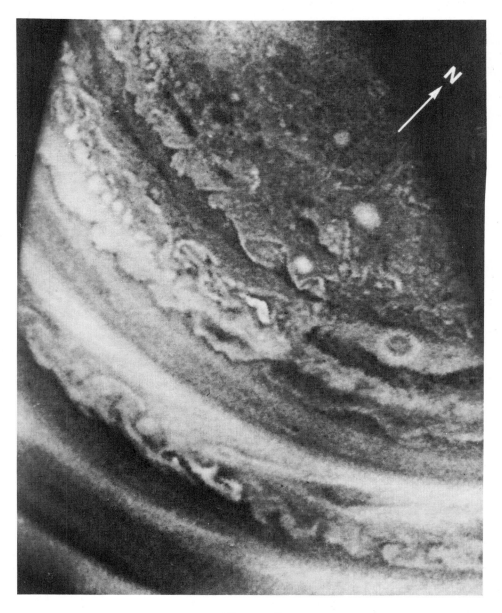

Figure 7

Pioneer 11   Picture of Jupiter and its
Atmosphere Taken From 600,000 Kilometers,
1974.   Image Covers the North Temperate
and North Polar Region Where the Atmospheric Patterns of Belts and Zones Breaks
  Down Into Numerous Swirls and Eddys.

But despite the best of plans, space science, indeed all state supported basic research, found the justification of its efforts increasingly difficult. Acquiring fundamental knowledge to substantiate or disprove esoteric hypotheses is an activity confined to and understood by an elite few, without obvious utilitarian advantage. Other welfare, resource conservation, and energy programs demanded the government's attention, and in the 1960s and 1970s the leaders of NASA and the nation began to place more and more emphasis on the utilization of space for immediate practical benefits.

APPLICATION SATELLITES

The feasibility and utility of applications satellites had been early investigated by the United States Navy and Air Force. By 1950 these services had delineated a number of potential military uses: as Earth-orbiting platforms from which to conduct strategic aerial reconnaissance, relay radio messages, and serve as beacons for air and sea navigation. Because the Sino-Soviet bloc countries tightly restricted domestic and especially foreign travel within their borders, official interest naturally focused on the reconnaissance role. Nevertheless, military leaders could not justify the research and development costs needed to advance the state of the art and produce an operational satellite system for any one of these applications. But in 1954, when work began on the Atlas intercontinental ballistic missile that could also double as a satellite launcher, the Air Force reexamined the question.

On March 16, 1955 the Air Force issued General Operational Requirement Number 80 that called explicitly for a system of strategic reconnaissance satellites. After a design competition, a contract was awarded to the Lockheed Missiles System Division, and the effort was underway. In 1959-1960 the first developmental flights using Thor and Atlas launch vehicles and Lockheed Agenas as second stage booster-satellites, found their way into orbit. In the mid-1960s, ten years after its authorization, the first generation of strategic reconnaissance satellites became operational.

Needless to say, the Air Force reconnaissance satellite program is highly classified and little is known about the interest groups and conditions that influenced the course of developments.[15] However, we do know that in the early 1960s the program had differentiated into four primary classes of surveillance missions: visual imaging, missile detection and alarm, electronic surveys, and radar imaging. The visual reconnaissance payloads carry photographic cameras of varying focal lengths and different color filters, as well as infrared and television cameras. The product, recorded on film or magnetic tape, is either developed onboard, electronically scanned and then "read out" to Earth stations over a wide-band radio link, or is deorbited inside a reentry capsule for recovery. It is said that some of these payloads obtain the remarkable resolution on Earth of two or three feet.

The missile alarm satellites are equipped with infrared cameras to detect the heat emitted by rockets rising through the atmosphere, and can provide early warning of a surprise attack. More recently, in the 1970s, these payloads are believed to have been augmented with high resolution television cameras, allowing controllers on the ground to observe, in real time, the sources of heat detected by the infrared cameras. Next, electronic intelligence, or ferret payloads as they are known, consist of equipment to locate air- and missile-defense radars and determine their signal characteristics and detection range. Other functions involve pinpointing military radio stations and eavesdropping on military communications. Finally, the radar imaging payloads employ a "side-looking radar" that, transmitting an electronic signal and receiving its reflection from the surface below, can "photograph" terrain with a resolution of about 100 feet. Although this system lacks the resolution obtainable with cameras, it has the advantage of being able to penetrate cloud cover. The Soviets have developed similar instrumented payloads and, taken together, these applied space reconnaissance devices make it improbable, if not impossible, that any major nation could prepare for and launch a pre-emptive thermonuclear attack undetected.

Though events in the instrumented reconnaissance program moved rapidly toward this conclusion, manned spaceflight remained the scene of the action, and by 1962 NASA could claim it all. Toward the end of that year, Air Force officials and their supporters on Capitol Hill mounted a vigorous campaign to secure a manned space program of their own, and on December 10, 1963, the Secretary of Defense announced approval of an Air Force Manned Orbiting Laboratory. In succeeding months, as the manned program got up to speed, the managers of the instrumented Air Force space projects, like their counterparts at NASA, began to feel the budget tension. But the MOL program as it came to be called, without a foreign menace to combat in space, running well behind schedule and ahead of anticipated costs, in 1969 was quietly cancelled. However desirable a manned reconnaissance system in space might be, Air Force officials had decided that that job could be accomplished more economically with their instrumented vehicles. The military thus avoided the sharp division of effort that characterized affairs between manned and unmanned space flight at NASA.

Besides reconnaissance applications, after 1958 the armed services developed other instrumented satellites to detect above-ground nuclear and thermonuclear explosions, transmit communications, and furnish air and surface vehicles with precise information for navigation. The first of these, known as Vela Hotel (the first term after the Spanish word for "watchman"), was devised by the Atomic Energy Commission and Built under Air Force supervision. The Vela machines detect X-rays and gamma rays released in above-ground explosions of fission or fusion bombs. After a few trial experiments in the early 1960s, the Air Force orbited a Vela satellite in late 1963, and within a few years that system became operational. The military communications satellites, also developed in the early 1960s, relay radio, telex, telephone, and television messages for all of the

United States military services around the globe. They are also coupled to some of the surveillance satellite systems, and inform immediately of missile launches and, probably, of above-ground nuclear explosions. Completing the list, Transit navigation satellites were developed by the U. S. Navy and launched by the Air Force beginning in 1960. Acting as a fixed, active referent in space, these machines permit military air and surface vessels to determine their position in latitude and longitude within a few hundred yards anywhere on Earth.

When work began in earnest on the instrumented military satellite programs, and especially after the "U-2 incident" in 1960, many feared that space surveillance might turn the cosmos into another battleground, with the major states attempting to destroy foreign machines passing in orbit above their air space. In this country, the very high security classification assigned these programs in 1961 occurred in large measure, it seems, because of official concern over the possibility of military conflict in space and international protests on Earth. But far from proving a destabilizing influence, military applications satellites have become indispensable for policing the nuclear test ban treaty, the convention that prohibits the stationing of weapons of mass destruction in orbit, and have enabled leaders with some confidence to engage in negotiation of agreements for arms limitation and control.[16]

Thus, by 1976, leaders of the major states had tacitly, and in some instances openly, sanctioned reconnaissance satellites. For example, the treaty limiting antiballistic missiles states that "monitoring of compliance shall be by such 'national technical means of verification' as are 'consistent with generally recognized principles of international law.'" And since custom and precedent form a primary source of international law,[+] it is reasonable to presume that reconnaissance from outer space is officially accepted among the major states. However, while the technical details of this activity will likely remain secret, continued classification of the entire effort could jeopardize its status as custom and, over the long term, could very well prove counterproductive. (For a synopsis of the instrumented military applications missions, see Appendix B.)

NASA'S APPLICATION SATELLITES

Among the United States applications satellite projects, only those of the civilian space agency remain unclassified and open to public scrutiny. These projects consist of meteorological, communications, applications technology, Earth resource survey, and geodetic

---

[+]Custom and precedent derive from actions conducted over a period of time which, in the absence of formal protests and overt attempts by states to thwart the activity, are accepted as legal even though treaty law does not specifically address the subject.

missions. NASA inherited the meteorological project from the Department of Defense. The remaining missions were largely formulated and developed by the space agency, although their use is often shared with or assigned exclusively to other agencies.

As early as 1951 Harry Wexler of the United States Weather Bureau had proposed launching meteorological satellites to provide rapid, global information about cloud and weather conditions. In 1956 the Radio Corporation of America sold just such a proposal to the Army. Transferred to NASA in 1959, the project was developed under the acronym Tiros (Television and Infrared Observation Satellite). This developmental series of meteorological vehicles brought the thorny issue of meshing a hardware product and a customer's desires forcefully to the attention of NASA's leaders. The data furnished by these new machines would be used primarily by the Weather Bureau in the Department of Commerce and the military services. Responsibilities had to be assigned and procedures established to ensure that NASA exercised the necessary technical direction over research and development, and at the same time met the customer's special requirements.

Before it was resolved, this issue nearly ended the Tiros project. Space scientists, NASA's customers in space exploration, had faced a similar problem; however, here NASA served as both product developer and, through contracts with the experimenters, as the customer. Although always a focus of tension, procedures to reconcile the differences between science and engineering had been achieved. But Congress had determined that the Weather Bureau would fund NASA's work on weather satellites. Compared to scientists, the Department of Commerce wielded real political clout, and in 1963 that agency announced it might withdraw from the program entirely unless NASA met the technical and managerial requirements it wanted.

In January 1964 Commerce Secretary Hodges and NASA Administrator Webb signed an agreement that essentially settled this issue and established a precedent for subsequent agreements between NASA and customer agencies. Under its terms, NASA would be responsible for developing meteorological spacecraft and associated ground stations, launching the spacecraft, and ensuring their successful performance. The Weather Bureau, later reorganized as the National Oceanic and Atmospheric Administration, would pay for these developments, set the overall requirements including the cost and schedule, monitor the work, control the satellites in orbit, and reduce and distribute the information obtained.[17] Under supplemental agreements, the meteorological satellite program has grown to become an integral part of the nation's weather service. No longer an experimental effort, more advanced operational meteorological satellites located in synchronous orbit provide advance warning of storms that threaten lives and property. Today, citizens view as customary the isobars superimposed on cloud patterns in the satellite weather report on the evening television news.

Civilian communications satellites comprise still another
space application that has had a pronounced effect on human affairs.
In late 1958, together with industrial firms, NASA initiated a research
and development program to build these machines. The first experimental
flight in 1960 placed a metalized balloon in orbit that served as a
passive radio mirror, reflecting signals transmitted by one ground station to the receiver of another. But active communications satellites
could best meet expanding communication needs, and in July 1962 NASA
cooperated with American Telephone and Telegraph to launch and test such
a device. Named Telestar, the AT&T satellite amplified signals it
received and retransmitted them, relaying television programs, telephone
calls, and wirephotos between the United States and Europe. This was
followed by a similar NASA satellite in December 1962, named Relay.
Continuing work towards an operational system, NASA funded and launched
three developmental communications vehicles designed to function in
synchronous, or geostationery orbits. The last two of these satellites,
known as Syncom 2 and 3, were turned over in 1965 to the Department of
Defense for military use.[18]

Meantime, after intensive study and national debate, the
President and the Congress acted to place the commercial use of communications satellites in the hands of private industry. The Communications
Satellite Act of 1962 authorized formation of the Communications
Satellite Corporation, called Comsat. The legislation also stipulated
that NASA would provide launching services and furnish technical advice
to the firm on a cost reimbursable basis. In addition, the space
agency was directed to continue research and development work in this
field. Subsequently, many nations joined with the United States to
form the International Telecommunications Satellite Organization, with
Comsat acting as the United States representative and technical manager.
Beginning in 1965, Intelsat, as the international organization became
known, initiated commercial operations with a series of progressively
more sophisticated communications satellites that now gird the globe.
On its part, NASA has continued communications research with its
Applications Technology Satellites. The most recent one, loaned to the
Government of India, has been used to transmit educational programs
on family planning, farming, and health measures into 2400 villages--
a start toward helping developing countries improve their economies
through the use of instrumented spacecraft.[19]

Earth resource survey and geodetic satellites conclude the
major, instrumented civilian space applications missions. In 1964,
with the Departments of Interior and Agriculture, NASA examined remote
sensing techniques that could provide useful environmental information.
Aircraft flights were conducted to define the most promising systems of
remote sensing and, after an extended debate about the cost effectiveness of employing aircraft or instrumented spacecraft for this purpose,
in 1969 the space project was approved. NASA built two instrumented
vehicles equipped with both imaging and spectral sensors that operate
over the entire electromagnetic spectrum, including the visible,
infrared, ultraviolet, radar, and microwave frequencies. Launched in
1974 and 1975, and designated Landsat 1 and 2, these machines have

since returned information of exceptional value to students of agriculture, forestry, geology, hydrology, oceanography, and urban growth.
Like meteorological satellites, NASA furnishes Landsat data to the
principal using agencies, in this case the Departments of Interior
and Agriculture. And, following a long-standing federal policy, Landsat
imaging and spectral data is offered for public sale in much the same
way as the United States Geological Survey has sold maps and aerial
photographs for nearly a hundred years.[20] (Figure 8)

    In the early 1960s, NASA also examined geodetic satellites,
vehicles that could assist the work of cartographers and also measure
gravity anomalies of the Earth. In 1965 and 1968 the first of these
satellites containing light beacons, transponders, and passive reflec-
tors, were orbited. Named Geos 1 and 2, they permitted very precise
position measurements to be made from ground observation stations, and
contributed to a unified world datum accurate to within ten meters. A
more recent NASA geodetic satellite, from which simultaneous laser
measurements can be made from Earth stations a continent apart, was
launched in 1976. It produced highly accurate measurements of the
Earth's rotation and the movements of the Earth's crust, and assisted
investigations of plate techtonics and Earthquakes.[21] (For a synopsis
of civilian applications missions, see Appendix B.)

    All of these instrumented civilian space vehicles, whether
used in public or private applications missions, have gradually become
indispensable to the welfare of the United States and its citizens.
Today they function as vital links in the systems of communications,
weather forecasting, mapping, and a large assortment of land use and
resource planning. But all of these instrumented machines have been
placed in space by expensive and expendable launch vehicles. Now, this
method of space launching is about to change, and that change can be
expected to effect the course of space exploration and utilization in
the years ahead.

IN RETROSPECT

    Since the authorization of the first United States instrumented
satellite projects in 1955, the space program has grown and diversified
in three principal stages: a formative period, 1955-1957; a period of
organization and action following Sputniks 1 and 2, 1958-1960; and a
period dominated by the commitment to a lunar landing and manned space
flight, 1961-19(79). During these periods various interests arrayed in
shifting alliances have moved in and around the civilian and military
space agencies. There were scientists intent on exploring the universe,
engineers caught up in the problems and prospects of building space
hardware, manned flight proponents desirous of bases in space, and the
users of space applications data who wanted results quickly and in a
format that suited them. But above and beyond exploring and utilizing
space, United States officials at first responded to the Soviet
Sputniks and manned Vostoks with missions aimed at restoring pride at
home and prestige abroad. That emphasis clearly favored the challenge
and human drama of manned space flight.

Figure 8

Landsat Picture of the San Francisco
Bay and Sacramento Delta Regions Showing Urban and Rural Land Use Patterns,
1975

An idea of the influence exerted by manned space flight can be ascertained in the following illustrations. Figure 9 shows the distribution of the NASA research and development budget, adjusted in constant 1964 dollars, among the agency's major offices. These figures include the cost of launch vehicle development. Even though the twin goals of space exploration and utilization have been realized mostly with instrumented vehicles, beginning in 1961 the spending for manned space flight within NASA ascended rapidly as the nation sought to conclusively demonstrate its technical superiority. Once established and endowed as the most affluent among the NASA offices, manned space flight has maintained a dominant position in the allocation of the agency's resources.

Figure 10 provides a similar but not identical breakdown for the Air Force. In this case the division is represented in terms of manned and unmanned space activity, rather than by major office; launch vehicles and tracking and data acquisition are included in these dollar amounts. Many Air Force officials were eager and worked hard for a manned space flight program of their own. However, having begun work in 1955, the Air Force instrumented satellite projects were well established in 1963. Furthermore, Congress had spared the Air Force the commitment of beating the Russians in manned space flight. Finally, most of the assignments for the Manned Orbiting Laboratory could be more economically performed by instrumented vehicles. Under these conditions, the proponents of manned flight did not prevail.

Attesting to their positions of influence within the respective agencies, figures 11 and 12 depict the share of the space research and development budget claimed by the manned and unmanned interests between 1961 and 1976. The contrast is a marked one both within and between the civilian space agency and the Air Force. But the goal of excelling in a competitive space race has now largely disappeared; at the same time new astronautical tools have become available. Another period in the exploration and utilization of space is about to begin. In the early 1980s, NASA, cooperating with the Air Force, will employ a space shuttle in place of the "throw away" launch vehicles developed in the 1950s. The orbit stage of the shuttle launch vehicle will fly into orbit and return to Earth to be used again (Figure 13). With the shuttle, the nation can place instrumented spacecraft in Earth orbit or on trajectories to the Moon and planets. Shuttle personnel can retrieve malfunctioning satellites in space and fix them onboard or return them to Earth for later refurbishment. And the shuttle itself can be used for manned scientific and applications missions.

With these capabilities near at hand, the nation's military and civilian space leaders face decisions on the important role of men and instrumented machines in space, and the proper balance between space science and applications. NASA, especially, must decide whether the flight of man in space will continue to be an objective for its own sake, or whether man in space will serve where he can best contribute to space exploration and utilization. In an era of inflation and a leveling of space appropriations, striking an acceptable balance between space

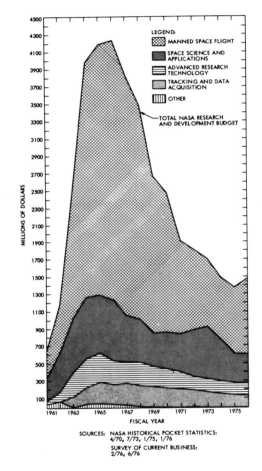

Figure 9

Distribution of the NASA Research
and Development Budget in Constant
1964 Dollars By Major Office,
1961-1976

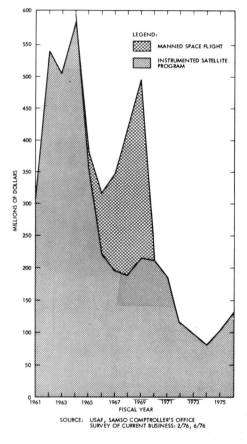

Figure 10

Distribution of the Air Force Research
and Development Budget in Constant 1964
Dollars for Manned and Unmanned Programs
1961-1976

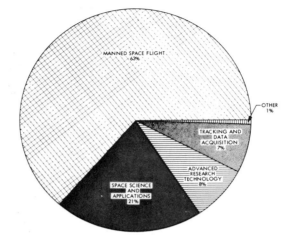

NASA RESEARCH AND DEVELOPMENT BUDGET SHARE BY MAJOR OFFICE IN 1964
CONSTANT DOLLARS, SUMMED OVER THE YEARS 1961-1976

MANNED SPACE FLIGHT
63%

OTHER
1%

TRACKING AND
DATA
ACQUISITION
7%

ADVANCED
RESEARCH
TECHNOLOGY
8%

SPACE SCIENCE
AND
APPLICATIONS
21%

Fig. 11

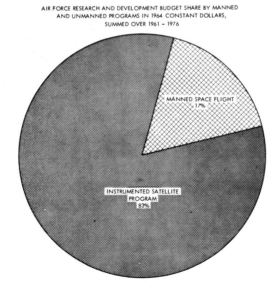

AIR FORCE RESEARCH AND DEVELOPMENT BUDGET SHARE BY MANNED
AND UNMANNED PROGRAMS IN 1964 CONSTANT DOLLARS,
SUMMED OVER 1961 - 1976

MANNED SPACE FLIGHT
17%

INSTRUMENTED SATELLITE
PROGRAM
83%

Fig. 12

208

Figure 13

Artist's Concept of Space Shuttle
Liftoff. The Manned Shuttle Orbiter
Will Return to Earth for a Landing
Similar to a Jet Transport.
(Courtesy of Rockwell International
Space Division)

exploration and utilization should prove equally as difficult a task. In the next few years we can expect to see increased emphasis placed on space applications to protect the quality of the environment, preserve nature's balance, and address the problems of overpopulation. "Congress," NASA Administrator James Fletcher recently observed, "reflecting the wish of the people, wants it that way and that became the direction we [NASA] took."22

Given mankind's earthly distresses, that direction cannot be faulted. And of course the distinction between exploration and applications is not absolute. For example, much scientific information has been acquired in the Vela, meteorological, and geodetic missions--and pure science has often had important applications, as was the case in the study of fluid mechanics, electricity, and magnetism. Where little or no information existed in much of the space sciences, we know today a good deal about objects beyond the solar system that emit X-rays, ultraviolet and gamma radiation, as well as about the solar wind and belts of radiation around the Earth, about the geology of the Moon, the structure of Mercury with its lunar-like surface and Earth-like interior, the curious surface of Mars with evidence for both wind and water erosion, and about the meteorology of Venus, Mars, and Jupiter, together with details of the Jovian magnetosphere. These data may prove extremely important in better understanding the Earth itself and the dynamics of the Earth's atmosphere; such an improved understanding could have profound implications for man's future welfare. Missions for the purposes of utilizing and exploring space must both be pursued, or we risk a space program that is far less challenging, innovative, and, ultimately, less valuable.

ACKNOWLEDGMENT

The author is indebted to William Kaufmann and Clayton Koppes for their valuable suggestions and critical comments, and to Gary Cox, who prepared the appendices.

REFERENCES

1. Outlook for Space: Report to the NASA Administrator by the Outlook for Space Study Group (Washington: National Aeronautics and Space Administration, NASA-SP-386, January 1976), p. 2.

2. R. Cargill Hall, "Earth Satellites, A First Look by the United States Navy," in R. C. Hall, (ed.), Essays on the History of Rocketry and Astronautics: Proceedings of the Third through the Sixth History Symposia of the International Academy of Astronautics, NASA Technical Memorandum to be published in 1977.

3. See Constance Mcl. Green and Milton Lomask, Vanguard: A History (Washington: Smithsonian Institution Press, 1971); also, R. Cargill Hall, "Origins and Development of the Vanguard and Explorer Satellite Programs," The Airpower Historian, Vol. XI, No. 4, October 1964, pp. 101-112.

4. John B. Medaris with Arthur Gordon, <u>Countdown for Decision</u> (New York: Paperback Library, Inc., 1960), pp. 101, 124.

5. Herbert F. York, <u>Race to Oblivion</u> (New York: Simon and Schuster, Clarion Book, 1970), pp. 106, 146.

6. DOD News Release No. 288-58, March 27, 1958; see also ARPA Orders No. 1-58 and 2-58 of March 27, 1958.

7. Robert Vexler (ed.), Dwight D. Eisenhower, 1880-1969, <u>Chronology, Documents, Bibliographical Aids</u> (Dobbs Ferry, New York: Oceana Publications, Inc., 1972), p. 41.

8. Among those most active in this regard: Alan Waterman, Director of the National Science Foundation; Edward Mills Purcell, Harvard University; James R. Killian, Special Assistant to the President for Science and Technology; Detlov Bronk, President of the National Academy of Sciences; Homer E. Newell, Naval Research Laboratory; James A. Van Allen, State University of Iowa; and Lee A. DuBridge, President of the California Institute of Technology.

9. Material in this section drawn from R. Cargill Hall, <u>Lunar Impact: A History of Project Ranger</u> (Washington: Government Printing Office), NASA SP-4210, Chapter 1, in press.

10. Berkner quoted in Harold M. Schmeck, Jr., "U.S. Held Leader in Space Science," <u>The New York Times</u>, May 28, 1961, p. 15.

11. See Swenson, Grimwood, and Alexander, <u>This New Ocean: A History of Project Mercury</u> (Washington: Government Printing Office), NASA SP-4201, 1966.

12. See Vernon Van Dyke, <u>Pride and Power: The Rationale of the Space Program</u> (Urbana: University of Illinois Press, 1964); and John M. Logsdon, <u>The Decision to Go to the Moon: Project Apollo and the National Interest</u> (Cambridge: MIT Press, 1970)

13. See Hall, <u>Lunar Impact</u>, Chapter 13.

14. See Richard S. Lewis, <u>The Voyages of Apollo: The Exploration of the Moon</u> (New York: Quadrangle/The New York Times Book Co., 1974); and Stuart Ross Taylor, <u>Lunar Science: A Post Apollo View</u> (New York: Pergamon Press Inc., 1975)

15. The material on military space applications in this section is drawn from the <u>Report to the Congress from the President of the United States, U.S. Aeronautics and Space Activities</u> (1959-1975); Philip J. Klass, <u>Secret Sentries in Space</u> (New York: Random House, 1971); and Herbert F. York and G. Allen Greb, "Strategic Reconnaissance: The State of Mind and the Art in National Security Affairs," to be published in the <u>Bulletin of Atomic Scientists</u>, Spring, 1977.

16. See, for example, the statement of President Lyndon B. Johnson, cited in Evert Clark, "Satellite Spying Cited by Johnson," _The New York Times_, March 17, 1967, p. 13.

17. See Richard Chapman, "The Politics of Research and Development: A Case Study of the Weather Satellite Program," Syracuse University, June 1965; also, Richard A. Bauer et. al., _NASA Planning and Decision Making, Final Report_, Vol. 1. Harvard Graduate School of Business Administration, 1970.

18. See Stockholm International Peace Research Institute, _Communications_ Satellites, Stockholm, SIPRI, 1969.

19. See Stephen E. Doyle, "Permanent Arrangements for the Global Commercial Communications Satellite System of Intelsat," IAF Report, September 25, 1971; also Agency for International Development, _Aidsat: Space Age Technology for Development_, Washington, D.C., 1976.

20. See J. R. Morrison, "Earth Resources Survey Program, New Results--1975," IAF Paper 75-143, presented at the 26th International Astronautical Federation Congress, Lisbon, Portugal, September 21-27, 1975; also J. Lehmann, "Remote Sensors--Prospects and Limitations," in _Management and Utilization of Remote Sensing Data, Proceedings of the Symposium, Sioux Falls, October 29 - November 1, 1973_ (Falls Church, Virginia: American Society of Photogrammetry, 1973).

21. See Henriksen, Soren, _et.al._, _The Use of Artificial Satellites for Geodesy_ (Washington: American Geophysical Union, 1972).

22. NASA Administrator Fletcher quoted in _Salt Lake City Tribune_, June 13, 1976, as reprinted in the _Congressional Record - Senate_, June 15, 1976, S9309.

V I I I

THE HEROIC ERA OF MANNED
SPACE FLIGHT

Edward C. Ezell[*]

Of all mankind's technological adventures, few have
been as spectacular when judged by contemporary or
historical standards as were the first steps of the
human species into outer space. For the United States,
the first phase of this national enterprise ended
with the 24 July 1975 splashdown of the last Apollo.
Ironically, the era of single-flight spacecraft, initiated by the fierce competitive rivalry between the
United States and the Soviet Union, closed with a
joint flight of Apollo and Soyuz. Subsequent American manned flight, utilizing the reusable Shuttle Orbiter, will have international cooperation built in,
as the U.S. searches for multi-national cargos for the
new craft. Since we have seen the end of one epoch
and the beginning of another (with the first Shuttle
"roll out" on 17 September 1976), it is fitting in
this bicentennial year to reflect upon the 32 flights
made by NASA's astronauts, to take a look at how the
hardware was developed and to understand how that
technological achievement fits into the nation's 200
years of space flight.

By the Mid-1950s, the idea of manned space flight emerged from the
realm of fantasy to become a topic of serious technical discussion. Frederick C. Durant III, President of the International Astronautical Federation (IAF), told the delegates gathered in 1954 at Innsbruck, Austria,
that "The feasibility of space flights is no longer a topic for academic
debate, but a matter of time, money and a program."[1] To illustrate his
point, Durant showed the Walt Disney Productions motion picture *Man in
Space* during the August 1955 Sixth Congress of the IAF in Copenhagen.

After an introductory discussion on the evolution of rockets, three
American proponents of "man in space" addressed different aspects of manned
space flight. Willy Ley described the prospects for utilizing rockets in

[*] Viking Project Historian under contract to NASA, has recently completed
a manuscript for NASA, "The Partnership: A History of the Apollo Soyuz
Test Project."

space travel and the steps required to build a space station that could orbit 1730 kilometers above the earth. Through the medium of an animated cartoon character, "Homo Sapiens Extra-Terrestrialis," Heinz Haber explained some of the questions raised by "space medicine," illustrating the physiological hazards--acceleration loads, weightlessness, cosmic radiation, meteorites--that the first space travelers would encounter. Finally, Wernher von Braun closed the film with a discussion of his conceptual design for a 55-meter tall, 1280-metric ton, 4-stage interplanetary rocket that could carry a crew of six into the cosmos. The IAF delegates were enthusiastic about this 33-minute movie, especially in the light of President Eisenhower's earlier announcement that the U.S. would launch artificial satellites during the International Geophysical Year.[2]

Among the viewers of *Man in Space* were Leonid Ivanovich Sedov and Kyril Feodorovich Ogorodnikov, the first Soviets to attend an IAF Congress. They spoke with Durant about borrowing the film for use in the Soviet Union, saying, it would be "very good to have here a copy of Walt Disney's excellent film for private demonstration."[3] It is likely that the Soviets viewed *Man in Space* as proof of growing American interest in solving the basic problems associated with manned space flight. Sedov and Ogorodnikov wanted to use the Disney picture to promote their own nation's efforts in rocketry and space research. To Soviet space enthusiasts, the movie was at once an encouragement and a warning.

Seven years after that Copenhagen meeting, both the USSR and the U.S. orbited and returned their first space pilots. Vostok and Mercury were possible within such a short span of time because engineers and scientists had amassed a wealth of basic engineering and scientific data directly applicable to the questions posed by manned space flight. In those early years, much of the work was duplicative, as security restrictions forced Soviet and American researchers to repeat the same fundamental investigations; but if the competitive environment was wasteful, it also spurred the development of space flight technology. Seemingly, man would have crossed the barriers of space frontier without the element of international competition, but it was precisely that element that did give rise to the space program--and made funds available. Fantasy yielded to reality; and that reality was orbiting hardware.

The Challenge of Space Flight

Vostok and Mercury were first steps, designed to explore the concept of manned space flight. Maxime A. Faget, chief designer of the Mercury spacecraft, summarized their importance:

> Since these flights were initial efforts, the purpose of the
> flights was limited to the basic experience of launching the
> spacecraft and crew into orbit, having them remain there for
> a period of time, and then having them return safely to Earth.
> These flights were made at low altitude with the spacecraft
> barely high enough to avoid appreciable drag from the upper
> fringes of the atmosphere. . . . the amount of energy re-
> quired for launching was minimized, and the flight was made
> safer, since the difficulty of making a reentry maneuver was
> also minimized. . . . these flights . . . proved that it was
> practical for man to fly in space.[4]

While providing valuable lessons in the design and operation of spacecraft, Vostok and Mercury also demonstrated two different approaches to accomplishing the same tasks.

The rapid onset of multi-gravity forces accompanying the rocket launch was one of the primary concerns that faced the two technical teams. During the powered ascent from Earth, crew members had to be protected from the increased "g-loads," vibration and noise. It was known that human tolerance to increased gravity forces varied with the duration of exposure and the attitude of the body with reference to the force. Soviets and Americans agreed that the reclining position permitted a pilot to absorb heavy acceleration loads more comfortably than in any other posture. In both countries, engineers decided in favor of a couch contoured to the form of each individual to protect him from g-loads, and all Mercury and Vostok pilots rode semi-supine in their own tailor-made seats.[5]

Once a pilot overcame the initial acceleration forces of flight, he would encounter the phenomena of gravity balanced by centrifugal force, generally called weightlessness or zero g. Flight physicians contended that the absence of gravity might affect man's physical and mental performance, but in the face of limited information, the effect of zero g was mainly a topic of speculation. Some medical doctors wondered if the human organism, tailored to Earth's gravity would continue to function normally when suddenly deprived of that force. More experimental data was needed to permit a better analysis of the role of zero g in manned space flight.[6]

Since it was impossible to duplicate weightlessness on Earth, scientists conducted tests with animals borne aloft by rockets. In the U.S. in 1947, experimenters began launching live organisms with V-2 rockets. From these and subsequent Aerobee monkey launches, scientists concluded that weightlessness and acceleration forces did not adversely affect the animals.[7] Soviet rocket engineers and physicians also sent animals to high altitudes, and their canine experiments led them to the same conclusions that the Americans had reached with primates and rodents. At first, the Soviet tests were conducted using pressurized capsules; then they experimented with dogs wearing special space suits and traveling in unpressurized cabins. These experiments convinced the Soviets that acceleration and weightlessness did not pose impossible barriers to manned flight. The significance of this conclusion was made clear to the rest of the world when the Soviets sent Laika into orbit with *Sputnik II* on 23 November 1957. Although she was not returned to Earth, Laika ate, barked and moved about in her space cabin for seven days without apparent ill effects.[8]

Life Support Systems

But there were other questions raised by the unknowns of space environment. Man in space would be absolutely dependent upon an artificial environment. The atmosphere on Earth is a mixture of 80% nitrogen and 20% oxygen, with small quantities of water vapor and carbon dioxide, plus traces of other gases. Since the astronaut would continually breathe oxygen and generate carbon dioxide and water vapor, the spacecraft needed devices to replenish oxygen and to eliminate excess carbon dioxide. While both the Soviet and American engineers removed carbon dioxide and humidity by using lithium hydroxide canisters, they approached the problem of oxygen supply differently.[9]

The Soviets decided upon a cabin pressure equal to about one atmosphere (760mm Hg)* and an 80/20 nitrogen/oxygen composition, which would

---

*

The atmospheric pressure at sea level can be measured as equalling 760mm Hg (14.7 lbs/squ in.). The atmosphere of the Soviet craft was therefore called a sea level atmosphere, while the U.S. craft operated with an atmosphere 1/3 that of sea level, or 258mm Hg (5 p.s.i.).

FIRST U.S. ASTRONAUT TEAM

Mercury astronauts were named on April 2, 1959. They were (front row, left to right): Walter M. Shirra, Donald K. Slayton, John H. Glenn, and Scott Carpenter; (back row) Alan B. Shepard, Virgil I. Grissom, and L. Gordon Cooper. Slayton did not fly in space until the ASTP mission in July 1975. (VIII-1, NASA photo.)

be essentially the same as on Earth. The Americans adopted a cabin pressure of 258mm Hg, or the equivalent of approximately 1/3 atmosphere, and elected to use a pure oxygen environment. While the Soviet system had the advantage of simplicity and minimal danger from fire (always present with oxygen), it had the disadvantage of exposing the cosmonaut to potential decompression should he have to switch to his space suit life support system in an emergency. American cabin and suit pressures were similar, so that a switch from cabin to suit oxygen would not subject the crew to the "bends." Astronuats were required to prebreathe oxygen prior to launch to remove the nitrogen from their blood streams, reducing the possibility of decompression sickness, or aeroembolism. This absence of nitrogen in the atmosphere also generated the requirement for flameproofing all materials used in the cabin.[10]

Soviet and American technicians also differed in the manner by which they replenished spacecraft oxygen. There are three ways to store oxygen—as a high pressure gas; as a cryogenic fluid; or as a solid, chemically combined with other elements. Storage as a gas requires strong, high-pressure tanks, which are heavier than the oxygen with which they are filled. Liquid oxygen can be stored in lighter and smaller tanks than those required for gaseous oxygen, but it must be kept very cold, below 90 kelvins (-297° F); this would require special thermal insulation. Chemical systems that release oxygen upon contact with carbon dioxide and water vapor have three drawbacks—weight; volume; and variable performance, based upon a number of factors, such as the crewman's metabolic rate, cabin temperature and humidity.[11]

To replenish cabin oxygen, Soviet environmental control system designers selected a "chemical bed" system based upon alkali metal superoxides, which liberate oxygen as they absorb moisture and form more alkali, which in turn absorbs carbon dioxide. Despite the lack of precision control and the space required for the apparatus, the Soviets favored the chemical bed because it eliminated the problems encountered with high pressure bottles for gas and the precise temperature controls for liquid oxygen. In the U.S., engineers were successful in arguing for pure oxygen atmosphere at a pressure of 258mm Hg, since it met the weight and volumetric requirements imposed by the design limitations of the Mercury spacecraft. Although the development of the spherical pressure bottles for gaseous oxygen proved to be a challenge, the American designers felt that the effort was justified by their increased reliability.[12]

Reentry Vehicles: Spheres vs Blunt Bodies

The choice of reentry vehicle configuration reflected additional differences in approach. The central and most visible difference between the Vostok and Mercury spacecraft was their external configuration. Beneath the streamlined launch shroud, the orbital/reentry portion of Vostok was spherical, while the basic shape of Mercury was a truncated cone. The spacecraft designers studied the alternative shapes for reentry vehicles and made their choices based upon standards established within their own programs.

The Soviets, under the leadership of Sergei Pavlovich Korolev, chief designer of spacecraft, reviewed the different possibilities and chose the sphere for their reentry configuration. According to Korolev, among non-lifting shapes, the spherical reentry body alone possessed an inherent dynamic stability as it plunged back into the Earth's atmosphere. He rejected the conical-shaped craft, because its tendency to pitch and yaw would have required an elaborate attitude control system, plus greater reliance upon man as pilot rather than man as passenger.

The orbital configuration of Vostok consisted of a spherical cabin with an attached equipment cluster.[13] Prior to descent, the spacecraft was oriented for reentry by means of a solar sensor located in the equipment compartment. This maneuver aimed the retrorockets so that they fired along the line of flight, slowing the craft as it entered its descent trajectory. Upon termination of retrofire, the cabin separated from the instrument section, which subsequently burned up as it entered the atmosphere. Vostok was then a simple sphere, protected from the intense reentry temperatures by an ablative coating that shielded the entire craft.[14]

Vostok reentered like a bullet following the path dictated by the retrorocket impulse; there was no attitude control. By placing the sphere's center of gravity behind and below the cosmonaut, the spacecraft designers assured Vostok pilots from Gagarin to Bykovskiy and Tereshkova the proper orientation for ejection from the "lander" when it reached 7000 meters.

At that altitude, the bolts securing the pilot's hatch were severed explosively, and the hatch was blown away. Two seconds later the cosmonaut and his couch were ejected from the craft to begin a parachuted descent to 4000 meters. At that height, the cosmonaut continued his return by means of his own parachute.[15]

In their study of reentry, the Americans evolved their own theories regarding optimum spacecraft configuration. In June 1952, Julian Allen of the NACA Ames Aeronautical Laboratory addressed the problem of structural heating during atmospheric reentry. His research led to the formulation of the "blunt-body principle," a radical departure from the streamlined aircraft of the early '50s. Although his studies were directed toward resolving the nose cone reentry problem of the ballistic missile, they were later applicable to the Mercury spacecraft.

Beginning in 1954 and continuing through 1958, Allen and two associates, Alfred J. Eggers, Jr., and Stanford E. Neice, examined the relative merits of three types of hypersonic spacecraft--ballistic, skip and glide. For manned satellite missions, any of the three craft could be boosted to orbital velocity by a rocket and then be separated from the launch vehicle for either free flight or Earth orbit. The skip vehicle, which would reenter the atmosphere by an intricate series of dips and skips, would require the greatest boost capacity and would encounter excessive aerodynamic heating during reentry. The glider was a promising concept, but it would also be a long term project, since it would require extensive engineering and development. The third option was the ballistic shape, which was simply a blunt, non-lifting, high-drag projectile. Although without aerodynamic controls, its blunt configuration would provide superior thermal protection to the pilot, and its lighter weight would permit longer range missions. Moreover, the deceleration forces would be minimized if the vehicle reentered at the correct angle. The Ames researchers concluded that "the ballistic vehicle appears to be a practical man-carrying machine, provided extreme care is exercised in supporting the man during atmospheric entry."[16] By late 1957, Eggers was proposing a semi-ballistic vehicle in which the best elements of the glider and the ballistic shapes were combined. Further progress on manned spacecraft was to be influenced by the Air Force and by research in progress at the

Langley Memorial Aeronautical Laboratory.[17]

On 29-31 January 1958, the Air Research and Development Command held a closed conference at Wright-Patterson Air Force Base, during which 11 aircraft and missile firms outlined for Air Force and NACA representatives their classified proposals for manned satellites. These variations on the three basic configurations discussed above ranged in projected weight from 454 to 8165 kilograms and involved mainly the use of multistage launch vehicles. Since there was such a difference in technology among the various proposals, the estimated development time ranged from one to five years. Looking back on this period, Robert R. Gilruth[*] recalls:

> Because of its great simplicity, the non-lifting, ballistic-type of vehicle was the front runner of all proposed manned satellites, in my judgment. There were many variations of this and other concepts under study by both government and industry groups at that time. The choice involved considerations of weight, launch vehicle, reentry body design, and to be honest, gut feelings. Some people felt that man-in-space was only a stunt. The ballistic approach, in particular, was under fire since it was such a radical departure from the airplane. It was called by its opponents "the man in the can," and the pilot was termed only a "medical specimen." Others thought it was just too undignified a way to fly.[18]

While subject to considerable criticism, the concept of a simple ballistic manned satellite gained important support from a group of NACA engineers who started work on just such a spacecraft, borrowing on the experience and technology available in recent research on nose cones for intercontinental ballistic missiles. Max Faget was one of the key members of the NACA group interested in this effort. In January 1958, he had identified himself as a supporter of the ballistic reentry vehicle when he proposed to NACA Headquarters that a non-lifting spherical capsule be considered for orbital flight. Less than a week after an Air Force man-in-space conference in March 1958, Gilruth called Faget and a group of top Langley engineers together to discuss a NACA conference on high speed aerodynamics, scheduled to begin at the Ames laboratory on 18 March. The Langley position called for the development of a ballistic spacecraft

----

[*] Robert R. Gilruth had been Assistant Director of the Langley Aeronautical Laboratory since 1952 and was named Manager of the Space Task Group, which was assigned responsibility for Project Mercury on 5 November 1958.

SPACECRAFT INTERNAL ARRANGEMENT

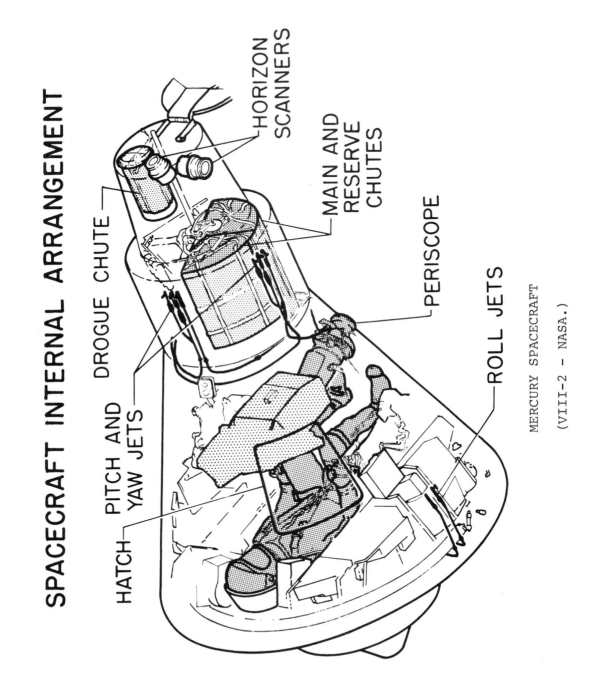

HORIZON SCANNERS

DROGUE CHUTE

MAIN AND RESERVE CHUTES

PITCH AND YAW JETS

PERISCOPE

HATCH

ROLL JETS

MERCURY SPACECRAFT

(VIII-2 - NASA.)

launched by a ballistic missile booster.[19]

The Ames conference was the last in a series of formal symposia; as such it attracted nearly 500 people from NACA, the military and the aircraft and missile industry. The 46 papers presented during the three-day meeting summarized the most advanced aerodynamic thinking within the Advisory Committee's laboratories on hypersonic, orbital and interplanetary flight. Faget presented the first paper, "Preliminary Studies of Manned Satellites--Wingless Configuration: Non-lifting," in which he and his co-authors pointed out the inherent advantages of the ballistic approach. The Langley engineers went so far as to propose a specific ballistic configuration--a cone, 3.4 meters long and 2.1 meters in diameter, protected on the blunt end by a heatshield. He concluded that "as far as reentry and recovery is concerned, the state of the art is sufficiently advanced so that it is possible to proceed confidently with a manned satellite project based upon the ballistic reentry type of vehicle."[20]

The Mercury spacecraft grew out of this 1958 conceptual study prepared at Langley. After an additional two months of design studies, preliminary specifications for a manned satellite were drafted during June by Langley personnel. Following a number of revisions and additions, these specifications were used for the Project Mercury spacecraft contract with McDonnell Aircraft Corporation. All this work occurred during the months in which the National Aeronautics and Space Act was being drafted and enacted by Congress.[21]

In designing the Mercury spacecraft, the key word was simplicity. The goal was a spacecraft that represented "the simplest and most reliable approach--one with a minimum of new developments and using a progressive buildup of tests." Employing these criteria, "It was implicit . . . that we use the drag-type reentry vehicle; an existing ICBM booster; a retro-rocket to initiate descent from orbit; a parachute system for final approach and landing; and an escape system to permit the capsule to get away from a malfunctioning launch rocket."[22] Although Vostok and Mercury emerged from the design process with different external configurations, their designers had met the same problems and had made some remarkably similar decisions. Undoubtedly, the key decision was to keep the first step into space a simple one.

Vostok and Mercury: The First Flights into Space

The years 1958-1961 were busy ones in both the U.S. and the USSR for the development of manned space vehicles. According to K. P. Feoktistov, Soviet designer, engineer and cosmonaut, the details for mockups and breadboard models of Vostok were worked out and then built during 1959. Final developmental work on the "carrier rocket" was being conducted simultaneously at the launch site.[23] By 15 May 1960, the Soviets had progressed sufficiently with the development of their spacecraft and the adaptation of their ICBM boosters as launch vehicles to commence a series of five unmanned test flights. These Vostok precursor flights, *Korabl Sputnik I* through *V*, were designed to collect additional data on the effects of space environment on biological specimens and to test the spacecraft systems. "In late 1960-early 1961 . . . revised technical documentation was used for the manufacture of the spaceships." The Soviets were ready to begin manned space flight operations.

Feoktistov summarized the rationale of the six Vostok flights. Yuri Gagarin's flight on 12 April 1961 was a single-orbit checkout of the spacecraft systems. Rather than the ballistic shots used at first by the Americans, the Soviets preferred an orbital mission to collect additional data on weightlessness, a topic of considerable concern to Soviet flight surgeons. Indeed, for the second mission, flown by Gherman Titov on 6 August 1961, the medical specialists had urged that the duration be held to just two or three orbits so they could judge the effects of zero gravity, but the designers and Titov wanted to go for a day-long mission, a goal that coincided with political considerations as well. Feoktistov also hinted that the one year hiatus in manned flight following *Vostok II* may have been related to the motion sickness experienced by Titov. A. G. Nikolayev and P. R. Popovich in *Vostok III* and *IV* completed their dual mission in August 1962. Though they did not actually rendezvous, they appear to have been within five kilometers of each other, thus giving the Soviet trajectory specialists an opportunity to study the problem of rendezvous and to track two spacecraft simultaneously. In June 1963, V. F. Bykovskiy's flight aboard *Vostok V* lasted nearly five days, and during the last three days he was accompanied in orbit by *Vostok VI*, piloted by Valentina Tereshkova, the only woman to fly in space to date. Vostok was the "necessary foundation for . . . further development of manned space vehicles in the Soviet Union."[24]

While the Soviet cosmonauts were monopolizing world headlines, work on Project Mercury continued. NASA had embarked upon a step-by-step program of spacecraft and booster qualification trials in 1959. The test program, divided into two parts, sought first to qualify the Redstone and Atlas missiles as launch vehicles for manned spacecraft, and second to "man rate" the Mercury spacecraft itself. The Mercury-Redstone phase of the program covered a 31-month period, during which six missions were flown. The results were mixed. On the very first launch attempt (MR-1), early separation of an electrical ground line to the booster aborted the mission. On the second flight (MR-1A), all systems worked satisfactorily, but problems again appeared in the primate "Ham" mission (MR-2), when over-acceleration caused a higher trajectory and longer downrange travel than had been anticipated. As a consequence, an extra flight was scheduled before a manned launch was attempted. Then on 5 May 1961, less than a month after the Gagarin mission, Alan Shepard became the first American in space, flying a suborbital trajectory in his spacecraft *Freedom 7*. Gus Grissom in *Liberty Bell 7* made the second suborbital flight on 21 July. The data gathered from these two successful missions justified canceling the remaining Mercury-Redstone flights.

Then came the step to orbital flight for which the Atlas missile had been selected as the launch vehicle. When the program was approved in October 1958, no other booster could have been chosen if the objectives of the program were to be accomplished in a reasonable length of time. So, as had the Russians, the Americans decided to "man rate" an ICBM. The 57-month flight phase for Atlas began with the launch of the Big Joe Atlas boilerplate model of the Mercury spacecraft on 9 September 1959. The first production spacecraft mounted on an Atlas launch vehicle (MA-1) was launched on 29 July 1960. After about 60 seconds, launch vehicle and adapter failed structurally. Because no spacecraft escape system was used, the spacecraft was destroyed upon impact. Following an intensive investigation, modifications were introduced to stiffen the adapter between the launch vehicle and the spacecraft and to otherwise improve the structural integrity of the entire upper part of the Atlas. An interim version of the alteration was used without difficulty on MA-2, and the final version was tested during MA-4 on 13 September 1961. More than two months later on 29 November, Enos, a trained chimpanzee, was launched on a planned three-orbit mission. During the flight of MA-5, the attitude control system performed abnormally, and ground control brought the spacecraft down after two orbits. The problem, as demonstrated on later flights, could have been corrected by an astronaut, thus confirming the American judgment favoring manual overrides of automatic control systems.

After a series of frustrating delays caused by unfavorable weather and fuel leaks, John Glenn became the first American to orbit the Earth. His flight was followed by a three-orbit mission flown by M. Scott Carpenter, in which the only problem was an attitude misalignment at the time of retrofire, causing a 402-kilometer landing overshoot. As the next step toward a day-long mission, Walter M. Schirra piloted a six-orbit mission on 3 October 1962. By drifting in flight, he conserved critical fuel and demonstrated the feasibility of longer duration missions. The 34-plus-hour mission of L. Gordon Cooper on 15-16 May 1963 was Project Mercury's last flight.[25]

Mercury and Vostok demonstrated the feasibility of placing a human in orbit, observing his reactions to space environment and returning him safely to Earth at a known point. While the Soviet designers assigned limited tasks to their cosmonauts, NASA went one step beyond to demonstrate that man could function as "an invaluable part of the space flight systems as pilot, engineer and experimenter." The next stage was the development of more flexible and multiplace spacecraft for the conduct of more intricate missions--the era of Gemini and Voskhod.

Voskhod and Gemini: The Intermediate Step

Even as the Vostok and Mercury programs were entering their operational phases, engineers in the U.S. and the USSR were undertaking the design of a second generation spacecraft. The Americans began with an effort to extend the capabilities of the Mercury, and ended up designing an essentially new vehicle capable of greater maneuverability, rendezvous and docking, and flights of a duration that would equal the period anticipated for the lunar missions of Project Apollo. The Soviets, apparently spurred by the goals set for Project Gemini, decided to modify their Vostok spacecraft for multi-man flights. Where Voskhod was an attempt to exploit more

GEMINI SPACECRAFT

Mockup of Gemini spacecraft at McDonnell Aircraft Corporation in 1964. (VIII-3 - NASA)

fully a tested design, Gemini became geared to the creation of new systems and to the testing of unproven flight concepts that would be applied to even bolder missions in the future.

By December 1961, Project Gemini received formal approval from Washington as the second major project in NASA's manned space program; however, much of the design work and many of the major decisions had already been made.[26] The character of the new effort was shaped by two converging lines of thought. The most influential consideration was President Kennedy's decision on 25 May 1961 that committed the U.S. to a manned lunar expedition before the end of the 1960s. NASA advance planners had been thinking about a mission to the moon, but in the time frame of the 1970s, dependent upon the development of a launch vehicle called Nova. This rocket would be capable of lifting a spacecraft that could fly directly to the moon, land and then return to Earth. This method of reaching the moon--direct ascent--was readily accepted because it would almost certainly work. However, within NASA there was a group of engineers who supported the development of an alternative route--the orbital rendezvous of two or more spacecraft.

John C. Houbolt of Langley and a group of his associates felt that orbital rendezvous promised significant savings in fuel, weight and time. A lunar expedition based upon rendezvous might be assembled with much smaller rockets than a direct mission, launch vehicles that would be available well before Nova. Orbital rendezvous had the disadvantage, however, of being a new and untested idea. No one could predict how difficult or hazardous a rendezvous and linkup in space might be. As long as there was no pressing deadline for a lunar mission, direct ascent offered the easier and safer approach, but with the Presidential creation of a specific timetable, the supporters of rendezvous could press their case for a quicker and cheaper path to the moon. The idea still had to be tried to determine its feasibility, and "Gemini was first and foremost a project to develop and prove equipment and techniques for rendezvous."[27]

Project Gemini was also influenced by a second important consideration, the desire to make a major jump in the state of spacecraft technology. The engineers who had worked on Mercury had seen a number of possible improvements that could have been used if they had not been held back by a combination of considerations--weight, time and the desire to keep the first spacecraft simple. While the Mercury designers were justifiably pre-occupied with solving the basic problems of manned space flight, it had taken too long to build and check out the handcrafted spaceship. James A. Chamberlin, chief designer of Gemini, described the difficulties in Mercury brought about by numerous design constraints:

> Most system components were in the pilot's cabin; and often, to pack them in this very confined space, they had to be stacked like a layer cake and components of one system had to be scattered about the craft to use all available space. This arrangement generated a maze of interconnecting wires, tubing, and mechanical linkages.[28]

Chamberlin saw an opportunity to make Gemini a more easily assembled and serviced vehicle. In an effort to eliminate some of the trouble spots identified in Mercury, he simplified his systems wherever possible. In one case, Chamberlin reduced the complexity of the relays that controlled the automatic systems on board the craft, relying upon pilot control with automatic backup flight systems. Another change was the elimination of the rocket-powered escape tower used in Mercury, cutting hundreds of kilo-grams of extra weight, numerous relays and much complex wiring. Gemini was equipped with pilot-actuated ejection seats.

Throughout the development period, 1962-1963, Gemini engineers and managers worked to solve technical problems and to meet a tight budget. "Within NASA and without, Apollo and the trip to the moon always held center stage." Toward the end of 1963, the first Gemini launch vehicle and spacecraft were being prepared for qualifying trials. Early April 1964 saw the first of Gemini's 12 flights, an unmanned test of the spacecraft and booster, which produced excellent results. Further test flights were postponed as hurricane season arrived on the Florida coast. Meanwhile, the Soviets had launched their first multiplace spacecraft.

When given the assignment to place three cosmonauts into orbit in the same spaceship, designer Korolev set about to redesign Vostok.[29] Apparently, the most important consideration in his decision to modify an existing design rather than to create a new one was the boost capacity of the launch vehicles at his disposal. It appears that by 1963 Korolev and his colleague L.A.Voskresensky were already well along in the design work of an advanced spacecraft capable of long duration earth orbital missions. This vehicle, which would later publicly emerge as Soyuz, was much heavier than Vostok, and the Soviets planned to launch it with the standard Vostok launch vehicle, plus a new and still untested upper stage.[30] As this design work progressed, the Soviet political leadership grew concerned that the U.S. might launch a two-man vehicle before the Soviets could do the same. Khrushchev wanted a Soviet multi-man space mission to maintain the Soviet lead in space.[31] Since Korolev could not hope to perfect his advanced spacecraft and uprated launch vehicle in time, he turned to the task of modifying Vostok.

Korolev had two problems of equal magnitude--how to make room for three persons, and how to keep the weight down. He eliminated the ejection seat, which saved weight and made it possible to accomodate three form-fitting couches. In order to make room for the crew, Korolev planned to have the Voskhod cosmonauts fly in a "shirt sleeve environment." The Soviet designer could risk eliminating spacesuits since he and his staff had created a virtually leakproof ship. Since the ejection apparatus had been removed, a spacecraft "soft-landing" system was devised. Korolev added two pieces of equipment--a second parachute, and a rocket-powered landing apparatus in the parachute shroud lines that would reduce the craft's velocity to less than one meter per second at touchdown.[32] "At Korolev's instructions, a series of Voskhod-type spacecraft were launched, until he was convinced that the soft-landing system worked impeccably."[33] This series included *Cosmos 47*, launched on 6 October 1964 and identified subsequently as an unmanned precursor to *Voskhod I*, which flew six days later.[34]

Voskhod I was another space spectacular. On board were Command Pilot V. M. Komarov; B. B. Yegorov, a medical doctor serving as flight physiologist; and the spacecraft engineer Feoktistov, who acted as an onboard technical scientist. The day-long mission, equivalent to three man-days for the life support system, was completed without reported difficulty. On 13 October, the retrorockets fired, and the craft began its reentry.

> As on the *Vostok* flights, the spacecraft's parachutes opened at an altitude of 7 kilometers. When it came close to the ground, the soft-landing system automatically went into operation. Streams of gases, expelled from nozzles in the direction of the ground, reduced the touchdown velocity to virtually zero. The cosmonauts did not feel the impact.[35]

Meanwhile, NASA was preparing for a second unmanned Gemini-Titan flight.

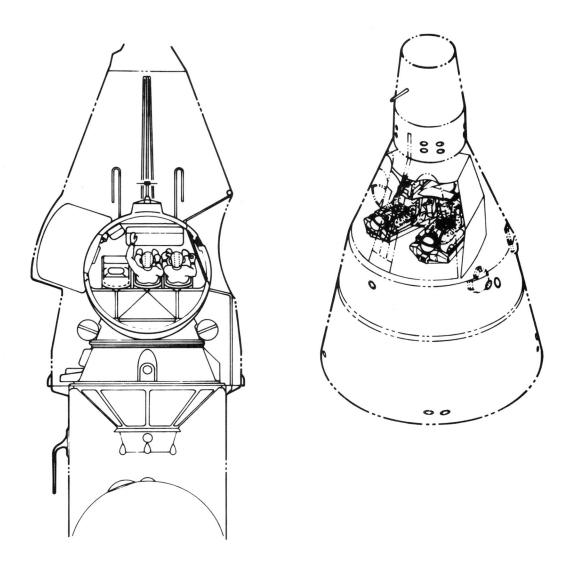

Simplified interior view of Voskhod and Gemini spacecraft

(VIII-4 - NASA)

231

Both space teams were fully occupied during 1965. The second Gemini mission was launched from the Kennedy Space Center on 19 January. This suborbital qual. test of the spacecraft's structure, onboard systems and reentry heat protection was a success; the spacecraft was recovered two hours after splashdown. Just over a month later, the Soviet launch crews sent aloft *Cosmos 57*, a rehearsal for *Voskhod II*, which flew on 18 March.[36] The two-man crew, P. I. Belyayev and A. A. Leonov, completed a 26-hour mission, during which Leonov took the first extravehicular steps into space.

Belyayev and Leonov had to land their spacecraft manually when the solar-orientation system malfunctioned. Reentry by means of the automatic-descent system had been planned for the 17th orbit, but when trouble was discovered, Belyayev undertook a manual reentry on the 18th orbit. Korolev counted off the seconds until retrofire, and the command pilot fired the retrograde rockets high over Africa. *Voskhod II* overshot the recovery area, landing in a dense forest on the snow-covered slopes of the Urals. After hours of searching, helicopters dropped supplies to Belyayev and Leonov who spent that night in the snow.[37] While the USSR celebrated the rescue of the crew and Leonov's 12-minute sortie into the void of space, the U.S. team was preparing for the first manned Gemini flight.

On 23 March, Gus Grissom and John W. Young flew their spacecraft "Molly Brown" in a four-hour evaluation flight of the craft and launch vehicle. Grissom and Young established a space flight first by maneuvering in orbit. With the basic success of the first flight, the project gained momentum, permitting a routine launch nearly every other month throughout 1965 and 1966. There were difficulties, to be sure, but the simplified manufacture and checkout procedure permitted the maintenance of this busy schedule. Beginning on 3 June 1965, James A. McDivitt and Edward H. White II conducted a four-day mission aboard *Gemini IV*. This was the first long-duration flight, best remembered for White's 20-minute space walk. But *Gemini IV's* difficulties with a practice rendezvous meant that the next Gemini crew would be concerned with practicing that capability before the full-dress rendezvous planned for the sixth mission. Andre J. Meyer, Jr., of the Gemini Project Office commented, "There is a good explanation on what went wrong with rendezvous. . . ." The crew and some of the flight planners "just didn't understand or reason out the orbital mechanics involved. . . ."[38]

ASTRONAUT WHITE'S EVA

    On <u>Gemini IV</u>, the second Gemini mission of ten
in twenty <u>months</u>, Edward H. White made his 20-minute
"space walk," and used a hand-held thruster. (VIII-5)

Gemini V's first day in space was a worrisome one, during which a wire to a heater used to raise the pressure for the fuel cell operations was found to be faulty. Gordon Cooper powered down the craft and consulted with the ground, but the rendezvous evaluation pod with which *Gemini V* was to maneuver had already been released and drifted away. The crew had to practice rendezvous with coordinates radioed to them by Houston. Charles "Pete" Conrad, Jr., and Cooper would rendezvous with a phantom vehicle. The success of these "phantom rendezvous" made the flight planners more confident about the feasibility of bringing two manned spacecraft together. The next step was a rendezvous with an Agena target vehicle.

But plans went awry when the target vehicle exploded before going into orbit on 25 October 1965. The flight of *Gemini VI*, ready for launch with Walter M. Schirra, Jr., and Thomas P. Stafford was postponed. But three days of intensive deliberation led to a decision for a *Gemini VII/Gemini VI-A* rendezvous mission. The two-shot mission was inspired by the concern that the Soviets might be planning similar flights, as well as by the desire to turn a minor defeat into a major accomplishment.

> That a plan of such scope could be suggested, thought about, decided upon, and announced in scarcely three days was a sign of the managerial and technical trust that Gemini had already come to inspire. . . . the President's Press Secretary . . . said the mission was targeted for January but gave no specific date. Back at MSC, however, everyone from Gilruth on down was working toward an early December flight.[39]

After 38 days of extensive crew training and spacecraft preparation, the dual mission began on the afternoon of 4 December. For 11 days, Frank Borman and James A. Lovell, Jr., aboard *Gemini VII* carried out their tests on the effects of long duration in space. On the morning of 15 December, Schirra and Stafford were launched on the fifth manned Gemini flight and the first genuine rendezvous mission. During the ensuing six hours, Schirra and Stafford executed a series of maneuvers that brought *Gemini VI-A* closer to the Borman-Lovell craft. At 05:56:00 ground elapsed time, the two vehicles met in space with only 37 meters separating them; the first manned rendezvous was a fact.

For more than three revolutions of the Earth, the two spacecraft flew together, separated by ranges of 0.3 meters to 91 meters, while the crew of *VI-A* tested stationkeeping and flyaround techniques. After a sleep

234

period during which they had "parked" 16 kilometers away from the other craft, Schirra and Stafford prepared to go home. With a brief transmission, "Really a good job, Frank and Jim," Schirra flipped *VI-A* around, blunt-end forward, jettisoned the equipment section and waited for the automatic retrofire.[40] Two days later after some anxious moments over the fuel cell, *Gemini VII* returned safely to Earth, proving that man could work and survive in space for the length of time (14 days) that it would take him to travel to the moon and back.

Each of the five remaining Gemini flights strengthened the conviction and technical certainty that an American could land on the lunar surface and return before 1970. On 16 March 1966, Neil A. Armstrong and David R. Scott conducted the first manned docking when they nosed *Gemini VIII* into the docking adapter of an Agena target vehicle. But after they freed themselves from the Agena, a spacecraft thruster stuck open, sending the two astronauts into a dizzying ride through space. To restore stability, they were forced to use their reentry control thrusters; ground control told the crew to prepare for immediate reentry. While the early termination of the mission was exasperating, the crew did return safely. And they had proved that docking two spacecraft in orbit was possible.

Tom Stafford and Eugene A. Cernan rode *Gemini IX-A* into orbit on 3 June to work further on orbital maneuvers, but when they completed their first rendezvous with the target vehicle, they discovered a problem with the docking adapter that precluded the docking phase of the flight. They did continue rendezvous exercises, however, simulating the meeting of an Apollo command module with a lunar module in lunar orbit. Cernan also left the spacecraft to perform some experiments in zero g to get the feel of this new environment.

The final three Gemini flights, complex missions with multiple maneuvers, were designed to test rendezvous and docking, to explore more fully the problems of extravehicular activity, and to conduct other experiments that would yield information for Project Apollo. *Gemini X* and *XI* reduced the worry about radiation, demonstrating that it could be avoided during trips into deep space. *Gemini XI's* first-revolution rendezvous with an Agena target vehicle simulated the meeting of an Apollo command module and lunar module. The automatic reentry of these last two flights gave additional proof that man could return from long missions in space with both manual and automatic control over the final approaches to home. Less than two weeks after the splashdown of *Gemini XII*, the Soviets on 28 November 1966 launched *Cosmos 133*, an unamnned flight of their new generation spacecraft--Soyuz.

Soyuz--Development of the Space Station; Apollo--Voyage to the Moon

While Gemini personnel analyzed their efforts and prepared for new tasks, the Soviets were beginning the flight phase of Soyuz. In the 18 months between the last flight of Voskhod and the first unmanned test of Soyuz, the Soviet space program lost three important advocates. Premier Khrushchev had stepped down from his post on 14 October 1964; Voskresensky, Korolev's top assistant, had died on 15 December 1965; a month later the Chief Designer himself was dead.[41] While the new Soviet leaders reviewed the competitive space program they had inherited, the space design group continued the development of Soyuz.

Two elements appear to have slowed the initial pace of the Soyuz project. Soviet engineers needed time to perfect a new upper stage to provide sufficient power to launch the heavier Soyuz. And the political requirements to launch a multi-manned Voskhod had diverted them. By the end of 1966, the Soviets resolved their various design questions and launched a series of four Cosmos flights that led to the 23 April 1967 launch of *Soyuz 1*. According to the Soviets, the basic purpose of Soyuz was the ultimate development of an earth-orbiting space station; others still speculated that Soyuz was the Soviet entry in the race to the moon.[42]

Work on Soyuz combined elements both old and new. The spacecraft had three major components--the cosmonauts' cabin (descent vehicle), occupied during the launch and reentry phases of the flight; an orbital module, separated from the descent vehicle by an airtight hatch; and an instrument assembly module. The descent vehicle had evolved from the earlier Vostok and Voskhod spheres but was fitted with a new heatshield, which gave the cabin a bell-shaped external appearance. Soyuz was designed to have a stabilized and controlled reentry. The Soviet design team retained the form-fitting couches and equipped the descent vehicle with landing rockets beneath the heatshield, which was jettisoned shortly before touchdown.[43]

Nearly spherical in shape, the orbital module was designed to house equipment for scientific experiments and serve as an airlock for extravehicular activity. The crew would eat, rest and sleep here. Cameras, food, medicine and personal hygiene gear were stowed in the orbital compartment, which also had an oxygen generation system typical of those used in earlier Soviet spacecraft.

The cylindrical instrument module housed the two 3.9-kilonewton space-craft engines, the attitude control thrusters and onboard equipment that otherwise would have cluttered the interior of the spacecraft. In the pressurized portion of this compartment were the temperature controls for the cabins, the radio and telemetry transmitters, and the attitude control system. A set of solar panels attached to the instrument/equipment section provided electrical power during the mission. Protected by a shroud at launch, these panels unfolded once the craft reached orbit. The radio and radar antennas, also folded at launch, deployed subsequently.

Soyuz 1, a test mission, was flown with a crew of one, Vladimir Komarov. This initial mission was fraught with trouble and ended in disaster. The first indication of problems came on the second day of flight, 24 April 1967, when the spacecraft began to tumble during the 15th and 16th revolu-tions. Komarov experienced difficulty in bringing his ship under control, and as with *Voskhod II,* the automatic orientation system did not function properly. After communicating with the ground, Komarov decided to attempt a manual landing, but he was unable to obtain the proper orientation for retrofire. By the 18th orbit, he succeeded in bringing his craft under control and jettisoned the orbital and instrument assembly modules and fired the retroengines at the proper moment. But the Soyuz reentry vehicle continued to revolve about its axis, causing the shroud lines to become entangled when he attempted to deploy the parachute at 70 000 meters. With no parachute, the descent vehicle crashed to Earth at a velocity of 450 kilometers per hour. At 6:15 am, Komarov was dead.[44]

President Johnson and Vice-President Humphrey expressed their sadness at the loss of "this distinguished space pioneer." Just three months earlier on 27 January 1967, American astronauts, Grissom, White and Chaffe perished when fire swept their Apollo spacecraft as it underwent tests at KSC. NASA Administrator Webb suggested that Komarov's death and those of the Apollo astronauts indicated the need for closer cooperation between the two space programs. "Could the lives already lost have been saved if we had known each other's hopes, aspirations and plans? Or could they have been saved if full cooperation had been the order of the day?"[45] But the competitive motivation behind manned space flight still outweighed the desire to cooperate. While a special state commission investigated the Soyuz mishap, NASA and American aerospace industries were implementing the recommendations and changes contained in the report of the Apollo 204 Review Board.[46]

Apollo design and development had progressed with reasonable speed since the first consideration of that project in 1959. After 16 months of preliminary study and work, Robert Gilruth on 1 September 1960 called for the creation of an Apollo Projects Office, which would have the responsibility of defining the spacecraft configuration. The command center module became the crew quarters for all phases of the mission, and the propulsion module held all redundant and orbital maneuvering systems. This work preceded even the first manned flights of Project Mercury and the conception of Project Gemini.[47]

NASA and industry specialists were working to define Apollo when the President established the lunar goal. NASA had not yet issued spacecraft specs, selected a contractor, chosen a family of launch vehicles or settled the question of direct ascent versus orbital rendezvous for the voyage. During the next 18 months, several key decisions gave Apollo more form and direction. NASA selected the Instrument Laboratory of MIT to develop the guidance and navigation equipment. North American Aviation, Inc., was selected as prime contractor for the command and service modules. The Saturn C-5 was chosen as the Apollo launch vehicle. On 11 July 1962, the agency announced that lunar orbit rendezvous had been approved as the mission mode. Grumman Aircraft Engineering Corporation had already begun development of the second Apollo craft--the lunar excursion module.[48]

As it evolved through the processes of conceptualization, design and development, Apollo was composed of two parts, the command and service modules. Called CM for short, the command module was a multipurpose space cabin organized to function as a cockpit, office, laboratory, communications center, galley, sleeping quarters and personal hygiene center. It was constructed with an inner pressure shell to provide structural and environmental integrity and an outer wrap-around heatshield for thermal and

VEHICLES FOR DEVELOPMENT OF MANNED SPACE FLIGHT

REDSTONE   ATLAS   TITAN II   SATURN IB   SATURN V

MERCURY   GEMINI   APOLLO

radiation protection. This form of construction yielded maximum strength for minimum weight (5450 kg). Conical in shape, the CM was 3.23 meters high and 3.91 meters at the base. The service module (SM), which had an overall length of 7.54 meters and a launch weight of 23 950 kilograms, contained the main spacecraft propulsion system, reaction control system and most of the spacecraft consumables. Work on both the spacecraft and the launch vehicle during the years 1962-1966 progressed at a pace that permitted the first manned Apollo flight to be scheduled for February 1967. These plans were altered, however, when the flash fire occurred that year.

The End of the Space Race?

Both the Soviet and American space programs went through a period of appraisal and re-examination before they next sent men into space. After the Apollo fire, manned flight was delayed for 21 months while the command module was completely reworked. Unmanned flights were flown in November '67 (*Apollo 4*), January '68 (*Apollo 5*) and April '68 (*Apollo 6*) to check out the modified spacecraft. The Soviets carried out five unmanned launches prior to the joint *Soyuz 2* and *3* mission. On 27 October 1967, the USSR sent *Cosmos 186* into a low circular orbit, and three days later it performed an automatic rendezvous and docking mission with *Cosmos 188*, passing over Soviet territory in a docked configuration. The two spacecraft remained docked for 3.5 hours, after which they returned to Earth. A second automatic rendezvous and docking mission was conducted with *Cosmos 212* and *213* in April 1968, during which the docking was televised to ground control by onboard cameras. After a final check-flight with *Cosmos 238*, the Soviets launched *Soyuz 2*, which was to act as an unmanned target for G. T. Beregovoy, the pilot of *Soyuz 3*, who rode into orbit the following day on 26 October.[49] Beregovoy's mission remains unclear. After making an automatically controlled rendezvous, the cosmonaut took control of his craft and guided it from a distance of 200 meters to within only a few meters of *Soyuz 2*, but he did not dock.

In the wake of the successful October 1968 ten-day manned test flight of *Apollo 7*, with Walter M. Schirra, Donn F. Eisele and R. Walter Cunningham, NASA was planning to launch the first circumlunar mission. The December 1968 launch from Florida was a major step to realizing man's dream of traveling to the moon. *Apollo 8* demonstrated that the distance between the Earth and the moon could be safely traversed. On Christmas eve as they orbited the moon, Frank Borman, Jim Lovell and William A. Anders shared their impressions of the stark lunar landscape, read a few verses from the first chapter of Genesis and wished their Earth-bound viewers a Merry Christmas. In Houston, *Apollo 8* was viewed as the pivotal flight in the Apollo Program. Christopher C. Kraft, Jr., Director of Flight Operations, later stated:

> It proved so many things that had a bearing on the progress of the program--things that might have been disproved. The navigation to and from the moon, the ability of the spacecraft systems to survive the deep space environment, all hinged on the Apollo 8 mission.

He also believed that the flight changed the competitive position of the U.S. and the USSR in space. He had thought that "the Russians planned to fly a circumlunar mission, sending a manned spacecraft looping around and returning without orbiting the moon. That way they could say they sent the first man to the vicinity of the moon." Once *Apollo 8* made her voyage, "there was nothing left for them to do."[50]

But from the Soviet Union came another perspective. Academician Boris N. Petrov, Chairman of the Council for International Cooperation in Investigation and Utilization of Outer Space (Intercosmos) of the Soviet Academy of Sciences, called *Apollo 8* an "outstanding achievement of American space sciences and technology" and praised the "courage of its three astronauts." Petrov also indicated that the Soviet Union would continue to explore the moon, but with unmanned automatic spacecraft.[51] Had *Apollo 8* won the space race? Had the Soviets ever really been in the race to send a man to the moon?

Lunar Exploration, Earth Orbital Stations, and a Handshake in Space

During the six and a half years between the circumlunar flight of *Apollo 8* and the final mission of Apollo with Soyuz, both the United States and the Soviet Union continued their ambitious programs of manned spaceflight. American astronauts after the final orbital check-flight of *Apollo 9* made eight trips to the moon. *Apollo 10* went to within 13 kilometers of the lunar surface. With dress rehearsals and mission planning complete, *Apollo 11* touched down on the moon on 20 July 1969. After man's first historic steps on Earth's nearest neighbor, the NASA team sent seven

APOLLO 11
Astronaut Aldrin prepares to deploy early Apollo
scientific experiments package on the surface of the
moon during Apollo 11. (VIII-7 - NASA)

APOLLO 15
Astronaut Irwin with Rover vehicle, with Mount
Hadley in the background. (VIII-8 - NASA)

more expeditions to the moon. Six of these--*Apollo 13* was aborted due to an onboard explosion of an oxygen tank in the service module--conducted successively complex examinations of the moon.

Apollo 9	3-13 March 1969	McDivitt
		Scott
		Schweickart
Apollo 10	18-26 May 1969	Stafford
		Young
		Cernan
Apollo 11	16-24 July 1969	Armstrong
		Collins
		Aldrin
Apollo 12	14-24 November 1969	Conrad
		Gordon
		Bean
Apollo 13	11-17 April 1970	Lovell
		Swigert
		Haise
Apollo 14	31 January- 9 February 1971	Shepard
		Roosa
		Mitchell
Apollo 15	26 July- 7 August 1971	Scott
		Worden
		Irwin
Apollo 16	16-27 April 1972	Young
		Mattingly
		Duke
Apollo 17	7-19 December 1972	Cernan
		Evans
		Schmitt

In 1973-1974, NASA astronauts logged more that 513 man-days in Earth orbit during the three Skylab missions. Skylab had emerged from a desire to extend the usefulness of Apollo hardware in the post-lunar exploration period. Where the lunar expeditions had given man an opportunity to examine the moon first-hand, Skylab permitted three crews of three men each to conduct lengthy scientific studies of man in zero gravity, the planet Earth and its environment and resources, and a number of aspects of the solar system.[52]

In the same span of time, Soviet cosmonauts flew 15 Soyuz missions. *Soyuz 10* and *11* docked with the Soviet space station *Salyut 1*, which was about one third the size of Skylab. The deaths of the *Soyuz 11* crew caused by the failure of a pressure equalization valve during reentry resulted in a 15-month hiatus in flights while the problem was studied and

SKYLAB

Launched into orbit by a Saturn V, the Skylab
Orbital Workshop was the S-IVB third stage. Three
Skylab crews inhabited the orbital station, the last
one of which resided there for 84 days. (VIII-9)

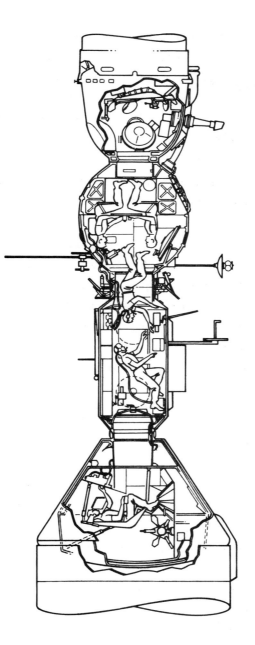

DOCKED APOLLO-SOYUZ TEST VEHICLE

Cutaway diagram showing crew transfer.
(VIII-10 - NASA)

alterations were made to the spacecraft. After the September 1973 checkout flight by the *Soyuz 13* crew, *Salyut 3* was successfully orbited and visited by the *Soyuz 14* and *15* crews. *Soyuz 16*, flown in December 1974, was a hardware test of the spacecraft as configured for the Apollo Soyuz Test Project. Talks concerning a joint mission had begun in October 1970 by representatives from NASA and the Soviet Academy of Sciences. Official government approvals of the project came at the May 1972 Nixon-Kosygin Summit. While work continued on the preparation for the first international rendezvous and docking mission, the Soviets also continued their Salyut-Soyuz flight program. By mid-1976, they had flown four more Soyuz missions, two each to successively updated space stations.

When Tom Stafford and Alexi Leonov shook hands high over Europe on 17 July 1975, they effectively brought to a close the age of rivalry in space and opened a hatchway to greater cooperation between the United States and the Soviet Union. The cornerstone had been laid, but it remains uncertain if the two nations will build anything upon this foundation. ASTP was also the final flight of Apollo--the end of an era in American flight history.

Shuttle: The Next Stage

The next time an American flies into orbit (March 1979), it will be aboard the Shuttle Orbiter. All three previous generations of U.S. spacecraft--Mercury, Gemini and Apollo-- have been single-flight vehicles, carefully tailored to specific missions. In these essentially experimental craft, the NASA team has mastered the problems of orbital and cislunar flight and has proven that man can work effectively under zero gravity conditions if provided with the correct hardware. But knowing that truly economical space flight would be possible only when spacecraft could be flown on multiple missions, NASA had begun the search for a reusable vehicle in the late 1960s. Space Shuttle grew out of that quest.

About the size of the DC-9 jet, Shuttle has been called the DC-3 of space because it promises to bring into being economical, routine and reliable space flight. Consisting of three major elements--an orbiter; an external booster; and solid-rocket, strap-on boosters--Shuttle is designed for a crew of four and up to six payload specialists. With a payload bay

SPACE SHUTTLE

Artist's rendering in 1974 of the Space Shuttle (now named "The Enterprise"), which is placing a Tug and payload into earth orbit as a prelude to the Tug placing the payload into synchronous orbit. (VIII-11)

18 meters in length and 4.5 meters in diameter, Shuttle will have the capacity to carry a 30 000-kilogram cargo. Shuttle will carry cargoes from many nations--most notably the European Space Agency's Spacelab, now under development. Initially, the orbiter will be able to stay in space for seven days at a time; ultimately that period will be expanded to 30 days. If anything like the 60 flights a year now predicted for Shuttle actually are flown, then space flight will become common place instead of spectacular. As yesteryear's barnstormers yielded to professional commerical pilots and engineers, yesterday's astronauts will yield to Shuttle flight crews and mission specialists.

SOURCE NOTES

1. Frederick C. Durant III, "Space Flight Needs Only Money, Time," *Aviation Week*, 27 September 1954, p. 46. On 14 July 1952, the executive committee of the National Advisory Committee for Aeronautics passed a resolution that "NACA devote modest efforts to problems of unmanned and manned flights at altitudes from 50 miles to infinity and at speeds from Mach 10 to escape from the earth's gravity." Letter, NACA to High Speed Flight Research Station, "Discussion of Possible Changes to the X-2 Airplane to Extend Its Speed and Altitude Range," 30 July 1953, which contains the NACA directive

2. Von Braun, Haber and Ley had been long-term advocates of space flight, and as early as 1952, they had contributed articles to a *Collier's* symposium entitled, "Man will conquer space soon." The articles included Wernher von Braun, "Crossing the Last Frontier," pp. 24-29 and 72-74; Willy Ley, "A Station in Space," pp. 30-31; Fred L. Whipple, "The Heavens Open," pp. 32-33; Joseph Kaplan, "This Side of Infinity," p. 34; Heinz Haber, "Can We Survive in Space," pp. 35 and 65-67; and Oscar Schachter, "Who Owns the Universe?" pp. 36 and 70-71, *Collier's*, 22 March 1952.

3. Letter, Kyril F. Ogorodnikov to Durant, 23 September 1955; letter, Leonid I. Sedov to Durant, 24 September 1955; Durant, "Impressions of the Sixth Astronautical Congress," *Jet Propulsion* 25 (December 1955):738; and interview (via telephone), Durant-Edward C. Ezell, 13 December 1974.

4. Maxime A. Faget, *Manned Space Flight* (New York, 1965), p. 8.

5. Loyd S. Swenson, Jr., James M. Grimwood and Charles C. Alexander, *This New Ocean: A History of Project Mercury*, NASA SP-4201 (Washington, 1966); and S. P. Umansky, *Chelovek na kosmicheskoy orbite* (Moscow, 1974), pp. 31-32, available in translation as *Man in Space Orbit*, NASA Technical Translation F-15973.

6. Swenson, Grimwood and Alexander, *This New Ocean*, pp. 36-39; and "Problemy nevesomosti" [The problems of weightlessness], *Nauka i Zhizn'* 22 (December 1955):17-20, translated in F. J. Krieger, *Behind the Sputniks: A Survey of Soviet Space Science* (Washington, 1958), pp. 127-133.

7. David G. Simons, "Use of V-2 Rocket to Convey Primate to Upper Atmosphere," Air Force Tech. Report 5821, Air Material Command, Wright-Patterson Air Force Base, OH, May 1949; J. P. Henry, E. R. Ballinger, P. J. Maher and D. G. Simons, "Animal Studies of the Subgravity State during Rocket Flight," *The Journal of Aviation Medicine* 23 (October 1952):421-432; and D. G. Simons, "Review of Biological Effects of Subgravity and Weightlessness," *Jet Propulsion* 25 (May 1955):209-211.

8. Evgeny Riabchikov, *Russians in Space*, ed. Nikolai P. Kamanin, trans. Guy Daniels (Garden City, NY, 1971), pp. 140-142 and 149-151; and A. V. Pokrovskii, "Comment se comportent les animaux a 100 km d'altitude" [How animals behave at an altitude of 100 km], *Etudes Sovietiques*, no. 106 (January 1957):65-70, translated in Krieger, *Behind the Sputniks*, pp. 156-163.

9. Umansky, *Chelovek na kosmicheskoy orbite*, p. 49.

10. Ibid., pp. 50-54; Faget, *Manned Space Flight*, pp. 98-100; Swenson, Grimwood and Alexander, *This New Ocean*, pp. 231 and 558, note 21; and Eugene B. Konecci, "Soviet Bioastronautics--1964," paper, National Space Club, Washington, 15 December 1964, pp. 4-7.

11. Umansky, *Chelovek na kosmicheskoy orbite*, pp. 50-51; and Faget, *Manned Space Flight*, pp. 100-102.

12. Swenson, Grimwood and Alexander, *This New Ocean*, pp. 225-233; and Frank H. Samonski, Jr., *Technical History of the Environmental Control System for Project Mercury*, NASA Technical Note D-4126 (Langley, VA, 1967).

13. P. T. Astashenkov, *Akademik S. P. Korolev* (Moscow, 1969), available in translation as *Academician S. P. Korolev, Biography*, Foreign Technology Division edited translation HC-23-542-70, pp. 185-186; and Konstantin P. Feoktistov, "Razvitie sovetskikh pilotruemuikh kosmicheskikh korablei," *Aviatsiya i Kosmonavtika*, no. 11 (1971):36-37, available in translation as "Development of Soviet Manned Spacecraft," National Lending Library for Science and Technology, Boston Spa, Yorkshire, England, and available from NASA as N73-15876.

14. Astashenkov, *Academician S. P. Korolev, Biography*, pp. 185-186; letter, Hartley A. Soule to James M. Grimwood, 29 August 1965; Swenson, Grimwood and Alexander, *This New Ocean*, pp. 71-72; and Ames Aeronautical Laboratory, "Preliminary Investigation of a New Airplane for Exploring the Problems of Efficient Hypersonic Flight," 18 January 1957.

15. USSR Academy of Sciences, comp., *Kosmicheskiy korabl' Vostok* (Moscow, 1969), available in translation as *The Spaceship Vostok*, Foreign Tech-

nology Division edited translation HT-23-705-70, pp. 5-6; and Leonid Vladimirov, *The Russian Space Bluff*, trans. David Floyd (London, 1971), pp. 89-91.

16. H. Julian Allen, "Hypersonic Flight and the Reentry Problem," *Journal of the Aeronautical Sciences* 25 (April 1958):217-230; Alfred J. Eggers, Jr., "Performance of Long Range Hypervelocity Vehicles," *Jet Propulsion* 27 (November 1957):1147-1151; and Swenson, Grimwood and Alexander, *This New Ocean*, pp. 55-82.

17. Swenson, Grimwood and Alexander, *This New Ocean*, pp. 68-69.

18. Robert R. Gilruth, "Memoir: From Wallops Island to Mercury; 1945-1958," paper, Sixth International History of Astronautics Symposium, Vienna, Austria, 13 October 1972, pp. 31-32.

19. Swenson, Grimwood and Alexander, *This New Ocean*, p. 86; Grimwood, *Project Mercury: A Chronology*, NASA SP-4001 (Washington, 1963), p. 17; "How Mercury Capsule Design Evolved," *Aviation Week*, 21 September 1959, pp. 52-53, 55 and 57; and David A. Anderton, "How Mercury Capsule Design Evolved," *Aviation Week*, 22 May 1961, pp. 50-71 passim.

20. Faget, Benjamin J. Garland and James J. Buglia, "Preliminary Studies of Manned Satellites--Wingless Configuration: Nonlifting," in "NACA Conference on High-Speed Aerodynamics, Ames Aeronautical Laboratory, Moffett Field, CA., March 18, 19, and 20, 1958: A Compilation of Papers Presented," pp. 9-34, reissued as NASA Tech. Note D-1254 (Langley, VA, 1962).

21. Grimwood, *Project Mercury: A Chronology*, pp. 19-24.

22. Gilruth, "Memoir: From Wallops Island to Mercury," p. 37.

23. Feoktistov, "Razvitie sovetskikh pilotruemuikh kosmicheskikh korablei," p. 37; Astashenkov, *Academician S. P. Korolev, Biography*, pp. 187-190; Riabchikov, *Russians in Space*, p. 155; and Vladimirov, *The Russian Space Bluff*, p. 89.

24. Feoktistov, "Razvitie sovetskikh pilotruemuikh kosmicheskikh korablei," p. 37.

25. Swenson, Grimwood and Alexander, *This New Ocean*, pp. 341-511.

26. Barton C. Hacker and Grimwood, "On the Shoulders of Titans: A History of Project Gemini," NASA SP-4203, in press, p. xiii.

27. Ibid.; Hacker, "The Idea of Rendezvous: From Space Station to Orbital Operations in Space-Travel Thought, 1895-1951," *Technology and Culture* 15 (July 1974):373-388; and John M. Logsdon, "Selecting the Way to the Moon: The Choice of the Lunar Orbital Rendezvous Mode," *Aerospace Historian* 18 (June 1971):63-70.

28. James A. Chamberlin, "Project Gemini Design Integration," Lecture 36

in a series on engineering design and operation of manned spacecraft, presented during summer, 1963, at the Manned Spacecraft Center and to graduate classes at Louisiana State University, the University of Houston and Rice University. The series was later edited and published as Chapter 35 in Paul E. Purser, Faget and Norman F. Smith, eds., *Manned Spacecraft: Engineering Design and Operations* (New York, 1964), pp. 365-374.

29. The Soviets are relatively vague in their descriptions of Voskhod and its development. See Astashenkov, *Academician S. P. Korolev, Biography*, pp. 226-230; and Riabchikov, *Russians in Space*, pp. 207-211. Vladimirov, *The Russian Space Bluff*, pp. 123-127 argues that Khrushchev wanted a space mission that would surpass the accomplishments promised by Gemini.

30. Apparently, the Soviets employed the Venus upper stage to launch the Voskhod. Peter Sullivan, "The Voskhod Spacecraft," *Spaceflight* 16 (November 1974):407-408, speculates that Korolev and his colleagues had to extemporize due to the tight schedule imposed upon them.

31. Vladimirov, *The Russian Space Bluff*, pp. 125-126; and statement, Hugh L. Dryden to PAO (dictated via telephone), 12 October 1964.

32. Sullivan, "The Voskhod Spacecraft," pp. 4050406; and interview, Willard M. Taub-Ezell, 28 February 1975.

33. Riabchikov, *Russians in Space*, p. 208; and Astashenkov, *Academician S. P. Korolev, Biography*, pp. 227-228.

34. U.S., Congress, Senate, Committee on Aeronautical and Space Sciences, *Soviet Space Programs, 1966-1970; Goals and Purposes, Organizations, Resources, Facilities and Hardware, Manned and Unmanned Flight Programs, Bioastronautics, Civil and Military Applications, Projections of Future Plans, Attitudes Toward International Cooperation and Space Law; Staff Report,* 92d Cong., 1st sess., 1971, p. 186.

35. Riabchikov, *Russians in Space*, pp. 210-211. Also see memo, M. Scott Carpenter to Gilruth et al., "Cosmonaut Training," 24 November 1964.

36. There has been considerable speculation as to the cause of *Cosmos 57*'s disintegration; e.g., William J. Normyle, "Cosmos 57 Believed Destroyed by Soviets," *Aviation Week and Space Technology*, 12 April 1965, p. 34.

37. U.S., Congress, Senate, Committee on Aeronautical and Space Sciences, *Soviet Space Programs, 1962-1965; Goals and Purposes, Achievements, Plans, and International Implications; Staff Report,* 89th Cong., 2d sess., 1966, p. 207; and Peter L. Smolders, *Soviets in Space; The Story of the Salyut and the Soviet Approach to Present and Future Space Travel* (London, 1973), pp. 144-145.

38. Hacker and Grimwood, "On the Shoulders of Titans," p. 447a.

39. Ibid., p. 497.

40. Ibid., p. 528.

41. Vladimirov, *The Russian Space Bluff*, pp. 136-137, 140-141 and 145.

42. The "moon" or "space race" has been a topic of continuing debate and a subject of considerable speculation. A sample of views are included here in the absence of a definitive Soviet statement. The Novosti Press book by Riabchikov, *Russians in Space*, does not address the space race question but indicates that the Soviets were concentrating on earth-orbital missions that would lead to the development of a space station. This thesis is reemphasized in the 1973 edition of Smolders, *Soviets in Space*. The Soviet emigre Vladimirov wrote *The Russian Space Bluff* to argue that the limited technical capability of the Soviet space program could not have possibly sent men to the moon and that the whole program was inspired by Khrushchev's desire to gain a propaganda advantage over the U.S. Nicholas Danilov in *The Kremlin and the Cosmos* (New York, 1972), suggests that after Khrushchev's ouster there was a retreat from the competitive posture and that the Soviet leadership opted instead for a two-part space program--automatic spacecraft for lunar and planetary exploration and manned craft for earth-orbital missions.

43. A. Yu. Dmitriyev et al., *Ot komicheskikh korabley-k orbital'nymm stantsiyam*, 2d ed. (Moscow, 1961), pp. 24-25, available in translation as *From Spaceships to Orbiting Stations*, NASA Technical Trans. F-812; and interview, Faget-Ertel and Grimwood, 15 December 1969.

44. Dmitriyev et al., *Ot komicheskikh*, pp. 26-28; and Smolders, *Soviets in Space*, pp. 151 and 154-159.

45. Memo, Julian Scheer to HQ Program and Staff Offices, 24 April 1967; and NASA News Release, HQ [unnumbered], "Russian Accident Statement," 24 April 1967.

46. Smolders, *Soviets in Space*, p. 160; and NASA, Apollo 204 Review Board, "Report of Apollo 204 Review Board to the Administrator, National Aeronautics and Space Administration," 5 April 1967. Uri Marinin, "Where Does Danger Lurk?" *Space World* D-5-41 (May 1967):43-44, presents a Soviet commentary on the Apollo 204 fire and the dangers inherent in a 100% oxygen system.

47. The details of the Apollo spacecraft story will be documented in Courtney G. Brooks, Grimwood and Swenson, "Chariots for Apollo: A History of the Lunar Spacecraft," in process. Until that official history is available, there are four very useful chronologies: Ertel and Mary L. Morse, *The Apollo Spacecraft: A Chronology, Vol. I, through November 7, 1962*, NASA SP-4009 (Washington, 1969); Morse and Jean K. Bays, *The Apollo Spacecraft: A Chronology, Vol. II, November 8, 1962-September 30, 1964*, NASA SP-4009 (Washington, 1973); Ertel and Brooks, *The Apollo Spacecraft: A Chronology, Vol. III, October 1, 1964-January 20, 1966*, NASA SP-4009 (Washington, 1976); and Ertel and

Roland W. Newkirk, with Brooks, "The Apollo Spacecraft: A Chronology, Vol. IV, January 21, 1966-March 4, 1974," in process.

48. Ertel and Morse, *Apollo Chronology, Vol. I*, pp. 106, 128, 135 and 168; Morse and Bays, *Apollo Chronology, Vol. II*, p. 5.

49. Viktor P. Legostayev and B. V. Raushenbakh, "Avtomaticheskaya sborka v kosmose," paper, 19th Cong. of the IAF, New York,, December 1968, available in translation as "Automatic assmebly in space," NASA Technical Trans. F 12, 113.

50. "Apollo 8 Called Key Flight Space Program," *Baltimore Sun*, 24 November 1972.

51. "Soviet Scientist Hails Apollo 'Courage' and Skill," *New York Times*, 31 December 1968; "Soviet Cautious on Moon Flights," *Baltimore Sun*, 31 December 1968; and Boris N. Petrov, "O polete Apollona-8" [On the flight of Apollo 8], *Pravda*, 30 December 1968.

52. Edgar M. Cortright, *Apollo Expeditions to the Moon*, NASA SP-350 (Washington, 1975); and W. David Compton and Charles D. Benson, "Skylab: A History," in process. *

---

* Editor's Note: Details on all U.S. manned space missions are to be found in Appendix C, which was included as a concise chronological reference.

PART IV — COMMENTARY

IX - PERSPECTIVES OF A HISTORIAN OF TECHNOLOGY

Thomas Parke Hughes

THE NASA LOGO

(1959-1975)

I X

PERSPECTIVES OF A HISTORIAN OF TECHNOLOGY

A COMMENTARY

Thomas Parke Hughes*

        This is my first opportunity to visit the National
Air and Space Museum. After this short visit, it is to me an
extremely intelligent, very sensitive, and bold statement.
All of us can be proud of what we have here on the Mall. I
want to thank the host of this meeting. I also would like to
express the appreciation of the group, to Michael Collins,
and also Mr. Lopez, Mr. Durant, Mr. Garber, and others associated with the museum who have been interested enough to have
this symposium.

        It is something of a celebration during our
Bicentennial. It is also a workshop for historians. My contribution will be along the lines of a workshop. I am a
critic. I am not celebrating what I heard although I have
enjoyed it very much.

        By way of introduction to my comments, I want to
place what has been said today in a broader perspective.
Several of the speakers have lamented the chore of condensing
fifteen or seventy years of history into twenty minutes.
Seventy years is not a large amount of time. Nor is the
subject an overwhelmingly significant one; that is, aeronautics and astronautics. I am compelled to say -- perhaps
because Gene Emme reminded me that I have a degree in modern
European history -- that we should look in the other end of
the telescope. We are dealing here with a very short period
of time and one episode in a long history of man and technology. From this point of view, a few comments.

        For one, we can expect a number of changes. We
tend to be present minded and, looking at the beautiful and
complex devices in this museum, we say, as sophisticated as
we are, "gee whiz." We tend to think this is the end, we
are the generation that has arrived.

────────────────
*Professor of History, University of Pennsylvania.

257

It is good exercise for all of us to look at things in a longer perspective. Historians have the responsibility of asking you to take this exercise. Project ahead one hundred years. The spacecraft, the airplanes you have seen projected on the screen this morning, the 747, and this afternoon, the Soyuz and the Apollo -- look at them one hundred years in the future. They may look like a DC-3, or an American locomotive of the late nineteenth century, does today. Taking this perspective relaxes us somewhat about the present and our responsibilities, and, perhaps, introduces some needful humility.

What we are discussing today is but one episode in the use of the air for transportation. If one considers the use of water for transportation, there have been thousands of years of change. There were dramatic changes four hundred years ago, fifty years ago, seven hundred years ago, and there will be dramatic changes in water transportation in the future. If one looks at the land as a way of transportation, there have been millenia of changes in the use of it. There will undoubtedly be dramatic changes in air transportation and exploration in air and outer space. We have considered only a century or so of changes in this mode.

Another reaction from the long-range perspective: Over the long years, centers of activity have shifted. We have been talking about a period in which the United States, and to some extent when talking about space, the Soviet Union, has been the center of attention, the focus of our interest. This too probably will change. One interested in the history of technology will study Italy during the Renaissance, France during the Age of Enlightenment, Britain in the Industrial Revolution, and America in the heroic age of invention, and so on. The attention shifts with the significance and density of the activity.

So we must prepare ourselves intellectually -- and I think it interesting to do so -- to witness the change of the center of technology with regard to the use of air and space from one country to other countries.

Also from perspectives of the historian, I think enough has not been said about the conditions that influenced the shape of an artifact. An impression is left -- despite some of the speakers having introduced qualifications -- that technology has an internal dynamic. We have gone through a rather lengthy listing of this airplane and that airplane, this spacecraft and that spacecraft, as if these follow one from another. I think many historians would agree, and archaeologists, and cultural anthropologists would certainly agree, that these artifacts are expressions of culture. As the culture changes, the artifacts may well change in step with the culture rather than imagined internal dynamics or logic of technology. Therefore, if one looks at the changing configurations of the spacecraft, one might consider the possibility they are manifestations of changing political configurations, social configurations, and values. One cannot explain the evolution of technology simply by looking at the technology.

Finally, with regard to perspectives, we have not heard much about individuals today. There is a debate in the academic world, especially among young historians, about the role of the individual. They argue that we have given too much attention to individuals. Today, we have certainly not violated their sensibilities. Perhaps we should have heard more about individuals, thus introducing a human scale into our considerations. Individuals have a great deal to do with the particular shape of technology, with the way it has been used, with the miserable failures and with the courageous successes.

So my position and perspective as a historian commenting upon both a celebratory occasion and a workshop has generated a tension and caused me to see paradoxes. I suggested, for instance, that the tone today is present-minded and exaggerates present achievements. Yet I ask for more attention to the individuals responsible for the achievements. I argue that we should take a historical perspective, but then insist that the history of aeronautics and astronautics is such a short one that we must look into a distant future to obtain the proper scale for comparing air and space transportation with the land and water mode. I have obviously been delighted by the emphasis upon technical advances or sequences in this Museum and in the papers, but I lament the lack of more attention to the societal forces that intervene in and interrupt these presumed linear developments. Yet the paradoxes should stand, for the history with which we have dealt today is layered with all the complexity and contradiction that we easily accept in other human endeavors like politics, business, architecture, and art. Papers and discussion we have heard today are, I believe in sum, a contribution to the art of writing history of this kind.

APPENDICES

APPENDIX A: U.S. SCIENTIFIC SPACE MISSIONS

      . Lunar

      . Planetary

      . Interplanetary

      . Astronomical

      . Life Science

      Prepared by Gary Cox, Jet Propulsion Laboratory, who also prepared Appendix B.

APPENDIX B: U.S. APPLICATIONS MISSIONS

      . Military

      . Communications

      . Technology

      . Earth Resources

      . Geodetic

APPENDIX C: U.S. MANNED SPACE MISSIONS - A Chronology,

      1961-1976

      Prepared by Leonard C. Bruno, Science and Technology Division of the Library of Congress.

APPENDIX A

SCIENTIFIC MISSIONS

TYPE	NAME	DATE OF LAUNCH	USING AGENCY	REMARKS
	Pioneers 1-4	Oct. 1958–Mar. 1959	AFBMD-NASA ABMA-NASA	Pioneers 1-2 were joint NASA-AFBMD ventures; Pioneers 3-4 were joint NASA-ABMA ventures. Pioneer 1 failed to escape the Earth's gravitational attraction, it nonetheless furnished data on terrestrial micrometeorite density and radiation; Pioneer 2 similarly failed to escape; Pioneer 3 also failed to escape, but discovered a second belt in the radiation field; Pioneer 4 missed the Moon by 37,000 miles and entered solar orbit.
LUNAR	Rangers 3-5 (Block II)	Jan. 26, 1962 Apr. 23, 1962	NASA	Rangers 3-5 were designed to achieve lunar impact at a pre-selected site and test ground and spacecraft control systems; they carried an approach TV camera, gamma ray spectrometer, single-axis seismometer, and surface scanning pulse radar. Ranger 3 missed the Moon by 20,000 miles; Ranger 4 crashed on the dark side without returning data; Ranger 5 lost power and missed the Moon by 450 miles.

SCIENTIFIC MISSIONS

TYPE	NAME	DATE OF LAUNCH	USING AGENCY	REMARKS
	Rangers 6-9 (Block III)	Jan. 1964 – Mar. 1965	NASA	Rangers 6-9 were designed to return pictures of at least an order of magnitude better resolution than Earth-based cameras to benefit planetary science and the Apollo program. Ranger 6 impacted on the Moon but failed to return pictures; Ranger 7 provided the first closeup photos of the moon; Ranger 8 returned 7,137 photos; Ranger 9 provided the first live televised pictures of the moon, and 5,814 pictures.
LUNAR	Surveyors 1-7	May 1966 – Jan. 1968	NASA	Surveyors 1-7 were designed to demonstrate techniques of soft landing and gather data on the bearing strength and soil mechanics of the lunar surface. Surveyor 1 made a fully controlled automatic soft landing on the Moon and took 10,338 photos the first lunar day, and 899 in the second; Surveyor 2 crashed without taking photos; Surveyor 3 carried a soil scooper to test physical properties of the soil; Surveyor 5 took approximately 20,000 photos; soil analysis showed soil chemistry to be of basaltic origin; Surveyor 6 made the first liftoff from the moon; Surveyor 7 sent over 21,000 photos and detected a small amount of iron-

SCIENTIFIC MISSIONS

TYPE	NAME	DATE OF LAUNCH	USING AGENCY	REMARKS
LUNAR	Lunar Orbiters 1-5	Aug. 1966 – Aug. 1967	NASA	group elements.

Objectives: Orbit the Moon to obtain geographic and geologic data to confirm Apollo landing gear design, and locate candidate landing sites; also equipped to record micrometeorite hits. Lunar Orbiter 5 had the additional task of photographing 99% of the front side at resolution at least 10 times better than possible from Earth. |
| PLANETARY | Mariner Venus Missions (2&5) | Aug. 27, 1962 Jun. 14, 1967 | NASA | Mariner 2 was designed to study Venus' surface temperature, cloud structure, and magnetic field, as well as charged particles and cosmic dust in the interplanetary medium; it was the first machine to fly by another planet; it discovered a high surface temperature, and found no Venusian magnetic field. Mariner 5 carried similar instruments, and also measured the structure of the upper atmosphere of Venus. |

SCIENTIFIC MISSIONS

TYPE	NAME	DATE OF LAUNCH	USING AGENCY	REMARKS
	Mariner Mars Missions (4,6, 7 & 9)	Nov. 11, 1964 Feb. 25, 1969 Mar. 27, 1969 May 28, 1971	NASA	Mariner 4 flew past Mars and studied space radiation, dust, magnetic fields, and returned 22 television pictures of the Martian surface. Mariner 6 on a flyby trajectory obtained infrared and ultraviolet spectra of the atmosphere, and measured atmospheric pressures and densities, as well as surface temperature; it returned 76 pictures. Mariner 7 was identical to Mariner 6, and returned 126 pictures, 33 of the south-polar region. Mariner 9 was the first spacecraft to orbit another planet; it made measurements of the atmosphere, surface, and gravity field, and returned 7,329 photos of the atmosphere, clouds, and Martian satellites.
PLANETARY	Pioneer Jupiter-Saturn Missions (10 & 11)	Mar. 2, 1972 Apr. 5, 1973	NASA	Pioneer 10 used a gravity assisted trajectory, and will eventually escape the solar system; it investigated the interplanetary medium and the Jovian magnetosphere and atmosphere, and returned more than 300 pictures of Jovian clouds and satellites. Pioneer 11, after its Jupiter encounter in December 1974, is en route for the first Saturn encounter in September 1979, and

SCIENTIFIC MISSIONS

TYPE	NAME	DATE OF LAUNCH	USING AGENCY	REMARKS
	Mariner Venus–Mercury (10)	Nov. 3, 1973	NASA	will also exit the solar system. Mariner 10 was the first Mercury probe; its photos revealed an intensely cratered planet with a huge iron-rich core; the spacecraft also took over 4000 photos of Venus. Mariner 10 reencountered Mercury in September 1974, and March 1975.
PLANETARY	Viking Mars Missions (1 & 2)	Aug. 20, 1975 Sep. 9, 1975	NASA	Each Viking spacecraft consisted of one orbiter and one lander; the machines have studied the atmosphere, photographed the surface, and investigated the geology and chemistry of Mars, as well as tested the soil for signs of life; to date, some 5,000 photos have been returned by all 4 vehicles.
	Mariner Jupiter-Saturn Missions (11 & 12)	Launches scheduled for Aug. 1977 and Sep. 1977	NASA	The MJS missions are intended to study the two outer planets and their 23 satellites, and measure the interplanetary medium out to Saturn; 20,000 photographs are planned.
	Pioneer Venus Missions (12 & 13)	Scheduled launches for May 1978 and Aug. 1978	NASA	Pioneer 12 is planned to orbit Venus and study the interaction of the atmosphere with the solar wind over a 243-day period; Pioneer 13 will

TYPE	NAME	DATE OF LAUNCH	USING AGENCY	REMARKS
				release 3 small probes toward the surface to study the atmosphere before landing.
	Explorer 1-8 (Initial Series)	Jan. 1958 Nov. 1959	ABMA, ARPA, NASA	Explorer 1, launched Jan. 31, 1958, the first U.S. satellite, discovered one of the radiation belts around the Earth. The next successful Explorers 3 and 4, under the Advanced Research Projects Agency (ARPA was assigned temporary responsibility for the U.S. space program on February 7, 1958) provided data on the radiation belts, micrometeorite impact, and temperature. Explorer 6 fell under NASA jurisdiction, and acquired radiation data and transmitted crude cloud cover images. Explorers 7 and 8 studied geophysical radiation, magnetic storms, the ionosphere, and micrometeorites.
INTERPLANETARY MEDIUM	Vanguard 1-3	Mar. 17, 1958 Feb. 17, 1959 Sep. 18, 1959	NRL, NASA	Vanguard 1, the second U.S. satellite, determined that the Earth is slightly pear-shaped. Vanguard 3 surveyed the Earth's magnetic field and detailed the lower edge of the radiation belts; Vanguard 2 was unsuccessful.

SCIENTIFIC MISSIONS

TYPE	NAME	DATE OF LAUNCH	USING AGENCY	REMARKS
	Explorers 9-17	Feb 1961 – Apr. 1963	NASA	Explorer was chosen in 1958 to be a generic term for a series of scientific satellites designed to explore the space medium. Experiments included measurements of the radiation belts; atmospheric pressures, density, and temperatures; gamma radiation; solar plasma, and micrometeroids.
INTERPLANETARY MEDIUM	Explorers 18-28 30-35*	Nov. 1963 – Jul. 1967	NASA	Continuing investigations of the space medium, Explorers 18, 21, 28, 33, 34, and 35 were the first of ten Interplanetary Monitoring Platform (IMP) intended for high eccentricity Earth orbit or a lunar orbit to study the cislunar magnetic field, solar wind, and cosmic radiation. Explorers 24 and 25 were launched by the same vehicle to take atmospheric and particle data in the same region of space; Explorer 30 was a Solrad satellite developed by NRL and launched by NASA to study the Sun's x-ray emissions and compare the intensity vs. time history of solar flares, as a contribution to the IQSY.

*Explorers 29 and 36, designed for geodetic research, were renamed Geos 1 and 2; see Geodetic Civilian Applications Missions, Appendix B.

SCIENTIFIC MISSIONS

TYPE	NAME	DATE OF LAUNCH	USING AGENCY	REMARKS
	Explorers 37-41 43-47 48-52* 54-55	Mar. 1968 – Nov. 1975	NASA	Explorers 41, 43, 47, and 50 completed the IMP series; 37 and 44 were additional Solrad satellites; 39 and 40 were launched together in the same fashion with the same purpose as 24 and 25; 25 and 40, designed by the University of Iowa as part of their Injun series, studied particles trapped in the magnetosphere; Explorer 52 (also named Hawkeye 1) completed the U of I series.
	Pioneer 5	Mar. 11, 1960	NASA	Pioneer 5 measured solar flares, particle energies and distributions, and magnetic fields in the space between Earth and Venus.
INTERPLANETARY MEDIUM	Pioneers 6-9	Dec. 1965 – Nov. 1968	NASA	Pioneers 6-9 were intended to study the solar wind stream, magnetic field, and plasmas, as well as observe extragalactic cosmic rays and differentiate between those from outside the Solar System.
	OGO Series (1-6)	Sep. 1964 – Jun 1969	NASA	The Orbiting Geophysical Observatories carried a versatile set of experiments into Earth orbit; they concentrated on solar wind, solar

*Explorers 42, 48, and 53 were small astronomical satellites; see Astronomical Missions, this Appendix.

SCIENTIFIC MISSIONS

TYPE	NAME	DATE OF LAUNCH	USING AGENCY	REMARKS
INTERPLANETARY MEDIUM				flares, magnetic fields, radiation belts, atmospheric phenomena, plasma in interplanetary medium, near Earth environment, and the neutral, ionic, and electrical composition of the Earth's atmosphere. OGO 1, 3, and 5 were launched into highly elliptical orbits, OGO 2, 4 and 6 into near-Polar orbits.
	OSO 1-8	Mar. 1962 – Jun. 1975	NASA	Eight Orbiting Solar Observatories have been launched into Earth orbit to study the Sun and its influence on the Earth's atmosphere during most of a solar cycle. They examined successfully the solar atmosphere and radiation in the UV, EUV, and visible range, and took the first full-disc photograph of the solar corona.
ASTRONOMICAL	OAO 1, 2, 3	Apr. 18, 1966 Dec. 7, 1968 Aug. 29, 1972	NASA	The Orbiting Astronomical Observatories were equipped to study UV, and gamma radiation, stellar sources, and matter in interstellar space. OAO 1 failed after two days in orbit. OAO 2 took the first UV photographs of stars and the largest telescope ever placed in orbit. OAO 3 successfully continued the work of OAO 2.

TYPE	NAME	DATE OF LAUNCH	USING AGENCY	REMARKS
ASTRONOMICAL	HEAO 1-3	Launches scheduled in 1977, 1978 and 1979	NASA	The High Energy Astronomy Observatory is scheduled to make an x-ray survey. The second HEAO is to detail the x-ray studies, and the third HEAO is to survey gamma and cosmic rays. After the 1980s, space shuttle launches of HEAO will carry heavier gamma and cosmic ray experiments.
	SAS A, B, C	Dec. 12, 1970 Nov. 15, 1972 May 7, 1975	NASA	The Small Astronomy Satellites, A, B, and C, also designated Explorers 42, 48, and 53, respectively, were launched by an Italian team from the San Marcos platform off the coast of Kenya, and have observed and catalogued almost 200 x-ray sources as well as providing evidence bearing on the study of black holes.
LIFE SCIENCE	Biosatallites 1,2,3	Dec. 14, 1966 Sep. 7, 1967 Jun. 28, 1969	NASA	Biosatallite 1 carried fruit flies, wheat seedlings, frog eggs, and other specimens to study the effects of weightlessness and radiation; the capsules failed to deorbit. Biosatallite 2 carried the same payload, was successfully retrieved, and demonstrated that plants require gravity to maintain orientation, it also provided data on some of the effects of radiation. Biosatallite 3 carried

SCIENTIFIC MISSIONS

TYPE	NAME	DATE OF LAUNCH	USING AGENCY	REMARKS
LIFE SCIENCE				a pigtail monkey, instrumented so that scientists could study brain-wave patterns and the nervous cardio-vascular and metabolic systems.

MILITARY APPLICATIONS MISSIONS

TYPE	NAME	DATE OF LAUNCH	USING AGENCY	REMARKS
MISSILE DETEC-TION SATELLITE SERIES	First called Midas, later carried a numer-ical designation	May 1960 – present	U.S. Air Force/ DOD	The MDS series was developed to detect missile launches by the infrared radiation they emit; the system became operational in the mid-to-late 1960s.
RECONNAISSANCE SATELLITE SERIES (GROUND OBSER-VATION: VISUAL, ELECTRONIC, AND RADAR SURVEIL-LANCE)	First called Dis-coverer and Samos, they later carried numerical designations	Feb 1959 – present	U.S. Air Force/ DOD	The reconnaissance satellite series became operational in the mid-1960s, and has geodetic and satellite detection functions in addition to its reconnaissance capability.
NUCLEAR TEST-BAN ENFORCEMENT SERIES	Vela Hotel	Oct. 1963 – present	U.S. Air Force/ DOD/ERDA	The Vela Hotel system detects above-ground fission and fusion explosions; it became operational in the mid-1960s.
NAVIGATION	Transit Naviga-tion Series	April 1960 – present	U.S. Navy/DOD	The Transit navigation satellite sys-tem aids ships in determining their latitude and longitude; it became operational at the end of 1963. In 1966 military aircraft could use the system to determine their position to within 500 yards.

MILITARY APPLICATIONS MISSIONS

TYPE	NAME	DATE OF LAUNCH	USING AGENCY	REMARKS
NAVIGATION	Timation 3	Jul. 14, 1975	U.S. Navy/DOD	Timation 3 is a Navigation Technology Satellite.
	NAVSTAR	1976-1977	DOD	The operation NAVSTAR Global Positioning System is envisioned as replacing other navigation systems in the 1980s.
COMMUNICATIONS	IDCSP Communications Series 1-7 8-15 16-18 19-26	Jun. 16, 1966 Jan. 18, 1967 Jul. 1, 1967 Jun. 13, 1969	U.S. Air Force/ DOD	The Initial Defense Communications Satellite Program was intended to establish a global military communications system; 1-18 formed the system, 19-26 were supplements.
	TACSAT 1	Feb. 9, 1969	U.S. Air Force/ DOD	TACSAT 1 was an experimental Tactical Communications Satellite to evaluate tactical communications by satellites and establish an initial capability.
	DSCS 1,2 3,4 5,6	Nov. 3, 1971 Dec. 1973 May 20, 1975	U.S. Air Force/ DOD	DSCS 1-6. The Defense Satellite Communications System comprised second generation military communications satellites that replaced and upgraded the IDCSP series. DSCS 1 and 2 are no longer operating. DSCS 3 and 4 are in geosynchronous orbit. DSCS 5 and 6 failed to achieve orbit.

MILITARY APPLICATIONS MISSIONS

TYPE	NAME	DATE OF LAUNCH	USING AGENCY	REMARKS
METEOROLOGICAL	DMSP 1	May 13, 1975	U.S. Navy/ Air Force	The Defense Meteorological Satellite Program provides weather data on a real-time basis to the Air Weather Service and Navy ground and shipboard terminals around the world.

CIVIL APPLICATIONS MISSIONS

TYPE	NAME	DATE OF LAUNCH	USING AGENCY	REMARKS
COMMUNICATIONS	Echo 1, 2	Aug. 12, 1960 Jan. 25, 1964	NASA	Echo 1 and 2, metalized balloons 100 feet in diameter, passively reflected communication signals.
	Telstar 1,2	Jul. 10, 1962 May 7, 1963	AT&T	Launched by NASA for AT&T, the Telstars were the first privately funded satellites. Telstar 1 was the first active-repeater communications satellite, and relayed the first transatlantic telecast.
	Relay 1,2	Dec. 13, 1962 Jan. 21, 1964	NASA	Both Relay satellites were research and development active-repeater communications satellites; after testing, Relay 2 was turned over to the DOD for military communications over the Pacific.

CIVILIAN APPLICATIONS MISSIONS

TYPE	NAME	DATE OF LAUNCH	USING AGENCY	REMARKS
	Syncom 1,2,3	Feb. 14, 1953 Jul. 26, 1963 Aug. 19, 1964	NASA/DOD	Syncom 1 was the first synchronous satellite; syncom 2 operated successfully as an active-repeater satellite; Syncom 3 was placed into a true stationary orbit. Syncom 2 and 3 were transferred to the DOD in 1965.
	Intelsat 1	Apr. 6, 1965	INTELSAT	Intelsat satellites are owned and operated by the International Telecommunications Satellite Organization (INTELSAT). They were launched by NASA for the Communications Satellite Corporation (COMSAT), the U.S. representative in INTELSAT. Intelsat 1 was developed to obtain information for designing a global communications system; it became the first commercial communications satellite and was capable of transmitting 240 two-way voice channels for telephone, telegraph, television, or high speed data use.
COMMUNICATIONS	Intelsat II Series A-D	Oct. 1966 - Sept. 1967	INTELSAT	Launched and tracked by NASA, Intelsat II-A through D were placed in synchronous orbit transmitting transpacific communications; they had more than twice the capacity of Intelsat I.
	Intelsat III Series 1-2	Sep. 1968- Jul. 1970	INTELSAT	Launched and tracked by NASA, Intelsat III F-1 and F-2 were placed in syn-

CIVILIAN APPLICATIONS MISSIONS

TYPE	NAME	DATE OF LAUNCH	USING AGENCY	REMARKS
				chronous orbit transmitting trans-atlantic communications; the Intelsat III series satellites had more than five times the communications capacity of the Intelsat II satellites.
	Intelsat IV Series 1-8	Jan. 1971 – Nov. 1974	INTELSAT	Launched and tracked by NASA, the Intelsat IV series satellites were placed in synchronous orbit at various points over the earth, and have more than five times the communications capacity of the Intelsat III series.
	Intelsat IVA F-1	Sep. 26, 1975	INTELSAT	The INTELSAT IVA F-1 was placed in synchronous orbit over the Atlantic to provide increased capacity for the INTELSAT global communications network.
COMMUNICATIONS	Westar 1,2	Apr. 13, 1974 Oct. 10, 1974	Western Union Telegraph Co.	Launched by NASA under contract, Westar 1 and 2 formed the first U.S. domestic satellite communications system, and can relay TV, telephone, or multiple data signals.
	Marisat 1,2 A,B,C	Feb. 19, 1974 Jun. 9, 1973 3rd scheduled for Oct. 14, 1976	COMSAT General	The Maritime Satellite System of two spacecraft, one in synchronous transfer orbit over the Pacific, is capable of transmitting voice, data, facsimile and telex messages to and from ships at sea through stations on

CIVILIAN APPLICATIONS MISSIONS

TYPE	NAME	DATE OF LAUNCH	USING AGENCY	REMARKS
METEOROLOGICAL				shore. A third satellite is scheduled for launch on Oct. 14, 1976 into an orbit over the Indian Ocean.
	Tiros Series 1-8	Apr. 1960 – Dec. 1963	NASA	The Tiros developmental series using a television and an infrared camera, photographed the Earth's cloud cover and provided weather data for meteorologists and the U.S. Weather Bureau.
	Nimbus Series 1-6	Aug. 1964 – Aug. 1964 – Jun. 1975	NASA	The Nimbus research series, operating in polar orbits, provided photographs of much higher resolution than those of Tiros; they also carried research equipment testing a variety of weather-sensing and measuring devices.
	ESSA series 1-9	Feb. 1966 – Feb. 1969	ESSA	Launched by NASA for the Environmental Science Services Administration (which incorporated the Weather Bureau), the ESSA series formed an operational meteorological satellite system called TOS (Tiros Operational Satellite), based on Tiros research.
	ITOS 1	Jan. 23, 1970	ESSA	An improved Tiros, ITOS 1 could scan the Earth's nighttime cloud cover and doubled the daily weather coverage of the ESSA satellites; it was developed and launched by NASA for ESSA.

CIVILIAN APPLICATIONS MISSIONS

TYPE	NAME	DATE OF LAUNCH	USING AGENCY	REMARKS
METEOROLOGICAL	NOAA Series 1-4	Dec. 1970 – Nov. 1974	NOAA	The National Oceanic and Atmospheric Administration Series satellites were improved Tiros spacecraft. Funded by NOAA (formed Oct. 3, 1970, it incorporated ESSA), these satellites will provide operational weather coverage through the late 1970s.
	SMS 1, 2 GOES 1	May 17, 1974 Feb. 6, 1975 Oct. 16, 1975	NOAA	The Synchronous Metorological Satellites SMS 1 and 2 were developed and launched by NASA; following check-out they were turned over to NOAA. These machines formed the nucleus of a system capable of providing coverage for a long-range weather forecasting. After SMS 1 and 2, successive satellites have been called GOES (Geostationary Operational Environmental Satellite), and are funded entirely by NOAA.
APPLICATIONS TECHNOLOGY	ATS Series 1-6	Dec. 1966 – May 1974	NASA	The Applications Technology Satellite developmental series was designed to test the technology and experiments for advanced applications satellites; ATS 1 took the first high quality photographs of the Earth in 1966, showing changing cloud-cover patterns, meteorological, and navigation experiments; ATS 6, launched May 1974, was the first satellite to broadcast

CIVILIAN APPLICATIONS MISSIONS

TYPE	NAME	DATE OF LAUNCH	USING AGENCY	REMARKS
APPLICATIONS TECHNOLOGY				TV photos to small local receivers, used to support public health and education experiments in the U.S. and India.
	ERTS 1,2 (renamed Landsat 1,2)	Jul. 23, 1972 Jan. 22, 1975	NASA	In low polar orbits, the Earth Resources Technology Satellites ERTS 1 and 2 conducted radar, optical, and other surveys of Earth resources, pollution, and environmental conditions useful in agriculture, forestry, hydrology, geology, geography, and oceanography; on January 14, 1975 they were renamed Landsat 1 and Landsat 2.
EARTH RESOURCE SURVEY	Seasat	Scheduled in 1978	NASA	Seasat will study the oceans and seas with microwave devices; the information will be distributed for weather predicting, shipping, routing, and issuing iceberg and weather warnings. The first launch will be a proof-of-concept mission, followed by later operational missions.
	EOS A,B	Tentatively scheduled for 1979 and 1981	NASA	The Earth Observatory Satellites EOS A and B are multipurpose satellites planned for low Earth orbit to survey the Earth, oceans, pollution, and weather, and supply

CIVILIAN APPLICATIONS MISSIONS

TYPE	NAME	DATE OF LAUNCH	USING AGENCY	REMARKS
EARTH RESOURCE SURVEY				improved information for urban planners and predictors of agricultural yields; they are capable of being launched, served, etc., by the manned Space Shuttle when it becomes available.
	SEOS	In study stage	NASA	The Synchronous Earth Observatory Satellite will use a large telescope with an infrared atmospheric sounder for experimental meteorological and Earth resource observations.
	Anna 1B	Oct. 31, 1962	Army-Navy-Air Force-NASA	Anna 1B was equipped with solar cells which supplied power for 4 flashing beacons that were photographed from the ground at night to obtain the apparent night ascensional declination of the satellite from each camera; used in the field of cartography.
GEODETIC	GEOS 1,2,3	Nov. 6, 1965 Jan. 11, 1968 Apr. 9, 1975	NASA/DOD/DOC	The Geodetic Satellites Geos 1,2 and 3 were equipped with electronic beacons and optical reflectors for lasers and radar targets; they refined knowledge of the Earth's shape and gravitational field, and developed a unified world datum.

CIVILIAN APPLICATIONS MISSIONS

TYPE	NAME	DATE OF LAUNCH	USING AGENCY	REMARKS
GEODETIC	PAGEOS 1	Jun. 23, 1966	NASA/DOD/DOC	The Passive Geodetic Satellite Pageos 1 was an uninstrumented (passive) balloon, 30 meters in diameter, which reflected sunlight and, when photographed, enabled the determination of the relative position of islands and continents to within 50-100 feet.
	LAGEOS	May 4, 1976	NASA/DOD/DOC	The Laser Geodetic Satellite LAGEOS in the shape of a dense ball covered with laser reflectors, permits highly accurate measurements of the Earth's crust; it will provide a stable reference point for decades, permit simultaneous laser ranging measurements from Earth stations a continent apart, and may possibly be used for Earthquake prediction.

APPENDIX C

U.S. MANNED SPACE MISSIONS: A CHRONOLOGY

The 43 American astronauts who flew in space during the past 15 years continued in a different medium the heritage of American balloonists and aviators. Theirs is a rich legacy of adventure, daring, and challenges met. The accomplishments of Orville and Wilbur Wright, Charles Lindbergh, and countless other Americans set standards of uncompromising excellence and dogged determination which became the hallmark of the American aeronautical experience.

The achievements of the American civilian manned space flight program are similarly impressive, especially in the light of its modest beginnings. When President John F. Kennedy announced to a joint session of Congress on May 25, 1961 that "we should go to the Moon", the entire American experience with manned space flight totalled a meager 15 minutes -- and that was a sub-orbital flight. The ballistic flight of this two-ton "man-in-a-can" marked the beginning of a series of manned space flights which culminated in an American first stepping on the Moon eight years later. This same modest flight of Alan B. Shepard, Jr.'s Freedom 7 spacecraft can be contrasted to the orbiting, twelve years later, of the 119-foot long Skylab 1 orbital workshop whose weight exceeded that of Columbus' flagship, the Santa Maria.

The number of firsts recorded by American astronauts in space far exceeds the space required to list them. In summary, American astronauts have spent nearly eleven months in space over fourteen years of flight. Thirty-one separate flights have been conducted by forty-three individual astronauts. Four of these men have made four flights each. Three American astronauts (Grissom, White, and Chaffee) perished on the ground in a command module fire. Twenty-seven Americans have conducted successful lunar orbits. The Moon has received twelve Americans on its surface and has surrendered to them nearly 400 kilograms of lunar material. Part of the Moon is now on the Earth, being studied under microscopes and growing cabbages. One crew (Skylab 4) spent over 84 consecutive days in space.

Last year's Bicentennial celebrations saw the beginnings of a new American space transportation system. Astronauts will soon fly in space in the reusable shuttle craft which will land like an aircraft after conducting its space missions. As the American technological progression in aeronautics advances from kites, balloons, propeller and jet aircraft to supersonic and hypersonic vehicles, so does the American adventure in space continue.

Leonard C. Bruno

APPENDIX C   U. S. MANNED SPACE MISSIONS

MERCURY

Name	Launch Date	Launch Vehicle	Crew	Remarks
Mercury-Redstone 3 (Freedom 7)	May 5, 1961	Mercury-Redstone	Alan B. Shepard, Jr.	First U.S. manned flight; sub-orbital, ballistic trajectory. Flight time 15 min.
Mercury-Redstone 4 (Liberty Bell 7)	July 21, 1961	Mercury-Redstone	Virgil I. Grissom	Ballistic, suborbital 15 min flight. Capsule sank in Atlantic after landing; astronaut recover-ed.
Mercury-Atlas 6 (Friendship 7)	Feb. 20, 1962	Mercury-Atlas	John H. Glenn, Jr.	First U.S. manned orbital flight. Three revolution flight lasted 4 hr 55 min.
Mercury-Atlas 7 (Aurora 7)	May 24, 1962	Mercury-Atlas	M. Scott Carpenter	Flight plan similar to Friendship 7. Landed 250 mi off target; flight time 4 hr 56 min.
Mercury-Atlas 8 (Sigma 7)	Oct. 3, 1962	Mercury-Atlas	Walter M. Schirra, Jr.	Five revolution flight lasted 9 hr 13 min.
Mercury-Atlas 9 (Faith 7)	May 15, 1963	Mercury-Atlas	L. Gordon Cooper, Jr.	Last Mercury mission. Long-endurance flight (34 hr 20 min) had no adverse effects on astronaut.

GEMINI

Name	Launch Date	Launch Vehicle	Crew	Remarks
Gemini 3 (Molly Brown)	Mar. 23, 1965	Titan II	Virgil I. Grissom John W. Young	First U.S. 2-man flight. Orbital maneuvers conducted in each of 3 orbits. Flight time 4 hr 53 min.
Gemini 4	June 3, 1965	Titan II	James A. McDivitt Edward H. White II	During four day mission, crew conducted scientific and engineering experiments. 21 min space walk by White. Flight time 97 hr 56 min.
Gemini 5	Aug. 21, 1965	Titan II	L. Gordon Cooper, Jr. Charles Conrad, Jr.	Eight day endurance mission confirmed physiological feasibility of Apollo mission. Flight time 190 hr 55 min.
Gemini 7	Dec. 4, 1965	Titan II	Frank Borman James A. Lovell, Jr.	Crew experienced no adverse physiological effects from 2 weeks in space. Flight time 330 hr 35 min.
Gemini 6-A	Dec. 15, 1965	Titan II	Walter M. Schirra, Jr. Thomas P. Stafford	Crew maneuvered spacecraft to within 1 ft of Gemini 7 craft. Flight time 25 hr 51 min.
Gemini 8	Mar. 16, 1966	Titan II	Neil A. Armstrong David R. Scott	Docked with unmanned target vehicle. Spinning of docked crafts caused early mission termination. Flight time 10 hr 41 min.

Name	Launch Date	Launch Vehicle	Crew	Remarks
Gemini 9-A	June 3, 1966	Titan II	Thomas P. Stafford Eugene A. Cernan	Multiple rendezvous performed with Target Adaptor. Total 2 hr 7 min EVA by Cernan. Flight time 72 hr 21 min.
Gemini 10	July 18, 1966	Titan II	John W. Young Michael Collins	First rendezvous with 2 different spacecraft. Docked with target vehicle and conducted maneuvers. Two separate EVA's made. Flight time 70 hr 47 min.
Gemini 11	Sept. 12, 1966	Titan II	Charles Conrad, Jr. Richard F. Gordon, Jr.	Docked with target vehicle and conducted extensive maneuvers. Two EVA's made. Flight time 71 hr 17 min.
Gemini 12	Nov. 11, 1966	Titan II	James A. Lovell, Jr. Edwin E. Aldrin, Jr.	Docked with target vehicle. Aldrin conducted extensive EVA activity (5 hr 37 min). Flight time 94 hr 35 min.

APOLLO

Name	Launch Date	Launch Vehicle	Crew	Remarks
Apollo 7	Oct. 11, 1968	Saturn IB	Walter M. Schirra, Jr. Donn F. Eisele R. Walter Cunningham	First U.S. 3-man mission; first flight of Apollo spacecraft. All systems checked out. Flight time 260 hr 9 min.
Apollo 8	Dec. 21, 1968	Saturn V	Frank Borman James A. Lovell, Jr. William A. Anders	First manned orbit of moon; first manned departure from earth's sphere of influence. Flight time 147 hr 1 min.
Apollo 9 (Gumdrop and Spider)	Mar. 3, 1969	Saturn V	James A. McDivitt David R. Scott Russell L. Schweickart	Successfully simulated in earth orbit operation of lunar module to landing and takeoff from lunar surface and rejoining with command module. Flight time 241 hr 1 min.
Apollo 10 (Snoopy and Charley Brown)	May 18, 1969	Saturn V	Thomas P. Stafford Eugene A. Cernan John W. Young	Demonstrated complete system including lunar module descent to 47,000 ft from lunar surface. Flight time 192 hr 3 min.
Apollo 11 (Columbia and Eagle)	July 16, 1969	Saturn V	Neil A. Armstrong Edwin E. Aldrin, Jr. Michael Collins	First manned lunar landing. First return of moon samples to earth. Deployed experiments on moon. Flight time 195 hr 19 min.
Apollo 12 (Yankee Clipper and Intrepid)	Nov. 14, 1969	Saturn V	Charles Conrad, Jr. Richard F. Gordon, Jr. Alan L. Bean	Second manned lunar landing. Retrieved parts of Surveyor 3 which landed on moon Apr. 1967. Flight time 244 hr 36 min.

Name	Launch Date	Launch Vehicle	Crew	Remarks
Apollo 13 (Odyssey and Aquarius)	Apr. 11, 1970	Saturn V	James A. Lovell, Jr. John L. Swigert, Jr. Fred W. Haise, Jr.	Mission aborted after explosion in service module. Crew used lunar module as "lifeboat", circled moon, and reentered in command module. Flight time 142 hr 55 min.
Apollo 14 (Kitty Hawk and Antares)	Jan. 31, 1971	Saturn V	Alan B. Shepard, Jr. Stuart A. Roosa Edgar D. Mitchell	Third manned lunar landing. Crew demonstrated pinpoint landing capability. Flight time 216 hr 2 min.
Apollo 15 (Endeavour and Falcon)	July 26, 1971	Saturn V	David R. Scott Alfred M. Worden James B. Irwin	Fourth manned lunar landing. First to use Lunar Roving Vehicle. Flight time 295 hr 12 min.
Apollo 16 (Orion and Casper)	Apr. 16, 1972	Saturn V	John W. Young Thomas L. Mattingly III Charles M. Duke, Jr.	Fifth manned lunar landing. Used Lunar Rover. Flight time 265 hr 51 min.
Apollo 17 (America and Challenger)	Dec. 7, 1972	Saturn V	Eugene A. Cernan Ronald E. Evans Harrison H. Schmitt	Sixth and final manned lunar landing. Lunar rover traveled about 22 mi on moon. Flight time 301 hr 51 min.

SKYLAB

Name	Launch Date	Launch Vehicle	Crew	Remarks
Skylab 2	May 25, 1973	Saturn IB	Charles Conrad, Jr. Joseph P. Kerwin Paul J. Weitz	Crew docked with and entered orbiting Skylab 1, activating first U.S. manned orbital workshop. Repaired damaged station. Flight time 28 days 50 min.
Skylab 3	July 28, 1973	Saturn IB	Alan L. Bean Jack R. Lousma Owen K. Garriott	Second U.S. manned orbital workshop. Conducted experiments and EVA's. Flight time 59 days 11 hr 9 min.
Skylab 4	Nov. 16, 1973	Saturn IB	Gerald P. Carr Edward G. Gibson William R. Pogue	Third and final U.S. manned orbital workshop mission. Longest manned space flight and longest single EVA. Flight time 84 days 1 hr 16 min.

APOLLO/SOYUZ TEST PROJECT (ASTP)

Name	Launch Date	Launch Vehicle	Crew	Remarks
Apollo	July 15, 1975	Saturn IB	Thomas P. Stafford Donald K. Slayton Vance D. Brand	First joint, international manned flight. Docked with U.S.S.R. Soyuz 19, exchanged crews, and conducted joint experiments. Flight time 217 hr 28 min. Last scheduled U.S. manned flight before Space Shuttle.

LIST OF ILLUSTRATIONS AND FIGURES

Chapter VIII: Manned Space Flight

INDEX

---

*Back note references (b.n.) indicate page and number

Brand, Vance C.: 291
Braun, Wernher von: 25, 26, 36, 214
Brick Moon: 10
Britain: Army of, 8, 54
  Battle of: 13, 18
  Jet transport, 167
  Military aeronautics, 140
  Seaplanes: 164
British Interplanetary Society (BIS)
  xiii, 30
British Overseas Airways (BOAC):
  167, 172
Bronk, Detlov: 211 (b.n.8)
Brooks, Courtney: 32, 252 (b.n. 47)
Brooks, Peter: 164
Brown, Arthur W.: 69
Brown, Margery: 118
Brown, Walter: 161
Bruno, Leonard C.: 261, 285
Bryan, John R.: 54
Bumper-Wac rocket: 20
Bunyan, Paul: 190
Burden, William A.: 120, 124
Burgess, Charles P.: 82, 83
Bush pilots: 115
Bush, Vannevar: 18
Business aviation: 116-18, 127
"Business of research": 14
Byrd, Richard: 118, 159
Bykovskiy, V. F.: 224

C-97 (Boeing): 165
Caldwell, Frank W.: 160
California Institute of Technology:
  xiv (See Jet Propulsion Laborat-
  ory)
Carnes, Peter: 6, 7, 29-30, 43-44
Cantilever wing: 17, 141
Cape Canaveral: 24, 28
Carpenter, M. Scott: 226, 227
Carr, Gerald P. 291
Centennial Exposition of 1876: viii
Cernan, Eugene A.: 235, 243, 288-90
Certification of aircraft and pilots
  15
Cessna 150: 126
Cevor, Charles: 56
Chaffe, Roger B.: 237
Chandler, Charles DeF.: 102 (b.n.12)
Chamberlain, James A.: 229
Chapman, Richard: 212 (b.n. 17)
Charles, Jacques A. C.: 42

Chennault, Clair: xv
Cheves, Langdon: 54
Churchill, Winston: 21
Civil Aeronautics Administration
  (CAA): 119, 162, 164
  Airways, 162
  Certified aircraft: 120
Civil War: 49-56
Clarke, Arthur C.: 30, 37 (b.n. 48)
Clauser, Milton U.: 36 (b.n. 41)
Clayton, Richard: 47, 48
"Cold War": 21
Collins, Michael: vii-viii, biog.
  xiv, 8, 243, 288, 289 (see,
  Apollo 11)
Colonies, in space: 5
Columbia (Goodyear): 100
Columbus, Christopher: 5, 285
Commerce, Dept. of: 14, 15, 120,
  122-24, 156, 158, 165, 200, 201
Communications Satellite Act of
  1962: 202
Communications Satellite Corp.
  (Comsat), 202
Communications satellites: 200, 202
  (see, projects by name)
Computers: 19, 22
Concorde SST (BAC-Aerospatiale):
  156, 170-75
Confederate balloons: 54, 56
Condor airplane (Curtiss): 158, 161
Congreve, William: 8
Conrad, Charles: 234, 243, 287, 289,
  291
Consolidated Aircraft Corp.: 20, 21,
  86, 159
Constellation (L-049): 156, 166
Convair 880: 168
Coolidge, Calvin: 15, 158
Cooper, L. Gordon: 226, 227, 234,
  287
Copernicus (lunar crater): 192
Corporal rocket: 20
Corsair (F4U): 141
Corson, Dale R.: 26, 36 (b.n. 41)
Cortright, Edgar M.: 253 (b.n. 52)
Cosmology: 30
Cosmonauts: 224, 230, 232 (see, by
  by name)
Cox, Gary: 261
Cretaceous period: 5
Crop dusting
Crouch, Tom D.: 14, 33 (b.n. 10)

XP-940 (Boeing): 144
XPS-1 (Dayton-Wright): 141

Yankee Clipper (Boeing 314):
  162
Yeager, Charles E.: 20
Yegorov, B. B.: 230
York, Herbert F.: 35 (b.n. 36),
  211 (b.n. 5 and 15)

Young, John W.: 232, 243, 287, 289

Zeppelin, Count von: 71
Zeppelins: 13f., 74f.:
    Luftschiffbau, 74, 81
Zeppelin-Staaken monoplane (E.4350):
    164

AMERICAN **A**STRONAUTICAL SOCIETY

PUBLICATIONS OF THE AMERICAN ASTRONAUTICAL SOCIETY

Following are the principal publications of the American Astronautical Society.

JOURNAL OF THE ASTRONAUTICAL SOCIETY (1954-   )

Published quarterly and distributed by AAS Business Office, 6060 Duke St., Alexandria, Virginia 22304.

AAS NEWSLETTER (1962-   )

Published bimonthly and distributed by AAS Business Office, 6060 Duke St., Alexandria, Virginia 22304.

ADVANCES IN THE ASTRONAUTICAL SCIENCES (1957-   )

Proceedings of major AAS technical meetings. Published and distributed by Univelt Inc. (P.O. Box 28130, San Diego, California 92128) for the American Astronautical Society.

SCIENCE AND TECHNOLOGY SERIES (1964-   )

Supplement to Advances in the Astronautical Sciences. Proceedings and monographs, most of them based on AAS technical meetings. Published and distributed by Univelt Inc. (P.O. Box 28130, San Diego, California 92128) for the American Astronautical Society.

AAS MICROFICHE SERIES (1968-   )

Supplement to Advances in the Astronautical Sciences. Consists principally of technical papers not included in the hard-copy volumes. Published and distributed by Univelt Inc. (P.O. Box 28130, San Diego, California 92128) for the American Astronautical Society.

Subscriptions to the Journal and the AAS Newsletter should be ordered from the AAS Business Office. Back issues of the Journal and all books and microfiche should be ordered from Univelt Inc.